THE
VIRTUAL REALITY
PRIMER

L. Casey Larijani

with illustrations by Herschel Stroyman & Anthony Marynowski

McGraw-Hill, Inc.

New York   San Francisco   Washington, D.C.   Auckland   Bogota
Caracas   Lisbon   London   Madrid   Mexico City   Milan
Montreal   New Delhi   San Juan   Singapore
Sydney   Tokyo   Toronto

Library of Congress Cataloging-in-Publication Data

Larijani, L. Casey.
    The virtual reality primer / L. Casey Larijani.
        p.   cm.
    Includes bibliographical references and index.
    ISBN 0-07-036417-6 — ISBN 0-07-036416-8 (PBK.)
    1. Human computer interaction. 2. Virtual reality. I. Title.
QA76.9.H85L37 1993
006.—dc20`   93-26466
                                                CIP

1 2 3 4 5 6 7 8 9 0 DOC/DOC 9 9 8 7 6 5 4 3

ISBN 0-07-036417-6 (HC)

ISBN 0-07-036416-8 (PBK)

The sponsoring editor for this book was Jeanne Glasser.

Printed and bound by R. R. Donnelley and Sons Company.

To

My Children

&

My Family

Contents

Preface

Virtual Reality — a new "high?" The idea's actually been around for over 25 years, but suddenly the term is cropping up all over the place — in trendy magazines, on cable news networks and cited as yet another threat from Japanese industry. Rumors abound of mobsters pouring millions into "VR" entertainment while universities grovel for research pennies. When called on by Senate committees convened to finally check it out, traditionally dry academic skeptics have exuded uncharacteristic passion. But what is it?

If you looked it up, the dictionary defines virtual as *"existing or resulting in essence or effect though not in actual fact, form or name."* Reality is *"the quality or state of being actual or true."* You can imagine the field day philosophers and lawyers would have with that! As a technology, however, virtual reality is being defined in very specific ways. A combination of sophisticated, high-speed computer power with images, sound and other effects, virtual reality (VR) has been defined alternately as

- a computer-synthesized, three-dimensional environment in which a plurality of human participants, appropriately interfaced, may engage and manipulate simulated physical elements in the environment and, in some forms, may engage and interact with representations of other humans, past, present or fictional, or with invented creatures. [Nugent91]

or

- an interactive computer system so fast and intuitive that *the computer disappears from the mind of the user*, leaving the computer-generated environment as the reality. [Goldfarb91]

or, simply,

- a cartoon world you can get into.

Roger Rabbit hopped into our world through advanced animation and film technologies; now, with the help of computer-related technologies, we can enter his sort of world. You use goggles or other devices to view and enter a computer-created representation of an alternate reality in which you are a player. As you move your head or give commands, this virtual scene becomes enslaved and changes accordingly. Your head or hand seems to be transposed into the head or hand that is displayed and moving within the computer-generated scene.

Virtual reality is neither intimidating nor the exclusive domain of arcade rats and techies. Neither are its applications restricted to the purely technical or purely scientific. It is a creative communications medium for everyone. It will influence how we design things and run our businesses, how we teach our children and treat our illnesses, as well as how we spend our leisure time.

Bring to mind the sensation of dreaming, and you get some idea of what the ideal virtual-reality experience is *supposed* to be. In the same way that sense and nonsense compatibly cohabit dreams, so can logic and ill-logic be freely mixed in the computer-generated worlds of VR. How would you put a dream together if you could hook up your imagination to a powerful computer engine? Immediately, visual images would come to mind. Then, you would interact with them. With the right setup — whether you want to solve problems or subject your senses to new experiences, virtual reality comes close to providing the opportunity.

The technology allows you to create an environment and participate in an experiential script of your choosing. You could become immersed in any way you wish. Issue a virtually possible command of "Fly me to the moon," and define yourself as part of the scene. Assign yourself Alice-in-Wonderland-type smallness, perhaps, or zero gravity or accelerated zooming power. You could also assign yourself (or virtual objects) logical attributes such as weight, physical appearance, gravity and mobility. Electronic feedback based on these qualities reinforces the experience, convincing you that something is really happening.

Daydreams, fantasies and concepts readily evoke emotional responses, but the plug is all but pulled for the other senses. Equally shortchanged are our night dreams — where the plug of our consciousness is pulled. Virtual-reality idealists hope to produce the best of both worlds, an arena for fully conscious interaction with our concepts and each other.

Virtual-reality environments or scenarios can be predefined and focused so that a user can gain specific skills or insight as if he or she were actually on the job. A language-independent or culture-independent virtual-reality environment can render borders transparent, a quantum leap forward — for anyone, from fighter pilots to brain surgeons to tradespeople — from the types of simulation programs now used for education and training.

Multiparty collaborators can create a temporary shared venue for cooperative design and exploration. In such a case, all participants would be identically equipped and able to feed their ideas into a common system — harbingers of the electronic town hall, perhaps? Rules would determine how these ideas are handled. Thus, individual ideas from decision makers in cities around the world or teams of construction workers from various sites are funneled into a common system that intelligently synthesizes the information, regenerates the environment appropriately and provides immediate feedback to other members of the group.

Virtual scenarios can promote dynamic brainstorming of factors that influence decisions. This is particularly important in business. In manufacturing, participants can go through an iterative process of design refinement without the costs or delays actual construction would entail. More detailed discussion of such systems is provided in separate chapters.

Customers and clients benefit, as well, from this new way of "experiencing" things. Virtual-reality scenarios offer people a chance to try out products or services before they buy or commit large sums of money for development. Thus, an automobile industry executive who must be convinced that a new car design warrants backing could, conceivably, be invited to "sit in and drive" a virtual realization of the proposed design. Depending on the elegance of the technologies used to create the particular VR product and scene, the executive is afforded either an approximate or a very realistic opportunity for a "hands-on" experience with whatever he or she is being asked to pay for. And, depending on the executive's reaction, the design can then be scrapped altogether, altered or regenerated so that it can be retested. Only after the product is approved is it put into a real stage of construction. Again, all this is done very fast, with minimal human resources and without the heavy costs and time delays of clay-model construction.

These are only a few of the applications that are rapidly becoming part of our lives. Even more exciting and interesting than these are the promises virtual reality holds for practical medicine and science. If measured by their potential for inspiring optimism among research diagnosticians and physical therapists alone, virtual-reality aids for the ill and disabled border on the miraculous. Virtual operating theaters provide safe, common areas for exchanges of knowledge and technique among practitioners and patients.

This critical convergence of imaging and computing power that we call virtual reality has opened up possibilities for shared expertise and experiences far beyond what any of us could imagine. It holds the potential not only of enhancing noble efforts to better the lot of humankind but also of reawakening the daydreams, night dreams and pipe dreams of all of us.

Though the learning effectiveness of real experiences will remain unmatched, intelligently designed virtual-reality experiences, can shorten the distance between what we must learn and what we are able to know through experience. By providing us with the means of "seeing" things invisible to us in the real world, VR techniques can sharpen our understanding of that real world. We will invent virtual experiences that are impossible in reality and may even extend the boundaries of our senses beyond those we already know.

It is no longer a question of whether such things can be done but of where they can be best applied. Each time VR technology is used is a variation on a theme, beginning from some entry point in reality. And there is plenty of room for all types of computer-generated worlds — from those that remain based in realism to those that abandon constraints for digressions into fantasy. Applications for surgical procedures or architecture or engineering require a high degree of realism and must remain faithful to the real world and its accepted standards. Others, such as virtual entertainment, provide escape from convention by exploiting the power of computers to generate new kinds of environments and giving us the means to explore them.

The official purpose of this short guide is to acquaint you, through relaxed descriptions of real applications and current research, with what virtual reality is and how we might be using it in the future. Its unofficial, true purpose is simply to pique your imagination and race your mind. It is for anyone whose curiosity about virtual reality reaches beyond cocktail party conversation or comments like "Oh, that thing I saw on television!"

Your interest is the only prerequisite; you need not be conversant in computer language. Most of the terms used throughout the book are defined in the Glossary (Appendix A). Please refer to it often. I hope you find that only a very modest strain of intellectual investment is required to greatly increase your understanding of this wonderful new technology and its potential significance in our lives.

Chapters 1 through 5 and Chapters 14 and 15 are devoted more to discussion than to detail. Chapters 6 through 13 address virtual-reality technology as applied to specific tasks. Depending on where your interests lie, you may choose to read the material in other than sequential order. However, the early chapters contain what I anticipate might help some readers better understand specific applications described later.

Acknowledgments

This is probably the most gratifying, yet the most difficult part of the book to write — gratifying because printed words serve as public attestation, difficult because they fail to convey the real influence others have had on anyone's work or life. That said, let me proceed to mention at least a few members of the stellar cast of this particular production.

Sincere thanks go to Professor Walter J. Karplus of the University of California at Los Angeles and Ms. Dolores May Casey — muses of very different disciplines but equally gentle persuasion. Messrs. Leland Freeman and Robert Gluck tolerated unfinished drafts and offered valuable suggestions. A special hats-off is also due the impressive cadre of researchers now active in the field of virtual reality. In all contacts with them, their enthusiasm, creativity and sheer competence shone through. Mr. Arden Strasser of Virtual Reality, Inc. was especially accessible, as was Dr. Carl Machover, Consultant and Editor of McGraw-Hill's Series on Visual Technology.

I am grateful to Ms. Jeanne Glasser, my editor at McGraw-Hill, and her colleague, Mr. Gerald R. Papke, for spotting the potential for a "primer" on the topic and for infusing strict professionalism with cordiality. I also wish to acknowledge their competent production staff.

My children — Leila, David, Jayron and Sheida — with dependable humor, accepted all the idiosyncrasies I deny ever having as a writer. They are wonderful, and I thank them.

L.C.L.
New York
July 1993

An Overview of Converging Technologies

Realistic, stereoscopic images are projected off tiny screens inside a helmet, and sounds are added to convince the wearer that he or she is in another world. Motion sensors in the glove and helmet of the wearer become the means of interacting with the new world.

It sounds rather straightforward, but creating the artificial three-dimensional environments that make up the "other world" has only recently been possible. Wrapping pictures and sounds around us and immersing our senses in such a way that the line between the real and illusionary worlds disappears are being done only through a dynamic convergence of many different technologies, each of which evolved and matured at its own pace.

Computer speed and power have had to be combined with advances in image processing, tracking mechanisms and intuitive human-to-computer communication to converge into the experiential medium called virtual reality.

Conventional computers work fast but not fast enough to display high-quality images quickly. There is always a trade-off of time or essence. A computer designed to display images well and in rapid succession has to have both great computing power and great speed, as well as good display features. At any given time, these technologies are at different stages of development. Interplay among them always involves costly trade-offs in time or quality. In order to create virtual worlds, each one of the technologies involved must have reached a stage at which its strengths and resources can be used effectively with the others. The convergence must result in immersion that exhibits the following characteristics:

- It is perceived as authentic.

- It allows intuitive interaction and responds to it quickly.

- It is defined and focused, even for entertainment.

- It facilitates the collection, perception and analysis of data.

COMPUTER SPEED, POWER & IMAGES

The current trend toward graphics and the use of visual images are among the important developments of this decade not only for technical people using computers but also for nontechnical people. Sensory immersion like that provided by virtual reality is becoming an option for studying humans under varied conditions in the way that sensory deprivation was used in the 1950s and 1960s.

A picture, a piece of animation or a video, if properly prepared and presented, is also a much more effective way to convey information than a piece of text. Whether the image is a simple line drawing, a picture, a graph, a photograph, a multidimensional figure, a symbolic spreadsheet or an expertly enhanced visualization of scientific facts, it helps people understand the underlying complex information. Images help people learn. It's as simple as that.

Seeing & Believing

Of all our senses, our eyes are the primary information gatherers. What we see is received as an image on our retinas, reduced to signals and fed to our minds. We then reconstruct and synthesize the information we have received with what we already know.

Reversing the process, when you want to convey an idea or image from your mind to someone else's, you translate it into signals (words, drawings, gestures, etc.) that can be understood and interpreted by others, either directly or indirectly, e.g., through the help of computers. Thus, a message is passed from one person to another.

Computers help this process by storing information (which has been reduced to signals) in ways that can be displayed — such as a picture on a screen. Display technologies are the systems and programs needed to electronically generate these computer pictures and images. A person can look at the display, mentally decipher the signals and recreate the idea in his or her mind — in other words, understand it.

But a message is not dependent on its content alone; it also depends on how it is received and what kind of knowledge its recipient has. Anything that comes between the sender and receiver, however elegantly designed or well meaning, threatens to jeopardize communication. So, computers can also hinder the process. How effectively the information is passed is greatly determined by how accurately the rendered version represents the original idea and then by how close the receiver comes to guessing the original meaning of the display. Virtual reality has the potential of becoming the means of a higher, more effective level of communication than ever before. Nonintrusive virtual interfaces may reduce the margin of error in interpretation between one user and another.

Visual Vocabularies

How, for instance, can we show barometric pressure in a way that makes sense to most people? What should speech look like? Or thresholds of anger? A visual vocabulary is vital. Graphic specialists and designers play important roles in the effective dissemination of information, and this conceptual challenge continues into program design. (For detailed discussions of fundamental principles underlying the quantitative and interpretive display of information, see [Tufte83&90].)

Different types of displays are employed for different levels of communication. They range from simple, black-and-white line drawings to complex, full-color, interactive virtual environments. A person wishing to transfer information chooses whichever medium promises to preserve and represent the original idea best.

Virtual reality exploits all current imaging techniques and extends them by ushering them into environments in which users can examine the displayed objects, interact with them and manipulate them. By doing so, researchers and users are able to use the images to convey not only information but interpretive expertise, as well.

Sophisticated multidimensional imaging systems facilitate the involvement of cross-disciplinary professional groups in how decisions are made and how companies are run, and companies that use the new technologies will gain a competitive edge in their global markets. Clear visual representations of a company's strategy, capability and goals, if presented early and continued throughout a project's cycle, heighten the awareness of company direction in everyone involved — planners, designers, venture capitalists, marketers and end users. These people constitute a valuable corporate resource. As informed collaborators, they can be tapped regularly for insight and suggestions and for promoting products or services.

Imaging, combined with high-speed computational capabilities, allows people to examine "what-if" alternatives, whether of a managerial, medical or manufacturing nature. These analyses provide a timesaving and cost-effective means of interaction among decision makers and implementors and propose optimized solutions to problems. Moreover, they can contribute significantly to the process of determining the technical, financial or economic feasibility of alternative-case situations.

Some of the choices available for displaying information and the basic differences among them are described briefly in following sections; in later chapters, however, discussion is restricted to those systems used for virtual-reality displays.

The Last 10 Years

The critical convergence of technologies that is making virtual reality possible has occurred only in the last 10 years. However, as early as 1965, Ivan Sutherland spoke of tantalizing virtual worlds and, in 1966, conducted preliminary three-dimensional (3-D) display experiments at M.I.T. Three years later, after what he called "one of the most exciting educational experiences" he had ever had, Sutherland demonstrated the first system developed to surround people in 3-D displays of information. [Sutherland68]

The VR paradigm and technology were then all but lost, bouncing around the United States, with few takers other than the military. There, in the military, millions were spent on developing virtual-reality displays as flight simulators, and for decades, the application of virtual reality to real problems was monopolized. Until the late 1980s, other countries showed little or no interest in the technology.

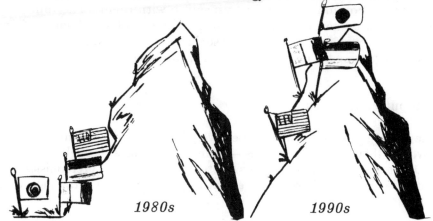

That situation has changed. The rash of technological advances during this last decade included great improvements in three areas that are particularly critical to independent virtual-reality research:

- Liquid Crystal Display (LCD) and Cathode Ray Tube (CRT) display devices (tiny television-like screens to show images);

- image-generation systems (high-resolution, high-speed graphics workstations to produce the images); and

- tracking systems (for converting position and orientation information into computer-readable signals that can be reflected in images).

These three technologies converged and became available on relatively affordable systems, allowing researchers to finally transfer and apply the technology in areas other than military and in places other than the United States — notably Japan, Germany and France.

Though the equipment needed to create virtual scenes is bulky and expensive, many experts predict a change in that situation. Indeed, today, all the hardware and equipment components of a virtual system are commercially available, and a number of applications are already in use — a vastly different scenario from that of 10 years ago. Still, many applications are being demanded but are not yet possible. This is due to tracking limitations and programming constraints. As the relevant technologies continue to evolve and become affordable, more diverse applications will be developed.

EVOLUTION OF DISPLAY TECHNOLOGIES

To better understand how advances in hardware and software provide impetus to the computer generation and display of information, it is useful to trace the evolution of display technologies and become familiar with terms commonly used in connection with them. The following sections discuss how the escalation of computer display technology, from graphics through imaging through visualization, has played an important role in advancing the creation of virtual environments.

Computer Graphics

The term "graphics" has always been very loosely used. For most people, anything that isn't text qualifies — from straight lines through elaborate, 3-D pictures made up of millions of little dots. The only prerequisites for computer graphics, it seems, are that they are made with the help of a computer and don't look like text.

Here, however, for purposes of comparison, the term graphics is confined to denote simple drawings — little more than electronic mimics of hand drawings, and computer graphics are merely those same types of simple drawings generated by computer. We can create, store, retrieve and manipulate graphic drawings electronically, and pictures or drawings can be entered into the computer by scanning or photographing.

The use of simple graphics can be likened to building sentences or sums using only simple words and numbers. Simple graphics are easy to produce and do not require a lot of computer power or speed.

But people usually want more than only rudimentary graphs or pie charts. They are beginning to demand pictures that convey more information. They require sophisticated, complex displays and interpretation of knowledge. For this, elements of syntax or style or computation must be brought into play. Image displays and other visualization techniques go that one step farther and allow wider ranging versatility of expression and interpretation.

Imaging

The similarity between image displays and graphics is that they are both manual, mental or computer-generated reproductions of the appearance of something and include pictures or drawings. However, computer graphics are often perceived as a geometric or line-based environment, whereas imaging is perceived as a pixel-based environment. [Machover93]

In addition, images are usually created and manipulated by more sophisticated systems than are needed for graphics. Captured as results of direct computation, real environments, models or documents, images are relatively realistic representations of the environment. Commercial applications of image displays are video systems, cameras and optical disks.

Though more versatile than simple graphics, images and the systems used to generate them also have limitations. To translate and display qualitative properties of data and information, researchers have had to enlist newer techniques and more advanced technologies — those of visualization.

Visualization

Basically, visualization is a sophisticated amalgam and extension of the many display techniques used over the years. The visualization process aims to present data and knowledge in an intuitive, comprehensible context, and its techniques are particularly valuable for displaying expert translations of huge amounts of complex data.

Early efforts to convey interpretive information often involved a programmer's creative manipulation of plotters, printers and animators. Today, computers and other technical devices incorporate these capabilities. Visualization techniques afford us views of things invisible to our natural sense of sight — as long as they can be converted into data reportable to the computer. These may be electrical fields or the night movements of troops, for instance. From the data, the computer generates "seeable" pictorial representations.

For example, a computer can be programmed to translate the detection of radiation waves by some device into a visual display; however, a human working with them is unable to see them. The visualization rendered may not only represent the radiation, but may imply its intensity, consequent effects on populations, food supplies, etc. In other words, visualization techniques help a user display in some invented form what he or she is working with, real or conceptual. This displayed form is what a user sees.

Visualization is done by very powerful, very fast machines that are able to transfer data quickly and store large amounts of information. It requires machines that can put together and handle very large amounts (gigabytes) of complex data. It also requires display units that can convert the signals into elegant renderings that not only include the data but also reflect their weighed significance and interpretation.

Scientific Visualization

Scientific visualization helps scientists by improving their perception of data describing our world. Knowledge extracted from the data is processed, interpreted and displayed very quickly; thus, many different kinds of visualizations can be invented and generated from one set of data. Each of these represents a unique way of seeing meaning in the data. Some of them provoke more insight than others. In this way, the technology helps us visualize concepts, as well.

Commonplace graphic display aids are often enlisted and work well — use of the color red for heat and blue for cold, and moving lines for flow, for instance, but these are de-facto rather than real standards, and arbitrary choices occasionally lead to confusion. From among the more effective views of data, libraries of optimally communicative ones can be compiled for use and enrichment by all researchers.

The visualization of scientific material began with hand drawings, then progressed through computer graphics to interactive computer graphics. However, data acquired from scientific investigation or mathematical calculations are of limited use if merely displayed; these data must be analyzed and interpreted, and it is the interpretation of data that must be displayed — and done so in such a way that it sparks insight.

From mid-cycle analyses of scientific processes, researchers often gain insight that they can exploit spontaneously to influence or alter the course of their research. Today's relatively fast processing and display of computed information enables scientists to halt a process and generate images mid-stream, allowing them to examine results at intermediate stages of the computation. Scientists can also run processes backward to gain insight often afforded by the perspective of reverse time. Slower, traditional methods of analysis and image generation preclude or, at best, discourage this kind of creative, hands-on approach.

Although visualization techniques are used primarily for physics, chemistry and medical applications that need expert interpretation and analysis, they are currently being recognized as indispensable teaching and learning tools in school curricula and for financial analysis, promoting new ways of seeing old things. (Chapters 9 and 10 include more on these applications.)

Many different types of image-delivery systems provide visualization features. These include computerized animation, medical imaging, painting programs, simulations of complex natural phenomena and architectural design packages, as well as initial designs of scenarios for virtual-reality environments. However, even with sophisticated visualization techniques and machines, the scientist remains outside the realm of the world he or she is investigating and is limited to a role of observer. The realizations achieved by virtual-reality systems attempt to remove this alienation of the user from the system by inviting him or her to become part of it.

Realization

Turning data into displayable objects that can be manipulated is called *realization*, and we refer to the objects as "virtual" objects. Realization is occasionally referred to as *virtualization*. Both also refer to a computer-generated world made up of such objects, in other words, the virtual world or the virtual scenario or environment.

Realization may be considered image-delivery one step higher than visualization. The interpretive visualization of information aims to dim the line between the machine and the thinker outside it. A virtual-reality display (a realization) tries to erase that barrier by ushering the user into an active, participatory role in a world created by the machine. It incorporates how the information should be represented in terms of boundaries, surfaces, transparency, colors and other graphical, image and geometric characteristics. [IBM91] The realization process and how virtual objects are displayed are the topic of Chapter 2, "Displaying Virtually Real Images."

THE HUMAN CONNECTION: INTERFACES

Human/Machine Communication ... & Lack Thereof

To solve problems with the aid of a computer, a user must be able to easily and accurately communicate to the machine and control what needs to get done. Designing the means to do so (i.e., the interface) is by no means trivial. A whole field of study has evolved around the problems of human interaction with complex machines and is alternately referred to as human engineering, human factoring, human factors analysis, human interface technology, man/machine interaction, etc.

Generally, the more an interface's features allow a user to tap into the system, the more resource-consuming or difficult it is to use; if it's easy, it's usually limited and limiting. For example, when all you want is a quick bite to eat, it is faster and easier to pick something from a menu that features the most popular items rather than from one listing every combination possible from the kitchen. If, however, you intend to eat a balanced meal, including portions from each of the food groups, or if you have dietary constraints, only a detailed and complete menu could give you enough choices. That requires more creativity and a lot more kitchen readiness.

Computer users often find themselves in similar straits. Someone needing only a quick "byte" is faced with option overload — a confusing, feature-rich menu of choices. Other users, forced to interact through a limited, overly simplified menu when they need to tap into many features, become frustrated, knowing there is so much more in the system than they are being given access to. Few users are so adept with the operating systems of their machines that they can avoid menus altogether and issue commands directly to the computer, much like going right into the kitchen.

Creative Obstacles

In application development today, on one side of the picture, we see remarkably advanced computing and image-generating power; on the other side are the enhanced intelligence and knowledge of the user. What has not kept pace with these increases in computing speeds and capacity is the *way* we communicate what we need done to a computing machine.

In between human and machine lie the real problems — interfaces exhibiting varying degrees of stupidity. No one yet has gotten it quite right.

Interfaces should be designed by persons with high-level multidomain (psychological, topical and technical) expertise, in order to minimize the loss of information or knowledge and get the maximum return on the human effort expended. They should serve as good communication venues and be easy to use by almost anyone.

Interfaces should also spare a user the constant interruption of his or her train of thought. Current "user-friendly" graphical user interfaces (GUIs) help by using pictorial formats. The road to amity has taken users from writing stilted commands to writing stilted commands in more natural-sounding language to "doing" their commands, i.e., pointing to, clicking, touching or speaking to graphic symbols called widgets, icons, mice and pull-down menus (WIMP). But even a WIMP approach, admittedly less intrusive and less demanding of a user than command-driven programs, doesn't solve the problem. The required keystrokes, clicks and cue combinations still impede anyone trying to get things done.

VR, the Ultimate Interface?

Because two-dimensional and three-dimensional graphical user interfaces have, to some degree, helped users communicate with the machines, a large investment of time and money is being made to improve them. For instance, expert systems are being embedded into interfaces to help people find information across myriad potential research sources. These systems assess and interpret profiles of individual users so that each user is provided with the right level of information for his or her unique background and needs.

However, some researchers and aficionados of virtual-reality technology see a natural progression from today's 2-D and 3-D windowing systems to virtual-environment interfaces as much more effective means of communicating with the system. [Park92b]

Just as pictures often transform information into insight better than words, so can the manipulation of virtual objects better convey subverbal interests (or "curiosity piques"), which can then be either disseminated or translated to a model. Being able to grasp and manipulate images of concepts we were previously unable to represent visually could usher in new types of graphically enhanced, computer-aided brainstorming and excite even the most staid among us.

Queries and orders to mathematical models are often best transmitted subverbally by picking, poking or pushing virtual objects. [Brooks88] The status of the economy and its trends, for instance, could be visualized as a sort of topological map incorporating pictorial renderings of factors involved — long unemployment lines, inventory pile-ups, a large deficit, full shopping carts, etc. — whatever would most effectively convey the meaning of the numbers and graphics to the user.

The realization could be "handled" or manipulated by a user to reflect his or her curiosities, such as, "What if Congress imposed a surcharge on this sector of the economy?" or, "What if the deficit were to be halved over the next 5 years?" Perhaps a push or pull on the model to force it to reflect the new conditions in that sector's area would be enough to feed back to the computer system the suggested changes in variables.

The computer system would then regenerate the visualization, and the user would observe the consequences as computed and displayed in the model — including a deficit pile half the size and, perhaps, shorter unemployment lines, less-full shopping carts, etc.

This is a far cry from amending documented streams of data and then trying to extract and analyze results. Because visualization techniques often clarify and aid interpretation of inordinate amounts of data, a user very quickly sees aspects of a situation that might otherwise be overlooked or would take too long to analyze. By eliminating the need for a person to understand *how* a computer has stored information in order to use it, virtual interfaces promise to free the user to focus on *what* is stored there — the knowledge or information.

It will take many more years, however, to develop the high-speed general-application systems that allow such spontaneous interactivity. Few systems today enable totally free interaction or impromptu modification of the model by users. Those that do are dedicated to special problems and cannot yet be easily adapted for use in other applications.

Neural interface technology in the form of biocontrollers (described in Chapter 6) may eventually give a user volitional control over electronic devices directly from nervous system signals. [Lusted&92] However, indications are that it will be quite a while before this technology appears anywhere near your desktop.

The Whole Body As a Sending/Receiving Device

So far, discussion has centered on a human getting information through enhanced visualization — images received via his or her eyes, but this is only one of many ways in which we receive information. The impact of any experience is heightened by increased involvement of all the senses, but because pictorial representation is usually so effective as a means of communication, it overshadows what we receive through our other senses.

Some researchers are concerned about our becoming photo-chauvinists and underline the importance of our other senses in collecting and assimilating information. They refer to the body as a "sensorial combinetric integrator" [Warner&92] — in other words, a receiver and processor of lots of different kinds of simultaneous sensory stimulation. Muscles, tendons and joints that respond to stimuli are called proprioceptors, and researchers refer to visual, proprioceptive and auditory experiences in VR environments.

Touch screens used as interfaces to a computer system generally rely on pressure, sound waves or infrared beams. Now, there are touch screens available that rely, instead, on the human body's ability to conduct electricity — subtle recognition of its potential as an interface. The various ways in which this and other means of receiving input are represented and realized in virtual-reality experiences are discussed in context throughout the book and in "Tactile Facilities" in Chapter 3.

COLLABORATIVE DESIGN:
PSYCHOLOGICAL & SOCIAL FACTORS

Virtual reality is, ultimately, a medium for communication and a means for fostering insight. Technical advances are only the beginning of this and sensory immersion only one facet. Social, emotional and cognitive factors comprise equally enriching dimensions to any human experience, and it is in incorporating these aspects into applications that the creativity and sensitivity of VR designers will be challenged. Virtual reality is, after all, experiential.

In much the same way that a telephone is merely a tool to facilitate the art of conversation, the physical technology of virtual reality remains primarily only a facilitator in the art of communication. A technically astute program designer (sometimes called an "author") cannot alone decide how people interact in particular situations. Psychological factors and knowledge of instinctual behavior are very important, and specialists need to be involved as collaborative authors in the design process.

How It Looks, or How It Walks?

A person can absorb and synthesize only so much information per second — even if a firehose of data is turned on — and different people doused by the same hose will intellectually and instinctively assimilate interestingly different combinations of bits. (Teachers sometimes make students aware of this by staging incidents during class, then pointing out the differences among their eyewitness accounts.) In creating complex virtual environments, determining exactly which bits are absolutely necessary to convey an idea is a difficult task. Designers can easily produce firehose-force streams of bits that drown an application or fail to exploit commonality among users.

Data are expensive to gather, generate and display. So, beginning in the planning and design stage of a virtual environment and continuing through its completion, designers must strive for data efficiency. They must know which kinds of data will most effectively convince most users to believe that what is happening is "real" and which data do little to reinforce the effect. Have you ever noticed that Mickey Mouse has only *four* fingers on each hand? Disney animators knew where to draw the line.

A genteel controversy is going on between researchers at both ends of a looks-vs.-walks spectrum. At one end are those who believe image perfection is the way to reinforce believability. At the other are those who feel that fluidity of movement is the crucial factor, however elementary the display may look. [Brooks88]

As technologies and the work of people at both ends of the spectrum progress, the gap between the fluidity of movement and detail will narrow. Ideally, the virtual scene created will both *look* real and appear to *move* realistically.

Domain Expertise

Programs that deal with specific problems need to incorporate the ways experts in that particular area of expertise do things. Therefore, the ability to mimic the communication and exploratory patterns of domain experts must be built into systems, and domain experts must be involved at all stages of the design process of VR applications. Only they can provide clues to the patterns of behavior underlying their skills and the types of communication required for their field of expertise. It would serve little purpose to simulate a polo match if real patterns of behavior and communication needs of polo players in a competitive setting were not anticipated and programmed into the system.

The ability to precisely mimic human movement must be built into all systems in which users play roles. These movements range from low levels such as those required for digging a hole to very high levels of detail such as a brain surgeon's technique for delicate intervention. For instance, planetary geologists routinely carry out aerial reconnaissance, and the relevant features for this have been built into the Virtual Planetary Exploration (VPE) system (described in Chapter 12). Other geologists sample outcrops in the field. The capability of mimicking the manipulation of tools and use of the hands by either type of real geologist must be incorporated, for instance, into virtual systems dealing with their domains.

REALITY & RETURN ON INVESTMENT

Costs

In this light of virtual reality as a means of communication and extension of knowledge, the efficacy of some technically superb applications must be questioned. Ongoing discussion among players in the field can be compared to a debate on the use of life-support systems — sure, it's possible, but is it always worth it? As developers drive to make virtual worlds more realistic and technically elegant, they must re-examine them at various stages to determine if the return on investment is, indeed, worth the expense and intensity of effort. Often, it is not.

There will always be the temptation to indulge a form of myopia in the bright light of each technical success, but technology is most effectively executed when held subordinate to a higher aim. Careful selection of the problems we want the experts to tackle is important. The energy and resources poured into applications must be focused and contained to obtain useful results. [Brooks91] In other words, is there a pressing, human problem that can be *solved* by this application of expensive, intellect-intensive technology? By demanding an answer to that question, research in virtual reality identifies itself as an applied science, parting company with pure science or basic research, which may spawn useful by-products but is driven primarily by a need to *know*.

Select Efforts

In any search to find the most effective VR means for the most valuable results, very specific questions arise. For example, can better results be obtained with head-mounted displays than with conventional screen displays? Before researchers can know, controlled experiments need to be conducted, and the significance of their results must be analyzed. One such test pits window display vs. head-mounted display for beam placement in the treatment of cancerous tumors. [Ming&89]

In some carefully chosen experiments, results have shown that the enhanced technology of virtual reality illuminated problems more clearly and cut solution times significantly. For example, for simple, six-dimensional (6-D) molecular docking maneuvers, virtual force-feedback displays provide better results than conventional visual displays. For assembly tasks, the addition of stereo effects to the displays increased user accuracy, and tactile response combined with head-mounted displays has made solutions a lot easier in enzyme-connecting trials than have previous window displays.

Displaying
Virtually Real Images

2

THE VR SYSTEM: MACHINES & THINGS

A VR system is actually comprised of many systems. Resting on a basic foundation of hardware, software and electronics are independent systems that have been developed to produce the kinds of visual, audio or tactile effects used in virtual environments.

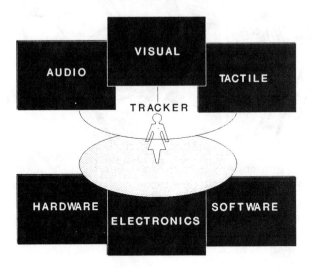

Each of these systems reinforces one aspect of a user's illusion of immersion within the virtual world. All of them draw from and are integrated with the available hardware, software and electronics setup so that they act in concert with each other. Their components are described in more detail in Chapter 3.

3-D IMMERSIVE GRAPHICS

Instead of the picture-to-look-at offered by conventional imaging, virtual reality provides a user with a world-to-experience. Admittedly, it is an electronic cartoon world.

As visual art, immersive graphics bank heavily on the user's wanting to believe. Nonetheless, it is one in which a person can feel immersed. Like operagoers who, engaged by grand scores and magnificent stage sets, readily forgive plots that today border on nonsense, users caught up in the clever graphics and interactivity of virtual worlds forgive their rather primitive achievement of reality and plot.

Opaque or Transparent

A displayed image can appear to the user in either of two ways: *opaque*, in which the view of the virtual environment blocks out and supplants the view of the real world; or as a *"see-through"* display, in which the virtual images seem superimposed on the real world, which remains visible through the visor.

In effect, an opaque display replaces the real world; an overlay enhances it. When a user chooses transparent display over opaque and continues to rely on the real world as a frame of reference, it is more "augmented" than "virtual" reality.

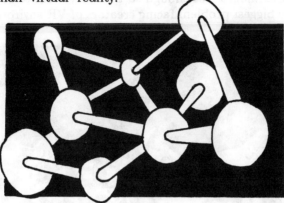

The transparent overlay is effected via half-silvered optical surfaces in front of each eye — in a visor-type setup. Images generated onto the visor appear as electronic etchings on surfaces of the real world — visual aids and notes that relate to and are seen as superimpositions on the real world.

The choice between opaque and transparent displays is often critical. In the following sections, the differences are discussed in the context of specific applications.

Real-Time Polygon Generation

The speed of the machine used to produce virtual images is important. Generating the images fast enough so that they seem to reflect real-time actions is the biggest problem facing creators of VR environments.

Each image is a mosaic of many small polygons, and each of these is generated separately by the computer. To approach realistic, near real-time visual sequences, a computer needs to generate more than 30,000 polygons per second, and the scenario must be updated a minimum of 6 times per second for even a borderline semblance of movement fluidity.

There is always a trade-off between speed and image quality. The algorithms to convert data points into little, lighted pixels on a screen or in a virtual scene are generally great consumers of computer resources.

Most high-quality machines *can* produce sharp, complex images, but slowly. Of course, they can produce simple, fuzzy ones fast. Few machines can produce high-resolution, complex images fast.

A lot of work is being done to speed up good image production and display. After his initial forays into virtual worlds 35 years ago, Ivan Sutherland ventured out to explore a number of other innovative ideas but did not abandon the VR scene completely. Evans & Sutherland, Inc.'s latest workstation device, a graphics "accelerator," purportedly produces images twice as fast as other systems. Other experiments with multicomputers are able to render up to 2 million polygons per second at a resolution of 1280x1024 pixels [Brooks91], slightly sharper than the screen of a good computer workstation.

Handmade screens customized for the secret Super Cockpit project of the U.S. Air Force display startlingly realistic flight conditions, and researchers have admitted to genuine fright when subjected to their simulated crashes. In fact, one trainee pilot fainted when an "approach" failed.

To date only the Super Cockpit and a few other military applications, such as the fighter plane environments used to train pilots for the Gulf War, approach a level realistic enough to completely fool users. The best quality most other applications offer is still only enhanced cartoon-quality. This does not necessarily sabotage a program, but efforts to minimize the distraction caused by less-than-realistic imaging include importing images of real-world backdrops and objects. Work is being funded for image "grabbing" systems to allow developers to capture, store and modify real scenes for use in virtual environments.

The ideal — photorealistic imaging displayed in real time — has an insatiable appetite for computer power, and the failure of most systems to be able to generate such high-quality images at such high speeds is the major roadblock to realistic virtual environments. What can be done computationally is still very far from what can be done photographically, and how effective such environments are hinges greatly on the willingness of the viewer to overlook imperfections. Fortunately, researchers have found most users remarkably eager to push skepticism aside!

Haptic Enhancement

Another type of virtual display, one that is used along with the visual, is the haptic display. In a haptic display, things seem to push, pull, radiate or sensate in different directions with varying degrees of strength. For instance, objects within the virtual world can be assigned force fields, torque, friction, heat and pressure, which become noticeable to a person interacting with them. Haptic displays are used in games to enhance feelings of speed or gravity and by pharmaceutical chemists to find optimal docking sites on molecules for things such as enzymes.

Interacting in a haptic environment requires patience and a keen alertness to clues. One system uses a "haptly" named mechanical device named GROPE. Indeed, in a spatial virtual setting, rather than real clues, one does seem to grope around randomly, blind-man's-bluff-style, until some sort of positive feedback is provided — much like being "it" in a game of hide-and-seek, with only hints of "getting warmer" or "getting colder" to help you out. Signals from a haptic display are meant to be interpreted by the user so that he or she can adjust movements to achieve some goal.

Participants in particular virtual worlds become accustomed to certain cues and use them to estimate real depth or force or distance. Practice improves both performance and the level of perceived realism. Designers help by including in the model lots of telltale lines and angles, forcing things to take on an orderly perspective. Exceptions to this would be instances in which some sort of order is sought from amidst disarray, such as when searching for parallel structures in atoms or molecules. In such cases, the addition of background grids may mask the structures.

Force feedback, even for the most simple of virtual objects, is a very difficult task, and haptic displays are not designed as "touch" machines but rather as environments from which a person is able to glean some knowledge of properties associated with the objects represented, such as weight or solidity, from signals delivered through the equipment. Despite the quality or intensity of the feedback, one still cannot sit on a virtual chair. Even with built-in "collision" software, it is easy to drift through walls.

Gloves and bodysuits are gradually being lined with areas that relay haptic and tactile effects to their wearers. These are connected to the computer and controlled to lend realistic effects to the displays. They are described in more detail in Chapter 3.

Real-Space Imaging

An image appearing in virtual space but totally dependent on something in real space is called a real-space image. A real-space image appears only under very specific conditions and in a specific location within the environment. These images, which can resemble almost anything, are informative and useful only when viewed in relation to real-world-based things or in the context of real-world conditions, and the user must share their virtual space to see it. The image, generated in virtual space but totally dependent on coordinates linked to real space, usually appears to the user as a type of transparent overlay on the scene.

As virtual objects are created, any real-world specifics upon which they might be based — e.g., relevant conditions, conceptual context, altitude, latitude and longitude — are catalogued and registered in a database linked to the system. Thus, they become "context-sensitive" images that are visible only when meaningful. When the coordinates of the images registered in the database fit within those of the virtual environment being explored, the images are displayed.

In other words, if the virtual object is a subset of any virtual environment and belongs there, it appears. It remains as long as the conditions of place and context are met. If the user moves out of that environment or if the context or conditions change so that the image is no longer relevant, the image disappears.

Current Limitations of VR Display Units

Regarding VR display units, there are many problems to be overcome. Among those cited in [Holloway&91] are:

- low image quality of small LCDs (i.e., low resolution);

- expense and availability of tiny CRT systems;

- elimination of the lag between user motion and system response;

- wide field of view in stereo that is superimposed on the view of the real world;

- superimposition of virtual objects on the real world in a way that makes sense to the human visual system;

- comfort vs. encumbrance of VR-users' head and body gear;

- performance of non-real-time operating systems;

- ability to model complex virtual worlds;

- image generation for complex scenes.

Depending on the application, any one of these can marginally dampen or completely thwart development efforts. Researchers are struggling to find ways to clear up as many of these problem areas as possible; otherwise, efforts will remain within the military for still more time.

DELIVERY

A VR delivery system needs to provide wide-angle, high-resolution and well-focused images to users' eyes. The image-delivery systems for virtual environments must create scenes that are realistically detailed. These must be displayed to correspond with scenes a user would see if moving around in that environment, were it real. Once realizations of virtual worlds are created, they can be stored electronically and be called up or transmitted across networks as needed.

Presentation Modes: User's Point of View

Images are usually presented either cylindrically or spherically. Some entertainment applications use projected imagery, in which players' movements and actions are detected, and real-time phantom images of them are superimposed upon a screen in front of them.

In cylindrical presentation mode, panoramic, 360-degree images appear to surround the viewer laterally but there are no ceiling or floor images. Even so, a user gets a good sense of being within a realistic environment.

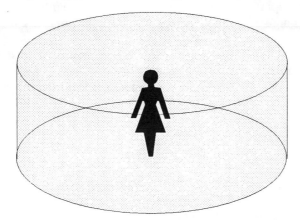

Alternately, images can be displayed in a visual hemisphere or dome around the user, in which case total vertical head movement is accommodated in a type of surround-sight. Occasionally, a type of grid is added as a ground plane reference.

Because the display must be computed and recomputed on the fly as the user turns, there can be noticeable latency — a lag between head movement and visualization, thus impairing the effect of realism. Put simply, a user turns his or her head, and the scene catches up. A major goal of product developers is to minimize latency, and millisecond differences are aggressively advertised.

In most cases, a user sees the virtual world from an egocentric point of view, i.e., he or she is central to it. Occasionally, however, a user may want to view things from an outsider's vantage point. In that case, his or her relative location could be marked and changed by a virtual arrow, like a movable "You are here" spot on a shopping mall or tourist guide.

Projected Displays

This type of display requires no helmets, gloves or suits. Instead, a video system merges a real-time image of the user with a 2-D computer-generated scene, which is then projected as a distant image that fills a user's field of vision. With projection systems, since the display device is not worn, user fatigue is low. Maintenance costs are generally lower, too, for projection systems, and image distortion is minimal when the display is hooked up to devices with high resolution, such as some computer screens.

Users integrate their movements with the display and appear to interact with each other and with virtual images portrayed there. Being able to observe one's own self as part of the screen environment promotes a user's sense of immersion. It is a technique used extensively in the government sector for wide-angle field weapons simulators.

COPING WITH COMPLEXITY

Precomputed Images

There is an advantage to limiting the image generation to only lateral-surround display. Panoramic displays are less subject than spherical displays to the trade-offs mentioned earlier between time and quality. By limiting a user's movement (but only to the extent that believability is not jeopardized), the toll on the machine is greatly reduced. Sparing the machine the overhead of generating even a few hundred polygonal image-pieces frees the resources to the point at which they can be allocated instead to prepare anticipated images and store them "on call" in memory. It then no longer needs to constantly recompute and generate an image in real time every time the user's head moves.

NASA has done it well. In their systems, a whole 360-degree panorama is preprogrammed and precomputed, then stored ahead of time in frame buffers — the computer's temporary storage. Since these images aren't computed on the fly, users aren't subjected to lags. Instead, they are presented with previously rendered images as soon as a change of position and orientation (i.e., movement) is detected. Also, because the immediacy factor is removed from the image-generating process, the precomputed images tend to be more detailed, complex and realistic-looking than those produced in rapid succession in real time.

Adaptive Refinement

Another way of coping with the computational complexity of a user on the move is to generate full-detail scenes only when the user becomes stationary. As the level of activity is heightened, the periphery seems to disappear or regress into simplistic form.

In a virtual display, a person traversing quickly from one location to another notices the level of reality drop and heighten again as soon as he or she "stands still." In other words, realism and interactivity play against one another.

This trade-off between image realism and interactivity, referred to as adaptive refinement, is made to some degree in all current systems. Any reduced need for interactivity allows for a higher level of realism. Also, by rendering only what would be within the view of the user, i.e., a subset of the whole model, the toll on the system is reduced; therefore, the display is speeded up, and the effect of realism is further enhanced.

The use of the technology and equipment is already refined enough to seem transparent to most users, and the tendency of our brains to fill in what's missing in near-complete sensations augments a VR system's power of suggestion. Even if being hooked up to a headset sacrifices some realism, a person perceives — as if by wishful thinking — that he or she is central to the computer-created environment and conducts his or her moves as an integral, active part of it. Users of virtual-reality systems are generally willing to allow their minds and eyes to be fooled — a lucky break for developers.

Levels of Immersion

Many different levels and degrees of sensory immersion are included under the umbrella of virtual reality. Each application can be designed to accommodate varying degrees of suspended belief or telepresent manipulation. Primitive 3-D spaces qualify, as do shadowy endoscopic images or objects.

By viewing a three-dimensional space, a person is subjected to an elementary level of virtual immersion. If, within that space, objects are defined for user perception and manipulation of the images is possible, the user is subjected to another level of immersion. "Total" immersion, however, requires that all reference to the real world be effectively blocked, substitute stimuli be provided, and a user be convinced it is real. This is immersion at an environment level.

Market potential and demand for applications exist at all of these levels — space, object and environment. Chapters 6 through 14 explore things being done to meet those demands.

Things You Need to Create a Virtual World

3

Software consists of the programs you buy, usually on disks that you insert into the front of your computer or on circuit cards that plug into the chassis. Hardware components for a system are usually obtained from several manufacturers. This chapter deals with what's special about a virtual-reality (VR) system; it does not address general aspects of operating systems, peripherals, processing units and so forth.

For purposes here, it suffices to say that hardware for virtual reality runs all the way from relatively inexpensive peripherals for a personal computer (PC) or MacIntosh to systems that cost several hundreds of thousands of dollars. It is important to realize only that they do come in all sizes, but speed and power are expensive. Even the smallest size can be pricy.

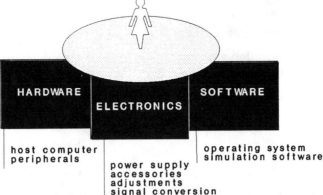

It may also be helpful to know how some of the basic components for VR tie in to a system. A number of independent systems tie in to the base of hardware, software and electronics, and others provide audio, visual and tactile effects.

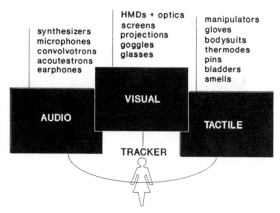

synthesizers
microphones
convolvotrons
acoutestrons
earphones

HMDs + optics
screens
projections
goggles
glasses

manipulators
gloves
bodysuits
thermodes
pins
bladders
smells

VISUAL

AUDIO

TACTILE

TRACKER

When it comes to operating systems, the manufacturer of whatever computer system you have will have specified one of a number of operating systems for it. UNIX is very widely used, especially in university research environments. Most manufacturers of peripheral equipment have adapted their products to these standard operating systems.

STANDARD INPUT/OUTPUT (I/O) DEVICES

Input devices are pieces of equipment used to put data or information into a computer. Early input devices were cards punched with series of holes that were meaningful to a binary machine, the computer. A later and still current input device is the keyboard on which we type.

Human frustration with these devices led to the development of other, more "friendly" devices for inputting data. Examples of these are:

- a mouse
- touch screens
- a pen or stylus
- knobs and joysticks

- scanners
- voices synthesizers
- head-mounted pointers
- biocontrollers

An output device is anything from which data or information are received via computer. Early output devices were very much like teletype machines; from computer-readable data, they produced ribbons of data that humans could understand. Later, the category included printers, video displays, synthesized voice and other devices that translate machine-readable data for delivery to the outside world. Some devices, called Input/Output (I/O) devices or channels, are dual-purpose, for two-way traffic, to and from the computer. A phone modem is an I/O device.

Many standard I/O devices are used for virtual-reality applications. However, an even more flexible, more powerful arsenal is needed if designers are to meet the unique challenge of creating and developing virtual environments. Since a virtual environment is primarily meant to be an arena of heightened communication, all means available must be explored for interacting with it. The degree to which flexibility and potential for qualitative input and output can be built into it greatly determines how well a developer realizes his or her design.

Standard input devices haven't provided the flexibility of nuance that creative designers need; so, new models and customized variations are cropping up almost daily. Eventually, these, too, will become relatively standard. The following sections describe some of the specialized equipment and I/O devices used for virtual-reality applications.

HEAD-MOUNTED EQUIPMENT

The angles from which we receive input to our senses — from behind us, beside us or ahead of us — influence our perception of the world around us. By synthesizing all the locational clues received through our sensory channels, we determine where something is in relation to our body. A number of these sensory channels, e.g., our eyes for sight, ears for sound, nose for smell and mouth for taste, are located in the head; so, it is not surprising that the headpiece is currently the most important part of the arsenal of gear for a visitor to a virtual environment. It is also one of the most complex. Ivan Sutherland noted that, when he started work on the head-mounted display, he had "no idea how much effort would be involved." [Sutherland68]

Headpieces are called head-mounted display units (HMDs). Some resemble helmets from which viewing devices are suspended in front of users' eyes. Another type resembles a diving mask without the pipe, and the simplest are shuttered glasses or goggles hanging from a head brace.

Full-color, wide-angle stereoscopic viewing devices give a slightly different image to each eye so that the images produced (i.e., the virtual environment) appear to have depth. Some units are fitted with earphones for audio accompaniment. Eventually, perhaps, the means to feed stimuli back to other senses will be built into the headpieces, as well.

Good headpieces are commercially available, but some research groups prefer to develop their own or customize those obtained from vendors for particular applications. Game developers are already selling a type of face apparatus for use with real-time adventure videos. These are gadgets that fit over the nose and mouth. A player's face gestures are mimicked by the animated character in the game. [MIRT] Japanese developers are pushing efforts to find technology to replace or minimize headpieces, or "face suckers," as they are sometimes called.

Headpiece Viewing Apparatus

Two types of viewing devices are currently being used to display virtual realizations — cathode-ray-tube devices (CRTs) and liquid-crystal-display devices (LCDs). CRTs, basically little televisions, deliver bright, high-resolution pictures but are cumbersome, especially for mounting on headgear; they tend to be heavy, bulky and thick. Because liquid-crystal displays are light and flat, like the type found on calculators or digital watches, developers of early versions of head-mounted displays preferred them, even though the best images they could produce were grainy and mosaic-like. LCDs were also inexpensive and used little electrical power.

Recent developments in technology, however, have made small, high-resolution CRT displays possible, and LCDs are now being replaced in many systems. Tiny, 1-inch television-like screens can now display clear images with a resolution of 1000x1000 pixels. (For comparison purposes, a good workstation displays images with a resolution of 1280x1024 pixels.) Until this year, most LCD resolution topped out at 100x100 pixels for 1-inch displays; so, there was a vast performance difference.

Preference will flip-flop again for many applications as the resolution gap narrows. Sony now has a full-color LCD panel only 0.7 inches square that displays well over 100,000 pixels.

Head-mounted displays are used for medical imaging, molecular realizations, architectural walk-throughs and some arcade games. As the wearer turns, the scene moves in the opposite direction, and the person feels as though he or she is within it.

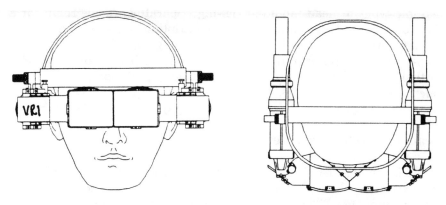

Field of vision improvements are complicated to specify and develop, and currently, a viewer has no peripheral vision. For high-performance HMDs, fields of view do not exceed 70 degrees per eye (and there is overlap). The goal is to improve the optical systems so that, ultimately, a user sees a 180-degree field of view displayed at any one time. Efforts are also being made to better control the generation of video images to left- and right-eye displays. The signals for both types of visual apparatus are standard, American-video NTSC signals generated by the computer.

Some HMDs aim to keep the actual computer-generated displays away from the head, instead relaying the high-resolution images via fiber-optics to lightweight lenses suspended near the eyes. A person may also waive head mounts altogether (forfeiting the sensation of total immersion) in favor of a "scene view," viewing the display on a large screen or through a terminal window. In this case, instead of headgear, which tends to feel heavy after extended wear, a person uses "shutter glasses" or goggles.

Glasses are used when viewing special scenes videotaped for television. The images appear three-dimensional (3-D) because each eye receives a unique picture. (When viewed without the goggles, the picture quivers.) This type of compromise is useful for small-screen virtual desktop setups.

Large-screen viewing is suitable for large-area or long-distance virtual environments such as architectural walk-throughs or bicycle touring. Small-screen or terminal viewing often suffices for small-area, focused applications (e.g., molecule building).

Some types of head-mounted viewing apparatus provide room for a user to wear eyeglasses; others don't. Descriptions for a few versions of viewing apparatus can be found in Appendix B. Initially, the EyePhone was the most popular and widely used. Now, other vendors, notably Virtual Reality, Inc., produce very sophisticated, special-purpose units for defense and medical purposes.

Headpiece Audio Facilities

Sound is important to a person's spatial awareness and is most effective when visual clues are minimal or absent. Sound effects also make visual effects come alive. Think how a thriller seems to lose its edge when its sound track is muted.

There are many instances, too, in which VR designers include audio features — for enhancing the visual and, because we tend to turn in the direction of sounds we hear, to help direct our eyes. Entertainment and game applications are the most visible examples, but among the other audio-augmented applications are control-tower or cockpit displays, telerobotic activity in hazardous environments, exploration and monitoring of multidimensional data and some kinds of teleconferencing.

Audio components containing a real-time signal-processing subsystem synthesize external, 3-D sounds. These recreate the filtering effects we experience from the irregular shape of our outer ears and give directional cues. But humans are not good at judging exactly how far away sound sources are and may even reverse back to front or up to down if the sounds are familiar. Developers try to produce unambiguous synthesized sound sources. How they accomplish this is interesting.

Small probe microphones are placed near the two eardrums of a real person seated in an echoless chamber. Sounds from as many as 144 locations are tested. From the different ways these sounds are filtered by a natural ear, a map of location filters is built. This allows researchers to recreate sounds that are similarly filtered and, thus, seem to be locational. [Wenzel&90] To render sounds this way and intertwine them to seem 3-dimensional is to "convolve" them. Systems that do it consist of components with formidable names like convolvotron and acoustetron.

Two different audio feeds are incorporated into headgear earphones, providing the wearer with simultaneous sounds from as many as four sources. They are synchronized with the program.

The sounds are usually selected from a CD-ROM library of prerecorded sound effects and generated by a computer used as a dedicated digital sound server. About 1000 sounds are available, e.g., clicks or thunks to signal contact between virtual objects; whooshing for flying effect, gurgling for water, etc.

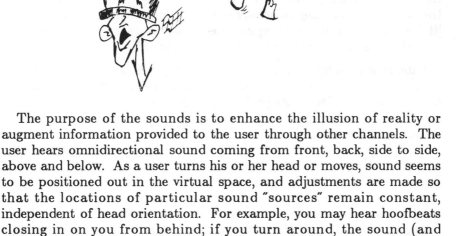

The purpose of the sounds is to enhance the illusion of reality or augment information provided to the user through other channels. The user hears omnidirectional sound coming from front, back, side to side, above and below. As a user turns his or her head or moves, sound seems to be positioned out in the virtual space, and adjustments are made so that the locations of particular sound "sources" remain constant, independent of head orientation. For example, you may hear hoofbeats closing in on you from behind; if you turn around, the sound (and probably an image of the horse!) will seem to be coming right at you. As you step aside, you may watch the horse pass you by, accompanied by a Doppler-effect rendition of the hoofbeats.

Not all systems have sophisticated, three-dimensional audio features. To adapt systems to incorporate audio effects, special control boards are needed for the computer. Often, software must be either written or modified to include sound. Occasionally, in the absence of device-mounted channels, loudspeakers are used.

This type of stereoscopic "surround-sound," sometimes called spatial sound, is being used in many nonvirtual systems, such as the navigation and tracking systems for pilots. What is picked up by radar is reinforced by directional aural clues, giving the pilot more to work with in potentially dangerous situations than just visual blips on a radar screen. Similar systems are being developed for flight controllers to augment the information displayed on their standard tracking screens. Some voice input is possible through speech recognizers. These allow users to issue some "no-hands" commands to the system — but at a price; they require separate processors but support only minimal multiuser communication.

TRACKERS

For tracking purposes, a physical device is attached to the object or user so that head or hand movements can be detected. This is usually done by electromagnetic or optical means. The movements are translated into position and orientation coordinates, which are deciphered by the computer. Then, images corresponding to that viewpoint are displayed.

Both types of position sensors, electromagnetic and optical, put constraints on the user. Currently, someone using an electromagnetic tracking device is restricted to a spherical working space of only 4 or 5 feet across. Ceiling trackers using light-emitting diodes (LEDs) extend the working space considerably — but do not yet exceed room size. [Holloway&91] Many tracking systems require a clear line of sight at all times between the sensor and the target or user.

Latency is a factor in both types of tracking, although the lag appears to be more problematic with electromagnetic systems than with optical ones. Users of electromagnetic trackers may also encounter noise interference or performance degradation from metallic distortion in certain environments.

Headpiece Tracking Features

In electromagnetic systems, the most popular device, Polhemus, keeps tabs on a user's change of position or orientation by reading alternating magnetic fields. For head tracking, the little sensor is stuck on top of the head-mounted display unit. Sensors can be mounted elsewhere, as well, such as on gloves or inside ball devices.

Due to diffusion of the magnetic fields at both ends, there is a fraction-of-a-second lag between a user's head movement and a corresponding response from the display generator. This lag needs to be lessened.

As the user moves, calculations are being done, and the images are constantly regenerated and updated. These images reflect changes in the virtual scene corresponding to what the user would expect to see if similar movements were made in a real environment.

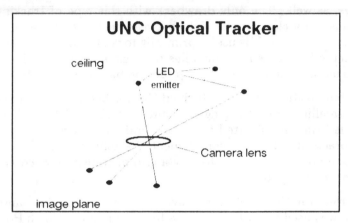

In optical systems, ceiling panels are embedded with as many as 1000 infrared LED beacons that serve as navigation beacons. Since the position of each light in the ceiling is known, the computer turns on those LEDs in the field of view of cameras mounted on top of the headgear worn by the user. Lateral-effect photodiodes make it possible for the cameras to gather information from the turned-on beacons. Then the computer uses a fancy algorithm called space reception by colinearity to calculate the position and orientation of the user's head and generate an appropriate display. Currently, the rate of updates depends on the number of LEDs that are visible. Rough calculations can be based upon as few as three lighted beacons.

Optical tracking is usually possible with minimal hardware, but the management of the information gathering elements requires great attention to detail. Exactly positioning the beacons, correctly mounting the cameras and calibrating the photodiodes to gather accurate information are crucial to the success of the application.

Alternate Tracking Research

Ultrasonic, gyroscopic and mechanical devices are also used for tracking purposes but comprise only a small portion of the tracking techniques used for virtual-reality applications. Ultrasonic devices are relatively inexpensive but are sensitive to outside noises and require obstruction-free paths between signallers and microphones; gyroscopic devices are accurate and compact but are expensive and suffer over time from drift; and mechanical devices are simple and inexpensive but physically limiting.

Shuttles could place many satellites into orbit, each of which would give out radio signals that a receiver and computer could convert into bearings. If two satellites are used, a two-dimensional map reading would be possible; three would provide enough data to include altitude readings, as well. The only drawback with this type of tracking is that there must be a clear line of sight between each satellite and the target being tracked. Thus, it is useful primarily for outdoor units such as those implemented by trucking companies to track and route vehicles. Dutch farmers use a version of this to keep tabs on bar-coded piglets.

A global positioning system (coined GPS) is being used by the military, and its satellite-based tracking is accurate to about 7 feet. This type of system is being investigated for public and airline use. However, it will not be practical until a full complement of satellites is in orbit and covers all surface areas (similar to the way a grid of transmitters covers ground areas for cellular phones).

Receivers for GPS are already available for several thousand dollars, and one was used recently to track a lone skier to the North Pole. Some luxury models of Japanese cars are being fitted with GPS units on the assembly line. When used more extensively, the units will work in conjunction with existing satellite communications terminals.

Research is being done combining systems. Self-tracking, optical radar and optical laser tracking are also being investigated and tested. They hold particular promise for advancing applications in which the user cannot be tethered to a laboratory — such as outdoors, in large spaces or for use with virtual desktop displays.

Positioning & Orientation: Absolute or Relative

Two types of values are used to determine where something is and how it "sits" in the virtual environment. If its position and orientation are measured from a single point of origin, for example, one "corner" of the virtual space, the values are *absolute*. Coordinates for tracking (loosely akin to values for altitude, latitude and longitude) are *constants* within that virtual space. If an object is moved, previous measurements don't count; its new position and orientation are remeasured each time from the "corner."

Some systems use no absolute points of reference for tracking but establish position and orientation values *relative* to a previous position and orientation. The coordinates of a virtual object are reset to zero after being moved and are calculated anew from there whenever it is moved again. Only the *changes* of position or orientation of a virtual object (relative to where it was immediately before movement) are sent to the tracking sensor.

BOOMs

BOOM stands for Binocular Omni-Orientation Monitor, a type of stereoscopic viewing device that has become a popular alternate to head-mounted devices. As a floor-standing device, the BOOM requires little customization and can be passed easily among a number of users. Using it is not unlike using an enlarged version of the View-Masters we played with as children.

A long rod, perched at its center, swings around upon a jointed gimbal with 6-degree-of-freedom movement. This means that any one movement may entail changes in as many as three different spatial positions or three degrees of orientation. Six-degree-of-freedom tracking techniques, by the way, are not limited to use with the BOOM. They are often used with other devices, as well.

Any tracking calculation is a composite of the measurements taken simultaneously of the three different positions and the three orientations. Optical encoders at each of the six joints of the BOOM feed the system this high-precision information about the position and orientation of the user's head.

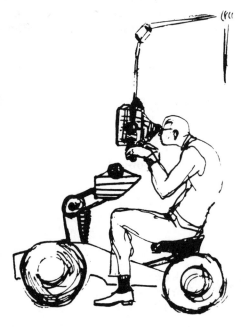

The viewing box is suspended from a swivelling frame at one end, its weight counterbalanced by a weight at the other. Two handles are located near the base of the box and are used for pulling and holding the box snugly to your face and steering it to display different views.

Current models present monochrome, color and "pseudo" color scenes in a cylindrical display space about 5 feet in diameter and 5 feet high. Its field of view, at any one time, is about 140 degrees horizontally by 90 degrees vertically. Its stereo effect is basically achieved by rendering red-shaded images to the left eye and blue-shaded images to the right eye.

The use of a BOOM has certain advantages over the use of a head-mounted device, especially if it is to be used for a long period of time. Because an HMD is actually worn by a user, there are limits to how heavy it can be or how long it can be used without becoming uncomfortable. (A few models, though, have attachable handles and need not be worn but can be held up like a costume-ball mask in front of the eyes.) Also, as noted before, most head-mounted displays are fitted with lightweight LCDs, and these produce only grainy, low-resolution (720x480-pixel) images. A BOOM's weight, however, is not worn and borne by the user; so, BOOMs can make use of CRT display technology — heavy little televisions with a resolution of 1280 by 1024 pixels per eye. This is good enough for sharp, detailed images.

The BOOM can be suspended over a person's workstation so that someone can access the virtual scene while seated at a terminal, yet easily swing it out of the way for other work. A BOOM's built-in mechanical tracking devices also eliminate the need for an electromagnetic tracking system, avoiding problems of distortion and latency often associated with magnetic interference.

BOOMs are best used for straight viewing or simple navigation and are particularly suited to projects such as scientific visualization and simulation and for building training and entertainment modules. Some research centers use BOOMs instead of head-mounted devices for molecular modeling and fluid dynamics studies. However, since hand devices are not usually connected to the setup, a BOOM is not suitable if users want to select or manipulate objects in the virtual environment.

CONTROL DEVICES

Early prototypes of control devices for VR use were jerry-rigged for experiments. At the University of North Carolina Chapel Hill site, researchers actually took apart little TVs and wired them up to use for eye displays. Today, widespread use and customer demand are provoking developers of VR components to consider packaging and ergometrics in the design process. Control devices are becoming increasingly elegant extensions to persons using them rather than unwieldy distractions. Ease of use varies among devices and types of applications, and practitioners tend to have favorites. All require getting used to.

Glove

Probably the most ubiquitous device for control and input to a virtual system is a glove "instrumented" with flexible fiber optics running along each of the hand joints. These sense changes in the position or movement of the hand and relay them to the computer. Gloves are separate devices that can be interfaced with any computer systems, and most early applications, from video games up through multimillion-dollar military research projects, used gloves developed and sold by one vendor. When these tended to have poor performance after a few months, other vendors jumped in with sturdier versions, and a buyer now has many choices.

At first glance, the glove looks like a wired ski glove; however, other, less cumbersome elastic types are being developed, perhaps spurred by programmers' not being able to type with the bulky versions. Among the newer models are fingerless gloves that allow the user to manipulate things in the real environment (such as a keyboard) while still hooked up to the virtual environment. Fingerless gloves are also more comfortable because areas of the fingers and palms are exposed and ventilated. Most gloves come in small, medium and large sizes and in left- and right-handed versions.

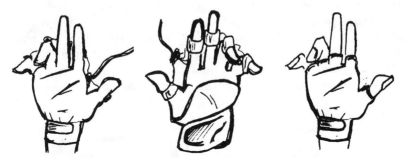

Currently, these glove connections are designed to measure flexion and extension of the major joints of the hand. Some can be customized to measure abduction and the minor joints, as well. Finger bends, pinkie or thumb rotation and the yaw and pitch of the wrist or arch of the palm are converted by flex sensors into computer-readable form. Some versions are adapted to convert fingerspelling or International Sign Language into synthesized speech.

The thin, fiber-optic cables running along the fingers are sectioned according to the joints of the hand. Each section protrudes a bit beyond its joint and is tipped with a light-emitting diode (LED). The amount of light detected passing through the fiber is proportional to the degree to which its corresponding joint is bent. This information is sent to the system, which determines which finger is being bent by how much, etc.

Also incorporated into the glove is a separate tracking mechanism that uses magnetic detection to determine the spatial coordinates of the hand's position, where it is in relation to the whole scene, and of its orientation, i.e., where it is in relation to the imaginary body. The two separate systems relay their information to the computer.

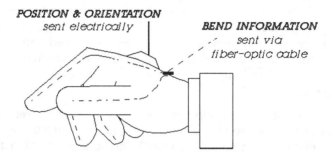

Bend information is sent via the fiber-optic cable, and the position and pitch information is sent electrically. Two-handed systems are possible, in which case each hand is an independent system requiring a separate control unit and separate computer channel.

As the combined position and bend information is received by the computer, the program generates and maintains an animated version of a similarly moving hand (usually floating) within the virtual environment. Its finger and joint movements correspond with those made by the user wearing the glove. The hand's coordinates are determined by movements made by the user relative to the virtual environment perceived.

Wiggle your fingers, and the animated fingers wiggle, too. Raise your hand, and the displayed hand appears to move up in the virtual world. It is through this animated hand that a user is projected into the virtual environment and works within it.

In a type of sign-language to the system, single movements by a user, such as pointing, or sets of movements combined as gestures are pre-set for giving commands to the program. The program interprets these and generates images that comply with these signals. For example, fingers clenched in a fist raised in the direction of an object could represent a command to zoom in on the object. The system will then generate a sequence of images that gives a person the sensation of zooming in on the object. Specific commands have not yet been standardized within the VR community; however, some hand signals are emerging as de-facto standards. These are described briefly in Chapter 5.

Gloves are used primarily to transmit one-way signals to the system; however, some are fitted to also transmit signals the other way — from the system to the user — to increase the believability of the virtual environment. This feedback can include tactile sensations, such as pressure or heat or texture, to enhance what the user experiences. For tactile feedback, real objects are grasped with a development glove. A pattern of forces is measured and stored, to be evoked at a later time to produce the same effect in a user glove.

Of the 20 or more sensors that a glove can contain, not all need to be active. Someone using the system may choose to utilize only those relaying data significant to a particular task, thereby conserving system resources. Also, depending on the nature of the feedback required, data may be sampled at intervals instead of being monitored continuously.

Most gloves require separate calibration or customization for each user, and the electromagnetic tracker may have to be adjusted for a room's magnetic peculiarities. Even though the data for each user can be stored in the computer for future use, pulling it up and reinstating it each time can be a nuisance.

There is another drawback to the use of gloves, as well. The highly instrumented joint-sensing gloves made for research applications allow so much freedom of movement and so many combinations of movements that they are probably overengineered for many programs. In such cases, other types of input devices are used. They are discussed in separate sections.

Applications suitable for glove input include:

- CAD/CAM design environments, so that the user can grab objects on the screen;
- biomedical training and collaboration when, for example, surgeons need to assess hand function and performance;
- robotics, so that gestures can be used to command a robot;
- telemanipulation, in which robot arm and grip actions can be practiced in real time;

- animation, for which a glove or other device's sensors can be "mapped" to computer-generated characters and control their actions;

- sign language and printed letter recognition research and training;

- simulation, in which the glove's signals can be incorporated to control data.

Typically, a glove allows the user to work with virtual objects in the same manner he or she would work with real objects — reaching for them, touching them and grabbing or otherwise manipulating them via the animated hand. A user can select objects and act on or with them in a very natural way, without having to resort to computer keystrokes or esoteric, formal interaction with the computer.

A very simple version of these gloves, called "Power Glove," is on the market for use with home video games [Lanier91S], and was sixth in dollar-amount toy purchases for the Christmas season in 1989. They already replace hand-held input devices or joysticks for over a million users. [VPL91b]

Representative of gloves at the top of the line are gloves lined with force-sensitive resistors on their inner surfaces. Whenever real objects are grasped, a distinct pattern of forces is generated to a person's hand. A pattern of the proportional pressure of these forces can be measured and stored as part of the environment database or in a database specifically maintained for this purpose. When that action becomes part of a virtual scenario, by dint of a user closing fingers around something, for example, most users experience a recognizable sensation — pressure in the same positions they would if grasping a real object with a real hand. [VPL91b]

Bodysuit

The bodysuit is basically a customized dataglove for the whole body. It is instrumented with the same type of fiber-optic cable running through a dataglove. As a user moves or bends or waves, the system collects spatial coordinates for each part of the suit, dynamically tracking a full range of actions. Currently, 20 or more sensors monitor all major body joints.

These digitized signals are translated by the computer into a realization — i.e., a virtual body that is displayed on a screen or in a virtual scenario. The generated image becomes enslaved to signals dictated by the movements of the user and is continually regenerated. A user identifies with the realization.

Applications particularly suitable for input and feedback via bodysuit include:

- movement assessment and testing, including ambulatory monitoring of movement and gait measurements, and physical assessment for occupational purposes;

- kinesiology and sports-medicine training and applications, especially for function and performance measurements;

- rehabilitation therapy for stroke or injury victims and preventive aids for repetitive strain injuries;

- biomechanics;

- sex therapy and erotica.

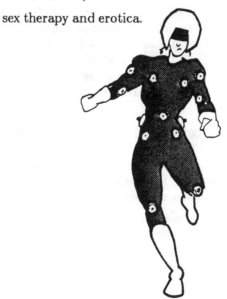

How a bodysuit is used to control the motions of a robot device can be seen in the film *FX 2*, in which the clown appears to be telemanipulated.

Remote Manipulator Device

A handgun-like grip attached to a mechanical arm device becomes the means by which simulated forces and torques are fed back to the user, who can manipulate the device over a fairly large space (about a cubic meter) to simulate grasping or placing objects in the virtual environment. This is the GROPE device mentioned in "Haptic Enhancement" in Chapter 2. Since visual images can be displayed independently of force feedback features, foot pedals are sometimes enlisted to turn the latter on or off.

Notable research using this device has included finding the minimum-energy docking configuration for drugs in an active site of a protein molecule, finding the minimum-energy position and orientation of a virtual bar suspended by springs and manipulating virtual blocks on and over a virtual table. [Brooks&90]

Billiard Balls

Some researchers hollow out a billiard ball, place a directional sensor inside it and stick it at the end of a rod or mechanical arm. Switches or buttons for particular commands are placed on the outside. These may include an activate button, fly command buttons or toolbox controls. Because the buttons can be made to define specific actions more precisely than gloves, customized billiard balls are generally favored by people creating virtual environments. Everything is wired into the program, and the ball's movements are interpreted by the program as input commands, enabling the person grasping the billiard ball to control or change the orientation of the virtual-reality scene.

The hand-held, joystick-like device, sometimes called a "geoball" or "servomanipulator," is simpler to use and maintain than a glove. It requires no or little calibration, and its positioning and actions can be accurately controlled and measured. Balls usually send relative position and orientation values to the tracking sensors.

Elaborate variations on the theme of billiard-ball-as-input-device are available. These feature enhancements such as hand rests, viewpoint selections and programmable keypads.

Force Balls

Some ball devices actually move very little. Instead, they are rigged so that directional forces (pushes, pulls and twists) applied to them by a user's hand are measured as input. Pushing hard intensifies the measurement; lessening it occurs when pressure is released. These are referred to as "force balls." Some force balls are customized with user-defined features — fitted, perhaps, with switches for emergency exit from the program.

Joystick & Joybox

Single or pairs of velocity-modulating joysticks, much like the controls on a helicopter, allow a user full freedom of movement. Architects prefer this as a control device.

Wands

Like a fairy wand with a sensor at its tip and a six-degree-of-freedom sensor at its base, this device is probably the simplest control device used within virtual environments. Some wands have switches or selection knobs attached. Brandishing a wand, a participant in a virtual world can use it to paint, interact with objects or issue a limited set of commands. Some versions emit a laser beam from the front. When aimed at an object in the virtual scene, it selects or retrieves it.

Finger Things: Picks, Rings & Vibrators

A number of devices have been developed for finger use. One, a small pick much like a ukelele pick, is fitted with a small, directional sensor and a tiny switch. The finger pick is easy to use and doesn't need to be grabbed or held. It can be used, for instance, by a biochemist to poke and move virtual molecular bonds around in order to gain a different perspective on the structure of the virtual model.

Another device mounted on the index finger or thumb is the finger ring. This device uses a pushbutton and sensor mounted on a ring. A vibrator ring is a variation of the finger ring. It contains a tiny vibrator to provide tactile feedback to a user.

Voice Controllers

Speech input and synthesized speech output are convenient, allowing relatively hands-free control of a procedure, and justifications for the development of voice controllers for applications often include the efficiency of dictated input by a physician performing surgery or split-second verbal commands by a soldier in the field. Thus, integration of speech into computer applications is being justified not only from a user-friendly point of view but also by dint of association with such sacrosanct areas as medicine and defense.

However, as with all new technologies, the convenience of speech recognition and synthesis must be viewed in light of a number of things:

- the high initial investment required to provide equipment for individual applications;

- the resources and talent diverted from other projects for its development; and

- the impractical bulk of systems currently available for such uses.

To date, these factors have discouraged widespread use of voice control.

TACTILE FACILITIES

"There's a love scene on a bearskin rug;
they say it's marvelous.
Every hair of the bear reproduced.
The most amazing tactual effects."
BRAVE NEW WORLD

Researchers designing the virtual environments strive to incorporate whatever features may enhance the realism of their design. The degree to which a user is convinced that a virtual world is real is a strong measure of how well the design has succeeded.

Factors generally recognized as contributing to tactile sensation are a feeling of pressure, a sensation of texture, an absence or presence of heat or cold and the sensation of odor, and means are being developed to relay these sensations to participants within virtual environments. It is done primarily through the clever customization of existing equipment. Configurations of physical accessories and transducers, devices that convert one form of energy into another, are used to enhance a person's illusion of full-sensory immersion.

Little Bladders & Micropins

Some models of gloves and bodysuits are lined with areas of micropins and little inflatable bladders that deliver haptic and tactile effects. They were first used in flight simulators to give the effect of gravitational acceleration (G-load). The pins and bladders are connected to the computer and controlled to change position and shape very quickly in synch with the program. Much like the air bulbs in Michael Jordan's high-tops, the bladders are inflated or deflated to exert or release pressure to give an effect of weight or tangibility to objects in the virtual world. Thus equipped, a user approaching and grasping a virtual doorknob, for instance, would receive not only visual feedback to heighten illusion of the act but programmed feedback through the pins and bladders of the glove that simulate the pressures on a hand when grasping and turning a real knob.

As the coordinates of the virtual hand meet those of the virtual knob, a unique blend of bubble and pin movement is actuated. The illusion continues in harmony with the action as long as virtual contact remains. Upon removing one's virtual hand from the knob, the microactuators are turned off, and the user notices an abrupt cessation of "feel."

Users lifting or maneuvering a virtual object can be made to "sense" its heaviness or lightness by the amount of pressure and movements of the pins in the glove or suit. Torque and resistance can be simulated by pressures and movements contrary to that enacted by the user, and sensors are available that transmit temperature, allowing a user to "feel" heat or lack thereof. Undoubtedly, creative refinements of this approach will be incorporated into entertainment and arcade applications.

Thermodes

Most virtual-reality applications do not need heat sensors. For some cases, though, the ability to simulate heat or cold, even if only over a limited range, is especially valuable. One way to do this is to slip little collar- or cap-like "thermodes" over a user's fingertips. These work like thermocouples. Each (of as many as eight) contains a temperature sensor and a little thermoelectric heat pump that moves heat in or out of a heat sink to produce the sensation of "hot" or "cold" to the user's finger.

Thermodes can be made to work the other way, as well, sending temperature and surface thermal signals from the human wearer to the system (like lie detectors); however, they are usually used for output from the system to the human.

Thermodes and other delivery devices need not be limited to the fingertips. Regardless of placement, their basic operation remains the same; so, they can be put anywhere. The body, as a whole, is more sensitive to variations of temperature than the fingertips, and a type of kinesthetic skin incorporating many tactile features is being investigated.

Whatever thermal device is used employs signals from the computer controlling the virtual environment. Temperature values are assigned to objects or locations or surfaces in the virtual environment and registered in the system program. As a user nears each, the system sends commands that trigger the appropriate corresponding response in the thermodes on his or her body. For telerobotic purposes, the temperature sensors are placed on the remote device, i.e., the robot. Real temperatures can be recorded and corresponding signals sent to the system, which then relays them to the user thermodes. Variations are being developed for use with prosthetic limbs. Signals from sensors placed on the limb are relayed to other parts of the body.

In some cases, real temperatures are not needed; instead, the computer program may use assigned temperature values. This is especially useful for training programs and in rehabilitation exercises. The amount of heat generated by the heat pump is controlled by both the computer system and an external circuit breaker. The temperatures felt by the user are usually limited to a safe, comfortable range between 10 and 40 degrees Centigrade (50-104 degrees Fahrenheit).

Scents & Stinks

Omnidirectional olifactors — smells from every which way — will, like omnidirectional sound, be included in some virtual environments. More than 30 basic smells have been identified; combinations of these provide researchers an even wider choice to work with. The generators and apparatus used today for aroma therapy need only to be augmented (to extend through the noxious) for possible incorporation into virtual applications. The odors and scents will probably be delivered through headgear channels, similar to the way audio features are delivered now.

Gustatory Illusion

Inclusion of "taste" in a virtual scenario is a luxury. Convincing users that they taste something, without their actually having eaten it, is not only difficult, but its contribution to the overall effectiveness of the experience is marginal. As smell greatly influences how we perceive taste, efforts will probably be made first in that direction, and cross-sensory substitution for taste will be made by enhanced smells. Today, even that is a bonus.

NAVIGATION DEVICES

A person can navigate within the three-dimensional space among virtual objects by moving and being tracked by sensors or by hand gestures. Foot-powered devices are also used to signal the system that we are on the move — and how fast we want to go. Treadmills and bicycles are most commonly rigged up for this purpose.

Treadmill

Some virtual areas, such as the architectural design for a building or hallways, are larger or longer than those that can be covered by a stationary tracker. For these, a treadmill like the one in your health club or doctor's office is used. A treadmill is often preferred by users who want a more natural (e.g., walking through, viewing) means of input. The device is modified to measure distance traversed, and the measurements are fed into the program.

These are then reflected in the virtual world that the walker sees. Handlebars (usually bicycle handlebars) serve as a steering device. As the user turns them, the virtual scene appears to change correspondingly.

Bicycle

Another navigation and control device is a stationary bicycle that is "pedalled" through a virtual world created to simulate an itinerary. For example, a user may choose a specific route through New England country in the fall or a surreal, twisting course through psychedelic galaxies.

The user views the scene either on a big screen placed in front of the bicycle or through a head-mounted device. The speed at which the virtual scenery passes is determined by how fast or slowly the rider pedals, and the direction of the handlebars determines the orientation of the scene.

Computer-controlled braking devices act on the rear wheel, providing resistant feedback to the rider to enhance the effects of steep or rough terrain. The computer charts a rider's progress by keeping track of the relative speed and distance he or she travels along the virtual road.

This type of setup is also used for flying simulations, in which case accommodation is made in the steering mechanism for simulated pitch and yaw effects.

Behind the Scenes:
Software, Databases, etc.

4

Early on, the world of computing was dominated by bulky, room-filling *hard*ware — machines that could compute. It very quickly became obvious that the big machines needed more than vacuum tubes and toggle switches to be used effectively. Thus evolved *soft*ware, the logical sequences of commands and documentation (known as programs) that completed the package.

Writing software is tedious, and talking or reading about it even more so. However, anyone who uses a computer is at the mercy of the people who write the programs.

Often ornery and compulsive, they've been likened to gamblers — neither is able to concede that some problems are just not computer-compatible or understandable, and neither is ever willing to give up. [Weizenbaum76] Compulsive programmers may even be worse since they create the very beasts of code that thwart them. If only they understand a bit more about what doesn't work, they can beat it, they maintain. In the world of computing, this is really bad news. It begets larger and larger programs that depend on smaller and smaller "fixes," only to get closer and closer to what's probably not what the customer wanted.

But not all are so addicted, and it is necessary here to acknowledge the importance of software in the creation and development of virtual environments and to understand how advances in dealing with it help or impede the effort.

A virtual-reality model is actually a huge chunk of software that demands the creation and maintenance of hundreds of thousands of lines of complex code that can be deciphered by a computer. [Brooks91] Whole sections of code representing commands and instructions must be refined and tested and protected against tampering. When changes or upgrades are made by numbers of people, the code becomes a mess.

Writing and maintaining such a large volume of unique, complex commands is a major part of any development effort and is what most often slows research and production. It is an important background responsibility of all virtual-reality research and development teams.

SOFTWARE: COMPUTER LANGUAGE

A computer can do nothing unless it is fed commands. These are nothing more than series of words "telling" it what to do. Groups of words are represented by code that can be read by the machine. The machine then "does" what it has been instructed to do. Each command or piece of information is entered as one line of code. Imagine prompting someone who "hasn't a clue" to perform a simple task such as picking up a book. After communication is established, i.e., the being is alerted, a number of lines of instruction (code) are needed to represent things that must happen or must be true. For example, the book is present; the being is alerted to find the book; the being recognizes book, approaches book, opens hand; etc., etc., etc. until the task is completed.

Behind every computer action lies just as grueling a process. A group of related commands (lines of code) becomes a "procedure" or "program" for a particular action or application. Programmers and application developers, the persons who write them, have been doing so for decades. Today in the United States, there are well over 100 billion lines in use, each of which has cost an average of $23 to produce.

And because people always want a computer program to do more, programmers fiddle with the original code (called "source" code) or piggyback new code onto it to upgrade the program — confusing the issue and often introducing "bugs" (programming errors) that sabotage other processes or start unexpected chains of computer-aided disasters. So, in addition to initial costs, each line of code incurs an average of over $3 per year in maintenance costs alone. [Haavind92]

Programmers' Shortcuts

Writing new code, playing catch-up with millions of changes and tracking down problems have created a development backlog that is being dealt with in a number of ways:

- Programmers store useful programs and reuse them as they are or with minor changes.

- A computer is used to automatically design and write error-free code for certain procedures — computer-aided software engineering (dubbed CASE technology).

- Old programs are reworked and streamlined; parts of them are replaced or upgraded so that they can be automated. This is called re-engineering.

- Small teams combine cross-specialty skills and automated tools to build complex applications quickly. This is called rapid application development (RAD).

Conversion software is available for converting existing CAD/CAM data into virtual-friendly code, and its use helps leverage some developers' investments and saves time. However, for most applications — except for architectural — converted code comprises only a very small part of what is needed.

Programmers' use of these shortcuts has made the coding task more manageable and will continue to do so, but constructing the block of code for any virtual application will never be easy. There is another technique, however, that looks like it might help. Whole blocks of code, as long as they are meaningful, can be defined as autonomous and thought of as programmed "objects." This approach is described below.

Object-Oriented Techniques

An object can represent anything that can be named, from something abstract (degrees of volatility) to something very concrete (a screw). In addition, objects or parts of programs can "inherit" or borrow features from other objects or from precoded, generic samples. For example, it would be necessary only to note that one object is like another *except for* certain features and then to stipulate the differences.

Increasingly, preprogrammed (canned) "things" that know how to "behave" are just being plugged into applications, with detailed instruction programming being reserved for manipulation purposes. The techniques of working with programmed objects is referred to as Object-Oriented Programming (OOP), Object-Oriented Software (OOS) or Object-Oriented Technology (OOT).

Japanese developers have combined object-oriented techniques with the popular programming language, C, to come up with a way to write programs with about one-tenth the amount of code required previously. The new language is called Concurrent Object-Oriented C (COOC). This could be important for large, complex applications like those of virtual environments.

The use of object-oriented techniques for creating virtual environments may be key to establishing its credibility as a real software-engineering breakthrough. On SIMNET, the U.S. Army's network of tank simulators, 1000 data objects are already in use, and the number is expected to increase to 10,000 within a few years and to 100,000 usable data objects by the year 2000. [Murphy92]

Still, building objects for virtual environments is by no means trivial. Many issues remain unresolved, including the incompatibility of many operating systems and the ways in which parts of a program "message" each other. Each independent, self-knowing module (such as a ball) must contain many rules of behavior (e.g., bounce patterns) for whatever it represents, and testing the contents of each module is extremely difficult. Developers have found that certain attributes, such as dynamics, are not easily transferred among graphics system formats.

In addition, because object-oriented technology is still relatively new, developers are often establishing precedent as they work, rather than relying on past programming experience. This sometimes results in programs that are reliable but slow.

Since most current virtual-reality applications are designed around dedicated machines, incompatibility is still a nonissue. Soon, however, virtual-reality software will have to be "device-independent," i.e., not limited to any particular type of computer or operating system. Only those programs and configurations that can be adapted and creatively massaged by users and developers are suitable for virtual-reality development purposes. As soon as these are available, many more applications will be created than are discussed here.

INFORMATION: DATABASES & KNOWLEDGE BASES

In creating a virtual environment, a developer feeds the design with material that helps him or her create realistic scenarios and that later helps reinforce users' believability in the system. Sometimes, this material is extracted from outside sources — from collections external to the system — and comes as "information" or "data" or "knowledge."

Generally speaking, databases provide content, and knowledge bases provide expertise. Both are needed for the development of effective virtual-environment applications.

Information, Data & Knowledge

These are terms that most of us understand and use — and very often interchange but rarely need to define precisely. However, for the purposes of this book, it may be helpful to make some distinctions among them.

Information refers here to random collections of unsynthesized, unanalyzed material. It is different from data, which are organized to facilitate analysis. Information also differs from knowledge, which is comprised of material that is empirical, inferred or interpreted.

We include in the definition of *data* any special-purpose facts and figures from which conclusions may be drawn. A data*base* is a collection of these facts and figures stored in some semblance of order. Order is important so that people accessing the database can find things. Databases are usually gathered, filed and stored electronically on a computer.

We refer to *knowledge* as an accumulated understanding that has been gained through experience or study. Its connotation is broader in range than that of unsynthesized information or collections of data. Knowledge represents the cognitive or intellective sum of what is perceived, discovered or inferred.

Knowledge bases can be stored in people's heads, but for our purposes a knowledge base is electronically recorded. Instead of being tacitly or verbally transmitted, it is accessed and transmitted via computer. Artificial-intelligence techniques are sometimes used to encode knowledge and store it in knowledge bases. Expert systems, where rules and data are used by computer programs to draw and store inferences, are examples of encapsulated knowledge.

Via virtual-environment interfaces, a user will become a part of the knowledge base, navigating through it and interacting with it to assemble those elements relevant to solving his or her particular problem. By visually encountering the knowledge, concepts and expertise residing there, a user can easily and intuitively discern which portions to select and which to disregard. (See "Expert, Intelligent Databases" below.)

Role in VR Applications

The designers of virtual environments need specific information for the virtual objects they build. They find it in either comprehensive or specific databases and dataset files. A developer working with a virtual molecule, for instance, refers to a scientific or molecular database for specific physical properties associated with that molecule.

Material kept in databases or knowledge bases is used both for building virtual objects and environments and for supplying information about those objects to users in the virtual environment. As applications are developed, current databases are upgraded, and specialized databases are compiled for more focused purposes. Database warehouses filled with virtual objects will become valuable, time-saving resources for others building the same types of applications.

Databases are increasing in complexity and size, requiring elegant, efficient interfaces and embedded intelligence (inference techniques) for a user to interact effectively with them. Sophisticated, real-time techniques that are used for lucidly displaying information from the database can be used to interface with the database itself. These help users understand what is available to them and help them more easily extract not only data but also knowledge relevant to the data. Virtual interfaces will help users apply new or extracted knowledge to data and will facilitate user interaction at levels higher than data manipulation alone.

Datasets

Datasets are files or parts of files that are kept as resources for particular subjects. For example, a mathematics dataset would contain definitions of all terms used in the field, any relationships among the terms, formulae, vocabulary, etc. — in other words, any facts or figures that would be of interest or use to someone doing mathematics. Scientific and technical applications often have arrays or tables of data that can be read by many types of computers. All data relevant to the topic are kept as a set and tapped into as a resource.

Hardcopy lists of datasets available to the general public would comprise many telephone books. From these, people can choose sets for banking and financial statistics, demographics, product information and specifications or data for the computation of complex fluid dynamics. The same holds for other types of datasets such as meteorologic, geometric, anatomical or planetary datasets.

New items on the list include gene and protein datasets, being compiled from ongoing genetic- and protein-engineering work. There are over 50,000 human proteins for which gene sequences can be coded, and many may be useful in the development of medicines. To date, however, only relatively few have been identified and isolated.

Scientific Databases

Scientific knowledge and facts have been recorded and archived on walls and tablets and in books for as long as humans have been able to write. As computer capabilities for building databases evolved and mass storage became cheaper, the bulk of scientific information, data and knowledge has been warehoused in many on-line databases. Some are broadly defined and encompass views across many disciplines. Others are narrowly defined datasets.

As chemists, physicists, biologists and astronomers continually add to their stores of data, scientific databases are enriched, as well, and serve as valuable resources to others. From large, general databases containing many datasets and relationships among them, researchers can extract what they need for their applications.

Task-Specific Databases

Collections of information, data and knowledge relating to techniques used to accomplish certain tasks are called task-specific databases. A task-specific database may be a collection of whatever data are relevant to car repair, for example. It would contain a compilation of what can go wrong with a car, how to diagnose a problem and specific steps that can be taken to fix it. A preventive maintenance database would be a database relevant to the task of anticipating potential problems and the steps necessary to prevent them.

Simply put, a task-specific database is a superset of all the instruction guides and procedure manuals on the topic. From it can be extracted what is needed to do a particular job or task.

Conceptual Databases

Conceptual databases incorporate the elements of information, data and knowledge that are relevant to a user's world and how he or she wants to use them. It is a high-level abstraction of the world in which a person is working and embodies the user's perception of how the material should be defined and stored.

Domain-Specific Databases

Designers of virtual environments (or anyone, for that matter) can buy access to databases through subscription. Then, by connecting to the on-line services via modem, they can gather the many bits of information, data and knowledge needed to make their virtual environment realistic. Knowledge and information specific to an area of expertise other than their own — international tariffs or Celtic crosses or documenting insect dance patterns, for instance — are gathered from databases customized for use by professionals in that area.

Government-compiled public databases provide easy-to-access, consistent sources of information to private citizens, the media and professional organizations. Both industrial and developing countries are consolidating information and establishing databases on issues such as health, security benefits, welfare, environment, public safety and law enforcement. Public databases may also serve as dispatching agents for federal-to-local assistance or communication.

Attorneys access and use electronic legal databases to search for precedents, tax information and contract and trade regulations, as well as U.S. and foreign laws. As resources, legal databases are so valuable that many law schools now require students to become familiar with them. The same holds for databases compiled and maintained by medical specialists and scientists.

Financial investment and financial services databases provide detailed information and data on quotes from the floors of the stock exchanges, business and economic news, prices of stocks, options and exchanges. Specific databases may contain corporate earnings estimates, Standard and Poor's ratings or summary data for corporations. Any virtual-reality real-time visualization of economic trends, for instance, would have to be connected to a database that contains that information and that changes dynamically in real time.

On-line, "live" access to commercial databases is expensive. Thus, it is used primarily for information that changes quickly or is not available from other sources, such as news updates or stock prices.

Expert, "Intelligent" Databases

Some databases and systems are extended to incorporate ways of representing knowledge and a capability to draw inferences from what is stored. Expert systems also help people find information across myriad research sources.

There are a number of ways you can recognize an "intelligent" database:

- The abstract, electronic data model that you see closely resembles a model of the real world in which you work.

- You can manipulate and manage the information, data and knowledge easily and in a natural way.

- It takes into consideration your profile as a user in order to facilitate finding the right level of information for your unique background and needs.

Virtual interfaces can augment intelligent databases and extend the ways in which you interact with a system. As a virtual participant in the system, you are able to focus more on the data or knowledge itself than on its arrangement. In many cases, particularly those in which responses to subverbal queries play vital roles in determining the course of further inquiry, virtual interface technology better accommodates a user's needs.

Real-Space Databases

Some things make sense only when viewed in particular context or in the right location. Pulling on your ear lobe at home might indicate nothing more than an itchy ear; by doing so at an auction, you could become the owner of a 17th-century footstool.

Likewise, certain virtual objects or overlays are informative and useful only when tied in to real-world-based things or events. As virtual objects are created, any real-world specifics upon which they rely — e.g., context, altitude, latitude and longitude — are also defined. Then, these real-space images that depend on fixed locations are catalogued and registered according to their real-world-based coordinates.

This collection of information, which can become part of a central repository of information available to all, is referred to as a real-space database. It is a collection of the details required for real-space imaging (discussed in Chapter 2).

A real-space database contains coordinates and data for real locations, for virtual space and for real-space images and also contains data on the relation and dependence among these. Whether a real-space image will be displayed or removed is determined by conditions specified by the creators and kept in the real-space database.

Multimedia Databases

As soon as networks permit the transmission of large, intense amounts of information, people will be able to access centralized stores of information in various media such as film, audio or video. As yet, this is not practical because high-capacity fiber-optic networks (which are planned for the future) need to be in place. When this is done, people will be able to link to or extract information in various forms from mass storage repositories similar to the National Archives or the Government Printing Office.

The U.S. National Geographic Society, for instance, has amassed an impressive photographic library of images for its own use in magazines and broadcasts. With regulation, these millions of static photos can be made available to outsiders and could be incorporated, along with moving images and other media forms, into a centralized multimedia database.

Select blocks of material from other countries, such as war film footage, interviews, music, art and drama, may also be obtained and made part of central multimedia databases that are accessible to everyone for study or use. Many such collections already exist, and a lot of them are in the public domain. Others are becoming available daily.

INTEGRATION: SYSTEM HARMONY

The extensive variety of computing, input and display devices that are the instruments for creating virtual environments must be integrated as a harmonic, interdependent system. This must be done so well that a user enjoys the illusion of being immersed in an interactive world.

Script-like production outlines become part of the process. Visual displays must be coordinated with auditory components, and tactile feedback must be integrated with both the visual and auditory segments. Then, to make it effective, timing, design, speed and power must be brought into play with them and each other in an extremely sensitive way.

Few applications have gotten to that point. However, as the different technologies evolve, applications are updated to exploit them at higher and higher levels.

Dedicated, wholly integrated systems are being developed and sold as single units, accompanied by ready-made application-building modules. However, since the separate technologies involved advance at different rates, many researchers prefer flexibility and assemble their own hybrid systems, upgrading individual components as fast as their different technologies allow.

TRANSMISSION: FACILITIES FOR SHARING

The resources available to most developers of virtual-reality applications are scarce and expensive, and investments must be leveraged. It would make sense for developers to arrange time- and resource-sharing with others doing the same kind of work. In addition, central virtual environments and repositories may be set up to be tapped into by many users. Connected sites of VR activity are called *networked immersion environments*.

Virtual Networks vs. Virtual-Environment Networks

Before discussing networks used to link virtual environments, it is important to note that they are very different from the virtual networks you may have seen advertised by telecommunications companies. Virtual networks are uniquely defined combinations of facilities that may actually be parts of real, hard-wired networks. Some vendors call them "virtual private" networks. AT&T refers to its version as a "software-defined" network (SDN). This is because software commands control the routes and necessary link transfers among the networks used.

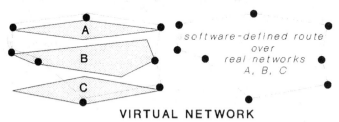

software-defined route over real networks A, B, C

VIRTUAL NETWORK

Many corporations establish private virtual networks because they can be cost effective and often offer fast response times and connectivity to other networks. Route segments are usually leased from private facilities that allocate bandwidth dynamically, on demand. Thus, a virtual network can be thought of as a special configuration, an innovative route over segments of networks that already exist — usually to take advantage of portions that offer lower rates or meet particular needs. This type of customized routing scheme has nothing to do with virtual reality per se.

Virtual-environment networks, on the other hand, are hard-wired transmission facilities that link user sites together for the purposes of sharing or developing virtual-reality applications. An example of one virtual-environment network is shown in Chapter 8. The figure maps the interconnected shared sites of the Virtual Art Museum created by a team at Carnegie Mellon University.

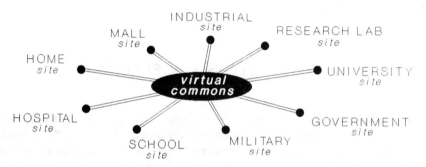

The teleoperation of robots is virtual-environment networking of a sort. The operator's telepresence at the remote site could be construed as a second user. (See "Telepresence: Being There" in Chapter 5.)

Bandwidth demands of virtual-environment networks preclude much exploitative use of today's existing networks. However, networks of the future will have sufficient bandwidth to accommodate the emergence of *virtual*, virtual-environment networks. Upgrading the usability of the information delivered and making it affordable may be more difficult.

Need for Bandwidth

It is expected that most shared applications would require ready-in-place transmission facilities and plenty of bandwidth capability. Some users are experimenting with narrowband ISDN but are waiting for broadband ISDN before making any major commitments. Others contend that bandwidth is not the problem and have concocted shared systems using currently available devices and modems. [Farmer92]

Major communication companies, as well, are hoping to bypass the need for higher-bandwidth optical cabling. Among others, AT&T is pushing a new technology that enables it to transmit images in real time over copper wire like the type used for telephone lines. IBM is also investigating how it can use existing cable lines for image transmission.

Regardless, in order to provide long-distance linkages of simultaneous users to common virtual spaces, it is crucial that high-speed networks eventually provide *ample* bandwidth and a sophisticated array of features for transmission and delivery. These are not yet in place.

Experimental Networks

Around the world, local support is growing for amateur and grass-roots networking efforts. [Loeffler92] On-line bulletin boards and services may be used as venues for shared virtual facilities. Users are documenting emerging protocols and conducting cost effectiveness studies, and de-facto standards of operating are emerging.

One experimental service, Reality Net, is being developed to connect primarily architects and clients but will eventually include other classes of users. All users share access to common virtual spaces in which they can communicate and collaborate even though they are not doing so from the same physical location. The Virtual Art Museum described in Chapter 8 is a networked facility for long-distance design and development of shared immersion environments. Another current project is called ExploreNet, established as an aid for teaching core disciplines in grade schools. Immersive jungle, cave and mountain environments compel students to query and interact with the presentation and with others who experience it. [Loeffler92] These projects could evolve into types of in-class Outward Bound experiences.

Team Work Station, a Japanese project for a paperless office, links multimedia workstations. The U.S. military used SIMNET, a networked, nonimmersive virtual training ground for personnel being sent to serve in Operation Desert Storm. Eventually, this will share its databases with a U.S.-government-owned visual simulator over a network.

Of interest to many manufacturers is the possibility of long-distance collaboration on the design and modification of products. Clay models can be transmitted as virtual models over a network for inspection or modification, eliminating the need for replicating facilities for shared collaboration at each site. Networked facilities for shared immersion environments at corporate locations enable manufacturers to design a product (a virtual car, for instance) at one site, create its virtual prototype at another site, test it at another and, finally, build it at the real manufacturing site.

Interpretation & Translation Facilities

Types of systems that transcend total dependence on spoken language could lead to the development of future shared global environments, where participants don't share the same language but share common purpose. Called automated interpreting telephony, this technology is only beginning to become commercially feasible. In Japan, government and private industry are jointly funding a 7-year, $130 million interpreting project.

Like virtual reality, instantaneous translator systems are dependent on other technologies, all of which are evolving at different rates. These are speech recognition, automatic translation and speech synthesis. Automated interpreters start with speech recognition — i.e., transcribing whatever is spoken (the input), analyzing the sound patterns and then converting them into digitized text (which can be displayed for review by the speaker). The text is then translated into another language and sent over telephone lines to another location. There, a device called a speech synthesizer processes it and produces output — synthesized, electronic speech in the target language at the target site. Because voice quality degrades more over long distance than does text, the computer generation of the electronic voice is done as close to the receiving end of the transmission as possible.

Currently, researchers from the United States, Japan and Germany are cooperating to develop a number of limited applications within a few years. There are many technical obstacles, among them a 12-second lag, for instance, between a "hello" in Japanese to its translation in English, a limited range of recognizable words and phrases and a requirement that utterances be grammatically correct. Some systems can recognize only voices for which patterns have been programmed into the computer.

Others, notably one being developed at Carnegie Mellon University in Pittsburgh, are versatile enough to accept any speaker's voice as input. The quality of the output voice can range from that of a human in a tunnel to crackly space alien.

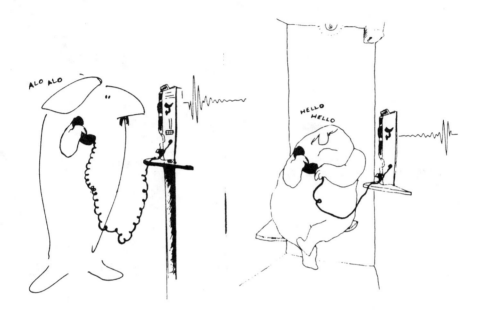

For dedicated use, such as that needed within a focused virtual application, these limited resources can be used effectively. Widespread, telephone-like communication with instantaneous interpretation will, however, take many years. Eventually, the possibility of instantaneous translation into various understood forms of communication may help dissolve some of the language, cultural and geographic barriers that today impede effective cooperation.

Virtual Mobility

5

SIZING & PERSPECTIVE

The intriguing option of nonorthodox perspectives is one of virtual reality's strongest hooks into our interest. However confident we may feel within a territory or subject, a change of perspective often yields surprise and insight. VR technology offers participants unlimited vantage points from which to experience both.

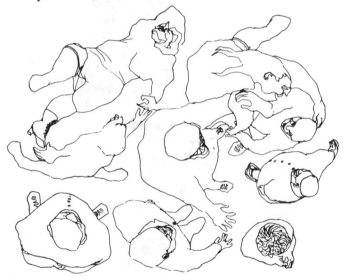

Sleeping in a frightened child's bed, for instance, can spark immediate understanding of what a child is not able to express. From a vantage point closer to the ground, shadows that appear harmless to us as grownups acquire ghoulish demeanor, and wind seems to howl so much more strangely at little-ear level.

You can, no doubt, bring countless other examples to mind. Take the perspective of time. Westerners generally think of time in linear, quantifiable terms — 8 o'clock is equidistant from 9, 9 o'clock is equidistant from 10, and an hour is an hour. Punctuality is rather cut-and-dry. In many other parts of the world, however, time is perceived globally and qualitatively, as if surrounding a person. Immersed in his or her unique sphere of unreal time, what is important emotionally to a person looms closer and larger, and lateness is a relative thing — an indulgent view that can be frustrating to outsiders.

Megamen, Microworlds

The ability of a virtual environment to block out constraints of the real world is similarly indulgent and actually ranks among its more alluring features. A tempting wish to be a "fly on the wall" can now be granted in a virtual world.

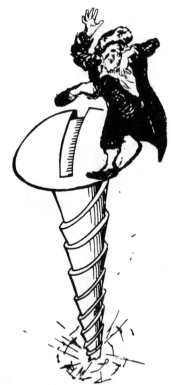

Imagine virtually shrinking to a point of perspective, being part of the world without affecting it by your presence — or, assuming shapes and identities foreign to our own, maneuvering in ways as clever and speedy as the little people in fairy books.

Free of the limitations of physics or the constraints of our conscience, we can zoom or loom upon command and examine virtual things from angles unheard, through infinitesimally keen computer-aided eyes. In a virtually lawless world, users can explore different perspectives, defying or denying speed limits, gravity or the laws of thermodynamics, answerable only to their imaginations and the speed and power of the computer being used.

CAN I GET THERE FROM HERE?

Modes of Travel

Travel modes may be preset, as they are in treadmill- or bicycle-driven applications, or they may be selected and activated via hand gesture, script, manipulation of a tool or selection from a menu within the virtual environment. Some systems accommodate limited verbal commands.

Walking and flying through the virtual space are the most common choices for navigating. Zooming, accelerating and braking features allow a user to exercise control over the maneuver. To "walk" through an environment, a user may activate a treadmill and be presented with images from the perspective of a pedestrian in the real world. "Flying," a user is presented with an aerial view of the scene and sequences of images that give the illusion of being airborne.

By electing to "zoom in" on something, a participant signals the system to generate a series of frames that produce a closer, enlarged look at the object. Zooming out produces the opposite effect, and a user is presented with a sequence of images that seem to distance him or her from the object or scene.

Specific Commands

Today, not only is there no standard for motion control of VR systems, there is none for *any* industry. Every game written and every application built have different input devices and different buttons for what the user needs to do. If remote controls for TV-stereo-VCR setups are any indication, the situation will probably remain a free-for-all for a long time.

Gloves can be programmed so that a unique set of motions or gestures runs each application, including navigational commands. Personal biocontrollers are best tailored for specific users.

For games, developers are borrowing ideas from video control pads and joysticks such as those used for Nintendo and Sega. (See Chapters 8 & 10.) Current discussions are rough guidelines, at best.

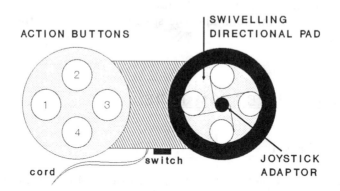

As more and more applications appear on the market, a few de-facto standards and devices will emerge, particularly among similar types of applications, but these will undoubtedly shift or fall from grace over the next few years. Once a user is familiar with one system, however, a transference of skills is relatively easy — like switching from softball to baseball or from one spreadsheet to another.

Within the virtual environment, a user navigates by issuing some sort preset command. Available choices may include:

- GO forward, backward, up, down, to the left, to the right, at an angle (usually 45 degrees), etc. as the program allows.

- WALK through environment in a designated direction.

- FLY through environment in a designated direction.

- ACCELERATE as the program allows.

- ZOOM IN for closer look at a selected view or object.

- ZOOM OUT for perspective from a distance.

- PAUSE & RESUME for pacing exploration.

- FORK to the system, i.e., temporarily interrupt program to communicate directly with the computer operating system, then reenter.

- STOP motion within environment.

- STOP & EXIT program, ending a session.

TELEPRESENCE: BEING THERE

When all of the design techniques and computer technologies work well enough together to fool the user into believing — if only for a short while — that he or she has been transported somewhere else, telepresence has been achieved. Telepresence requires that all the right stimuli trigger all the right responses in you. It is, in essence, the projection of a human mind to a remote site. The projection of several minds to a remote site can be effected by participants' sharing a virtual space. On-site disaster relief personnel, for example, may consult with teams of experts located, perhaps, far away from each other. Together, aided by a common view of the site and situation, they are able to decide on the best course of action before committing people and resources to the effort.

To build such a virtual scene, one that can be tapped into from remote sites, is a monumental but not impossible task. The job will become easier as developers from different disciplines begin a cross exchange of techniques and resources and as a repository of common, reusable modules is built up.

Teleoperation

Sometimes, telepresence is also referred to as remote presence. When this is used with robot technology to get something done remotely, teleoperation (or telemanipulation) comes into play. Simply put, teleoperation is remote control without the box; *you* are the control, directly coupled to the distant device. The system is hooked up so that a synchronized "you" in the form of a robot performs duties in a remote, perhaps hostile location.

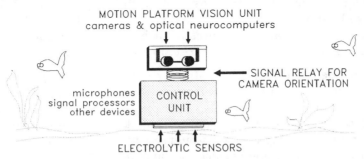

A teleoperated motion platform, fitted with microphones, cameras and other devices, transmits the sounds, images and signals of the remote site back to you, the user. Optical neurocomputers, used in conjunction with tiny lenses, constitute the vision units. Some tilting or rolling motion of the platform itself is possible through teleoperated head-movement control of electrolytic tilt sensors mounted on the platform.

Telepresence makes effective use of these real-time controls and computer vision by performing duties in places humans do not go or cannot survive for long periods of time — for instance, for monitoring and measuring levels of toxic, caustic or radioactive elements. If intervention is necessary, it can be done via telepresence combined with robotic systems.

Telemanipulation of Robots

Robots are ideal for many dangerous, effort-intensive jobs, from painting bridges to cleaning up radioactive waste, and virtual-reality interfaces facilitate their use. Workaholic robots don't complain and never go on strike — an appealing characteristic but outshone by the fact that they can be made to carry out tasks that tax and endanger human explorers.

How it works is that you, as an operator in a computerized mock-up, go through the motions of a task — ocean-floor sample retrieval, for instance. Your actions are mimicked by a robot at the real, perhaps hostile site. If your arms move, so do the robot's; bend, it bends, etc.

An area of current research focuses on increasing the ability of robotic systems to operate within unstructured hazardous environments. Because robots can be fitted with all kinds of sensors and measuring devices, they can be used to monitor levels of light, noise, humidity and pressure. They can be used to measure liquid flows, from raging rapids to lava. Armed with smoke detectors and heat sensors, robots can be sent to investigate fires. If equipped with infrared and optical detectors, a robot becomes a means for monitoring traffic or intrusions at a remote site.

Multimillion-dollar efforts to sweep the Kuwaiti desert of land mines entails sending squads of humans out in scorching heat to prod the sand, find the mines and defuse them. Aside from the vast amounts of money that have been spent, many lives have been lost. This is clearly an application in which an initial investment in teleoperated robots would have been safer and probably more cost effective in the long run.

Through telepresence in the robot, you can interact with whatever is in its environment — remotely, of course, with the system being the medium. If another robot is in the vicinity, for example, you and its real human can communicate. Some designers plan to project faces onto the robots so that a person interacting with one would see the human behind it all. But robots needn't be anthropomorphic, i.e., human-like; they can be any size, shape or material. (See "Micromachines & Micromotors" in Chapter 6.)

As we noted above, building a scene that can be tapped into from remote sites is a monumental task. However, when it has been done properly with adequate feedback devices, you feel as if you were in the place of the robot.

The Latency Factor in Teleoperation

Latency, the lag between user motion and system response, often impedes how well a user interacts with the remote environment. Initial studies indicate that lagging images degrade performance even more than slow image updates. [Loomis92] This is especially true for systems in which the robotic manipulator is located so far away that the signals for command, control and monitoring are significantly delayed, in which case effectiveness is critically jeopardized. For most on-site applications, a lag of 16 milliseconds is considered the maximum for realistic operation. For teleoperated procedures where a user is distanced from the remote operational site, however, the lag may increase to as much as 2 or 3 seconds.

There is a way around the problem. To give a user some semblance of timely response while waiting for a remote device to go into action after being given a command, researchers have developed predictive sequences of robot images to display while the system catches up. In other words, rather than make a user wait for the system to finish before providing visual or force feedback, the system quickly generates a ghost image of the robot that immediately reflects the user's motions. This image is superimposed upon the last available image of the real robot. Its data are then used to actually control the faraway robot. In this way, latency is minimized, and the user maintains a natural feeling of control over the process.

Pushy Robots

A good deal of trial-and-error is necessary before teleoperated tasks can be performed effectively. Responses by a mechanical robot are often disproportionate to (and usually stronger than) its human operator's actions.

This is because each of our senses perceives "presence" differently, and each combination of these different clues creates yet another degree of perception. Current systems' inability to accurately feed back degrees of resistance places a heavy burden on the user to learn specific reactions and adapt how he or she does things in the new "environment."

Getting used to the medium is akin to training astronauts under water in preparation for space walks; lots of adjustments must be made, and user performance improves with practice. If the user's actions are not monitored carefully and tempered appropriately, the simple task of adjusting a screw on a remote equipment panel may result in the robot arm pushing the screw right through the shell of the equipment.

Medical Applications

6

In the days of Avicenna, female patients were kept hidden behind a curtain, and physicians had to rely on nonvisual, nontactual sensorial impressions. These, combined with intuition, experience and a couple of well-chosen prayers, comprised the basis for their diagnosis and a course of treatment.

Even after doctors were permitted to extend their range of information-gathering senses to include seeing and touching their patients, a relatively holistic approach prevailed.

Eventually, the medical profession set the worry beads aside to welcome the advent of calibrated devices and objective testing. These tools eliminated a lot of the guesswork and efficiently quantified for healers what they had previously done judgmentally. Machines were objective and trustworthy, and results seemed all the more reliable and certainly more impressive when backed up by computer-enhanced techniques.

In so many ways, it was a blessing. No longer did doctors need to rely solely on their internal resources; technology was there to augment and reinforce them. Indeed, because of advanced technologies, today's physicians do have access to much more information and can now know much more.

That trend continues, and the current use of computer-based medical techniques is being boosted even further by the incorporation of elements of virtual-reality technology. Now, not only can medical researchers and practitioners access databases of extensive biological information, but they can interact with realizations of the digitized information itself.

Ironically, though, in the wake of technological advance, some of the trust historically placed in human expertise has migrated to the machines, and less credence is given the doctors — even by themselves. The addition of sensory receptors and haptic aids to virtual environments can, however, re-emphasize the wholeness of a physician. It attempts to reinstate within the person those assessors that may have been relinquished over time to external devices. In a way, as a participant in a virtual environment, a physician reclaims control, exploiting the technology to extend and expand his or her own abilities and talent rather than to supplant them. Often, skills suppressed from over-reliance on external devices or dampened by the aging process regain credibility within a virtual environment.

Virtual environments are becoming viable venues for the development of dramatic new medical applications, as well, ranging from prostheses for the handicapped to cyberspatial representation of war traumas. Also, medical exploration and intervention at the cell and gene levels are facilitated in a virtual environment since its micro- and macro-scaling features allow surgeons to work as if the areas were expanded (described further in "Telemanipulated Microsurgery," below). Virtual medical plants and facilities, virtual equipment and virtual patients give practitioners and students more opportunities for "hands-on" experience than has been possible till now, especially for high-risk cases.

Real applications exist. Stereo endoscopes can transmit three-dimensional (3-D) pictures to a physician's eyes through a head-mounted display unit so that he or she can perform minimally invasive surgery almost as if *inside* the patient. Anesthesiologists can see displays of vital signs such as heart rate or blood pressure superimposed on their patients.

CURRENT RESEARCH & DEVELOPMENT OVERVIEW

The medical community is aggressively developing uses for VR technology and has seized the new paradigm. Lively discussion pervades conferences convened to exchange ideas. As a result, environments and new aids are being adapted for the physically challenged, pharmaceutical researchers are conducting VR experiments to help them design new drugs, and surgeons are designing and practicing new medical techniques on virtual body parts in virtual operating theaters.

The basic virtual patient is a multidimensional, computer-generated image comprised of picture slices taken from different angles of a real person's body. The data used to create this image may be combined with data from other sources to enhance the model so that it may convey not only clinical information but also expert analyses and interpretation of the data.

Independent companies and university research facilities are already becoming providers of off-the-shelf virtual body parts, and Adam has been reincarnated as a software package (Animated Dissection of Anatomy for Medicine) in Georgia. [ADAM92] Laser disks containing detailed images of specific organs are available, and databases are sold for animations of organs, skeletons, muscular systems and vascular systems. As the relevant technologies evolve and databases are enriched, these renderings will appear more and more realistic. This may lead to the use of hybrid virtual bodies, genetic structures or immune systems for customized laboratory research. Assembled by kit, these may take the place of animal or human subjects for preliminary testing.

The advances in software, in hardware speed and power and in the visualization techniques discussed in Chapter 2 have made it possible for teams of surgeons, diagnosticians and practitioners to share virtual examination rooms for diagnostic and consultative purposes. There, they can explore and interact with the models and with each other to determine the most effective means for treating a patient. This all happens before surgery or other drastic measures are undertaken. In this way, doctors and medical researchers extend their knowledge and expertise without compromising patient well-being.

Interns benefit from virtual training scenarios. Through safe, shared virtual environments, high-risk surgical experimental procedures can be conducted and refined by teams of experts located, perhaps, far away from each other, and without the need of real cadavers. Physicians can collaborate via virtual operating theaters and decide on the best treatment and procedure before subjecting real people to surgery.

In a Real Doctor's Office

As a surgeon or physician works, he or she depends primarily on a personal assessment of the underlying structure of the part of the body affected. This personal assessment is aided by ultrasound, magnetic resonance or computerized images.

Now, a "see-through" virtual map can be superimposed on the actual area being looked at by the doctor to help him visualize what lies beneath. For example, via head-mounted display units with transparent virtual-image surfaces between their eyes and the real world, physicians will be able to examine a patient's stomach and "see" inside via a scanned image superimposed on the stomach. [Brooks91] At the same time, the real world is visible through the see-through eye units.

Arming the physician with a synthetic sense to see things that are normally invisible (like ultrasound readings), the VR system transforms image data from the ultrasound equipment to the visor. The images displayed are generated from datasets from the real patient.

A visualization system interprets and transforms the data collected into computer-enhanced images that show the anatomical structure and reveal details of the surrounding tissue. This transparent, ultrasound-generated image, placed between the physician's eyes and the real body, equips the doctor with a type of *ultra*vision (called x-ray vision by some researchers).

This "ultravision" is especially helpful, for example, to physicians planning facial or hip reconstruction surgery. A 3-D image of the actual bone is visible as tissue around it is manipulated.

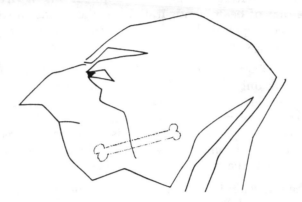

It is hoped that these ultrasound reconstructions in real time will aid the specialist in reinforcing, on the spot, what he or she feels physically or intuitively.

Visual Enhancement

Currently, interfaces between the surgeon and the surgical instruments he or she controls via the system leave a lot to be desired. There is always room for improving the accuracy of the feedback and calibration to physicians interacting with the system. To help, visual enhancement effects such as highlighting, shading and perspective are combined with stereoscopic techniques that intensify the 3-D effect. In many cases, they are not exact measurements; features are usually exaggerated — for the sole purpose of helping the physician visualize the situation. Pattern-recognition features and edge enhancements may be included, as well, to help a doctor discern differences and make comparisons.

However, data that are interpreted and displayed in enhanced images can be made even more valuable if they are augmented by expertise; so, more and more artificial-intelligence techniques are being embedded into the programs. These further enhance what the doctor "sees." For example, surgical cut planes that are optimally effective and minimally intrusive can be superimposed upon the images to guide physicians as they cut through the soft tissue to the bone. In a learning environment, various techniques can be used for nonsubject, nonintrusive experimental surgical procedures and for collaborative preventive and interventive experimentation.

RADIATION TREATMENT

One of the most exciting, within-reach applications of virtual-reality techniques is that of beam configuration for the radiation treatment of tumors. The technique of this type of treatment and therapy requires bringing very strong x-ray beams to bear on the tumor.

Traditionally, diagnostic radiologists and radiation oncologists who treat cancer have only two- or three-dimensional computer images to augment their expertise when delivering lethal doses of radiation to a cancerous tumor. Always present is the danger of exposing normal tissue surrounding the tumor, as well. The task is to put the beams through in such a way that they hit only the tumor and miss other sensitive parts of the anatomy, such as the spinal cord or the eyes. [ABC91]

Usually, the physician has, ultimately, to rely on an educated guess of the three-dimensional structure of the tumor or organ being targeted. Even the most highly skilled and experienced specialists find this difficult since each situation is unique. The targeted growth may be wrapped around an organ, may be embedded in sensitive tissue or may have offshoots threading into other areas. Anything that allows the doctor to better examine the out-of-control growth allows him or her to better decide on the most effective angles and means of dealing with it. Meeting the challenge is made easier by prepositioning virtual beams in a virtual mock-up of the actual affected area of the body.

How It's Done

The process begins with a traditional CAT-scan (or MRI) image of the patient. This is turned into 3-D model of the patient's body. This virtual-reality rendering of the patient's actual anatomy becomes the virtual patient (complete with tumor).

A head-mounted device becomes the means by which the physician is able to enter visually and interact spatially with the virtual world of the tumor. The physician — as part of the virtual environment — can examine the patient's condition from all angles, a definite advantage over techniques that allow only flat views or noninteractive models of the anatomy. This flexibility of viewpoint is a clear diagnostic advantage even if the image is cartoon-like or not as realistic looking as those produced by some static systems.

Then, armed with virtual arrows or beams of radiation, the physician (as a virtual participant) can explore the tumor and its surroundings from all angles. He or she can then place the virtual beams in positions deemed the least likely to damage healthy tissue.

Areas depicting healthy tissue can be computer-sensitized so that, if they are invaded by the virtual beams, the physician is alerted by noticeable audio or visual symbols (a bell or stop sign, for instance). The physician can then readjust the configuration.

In some cases, scaling his or her virtual size down in proportion to that of the virtual tumor allows better maneuverability and exploration of possible beam positions.

All this happens before actual radiation is applied; thus, the physician has every opportunity to change his or her mind or replace beams for more optimal effect. This is hardly the case with other techniques.

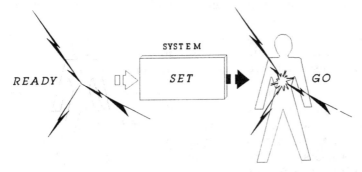

Only when the doctor in charge is satisfied that the radiation is directed at the tumor alone does actual radiation therapy begin — via feedback of the virtual beam positions to the program that controls the actual beams.

MICROMACHINES & MICROMOTORS

Micromachines are very tiny devices comprised of infinitesimally small motors, levers, gears, switches and pulleys — basically, conventional machines that have been miniaturized. Such devices are ideal for use in places too small or too hostile to accommodate conventional mechanical techniques, but because they, themselves, are so tiny, it is difficult to build them and work with them. Virtual models help in the manufacturing process and also act as interfaces to the microdevices themselves, facilitating a person's control of their various components.

The potential of using VR for advancing discoveries in the field of molecular electronics is remarkable, and research in that area is pushing the development of prototype micromachines. Current interest in applications is so keen that one U.S. manufacturing company has offered to build anyone's micromachine for $500 (if ARPA picks up the balance of the tab — which it has agreed to do for promising designs). [BusWk93] Proposals for microactuators (as they are sometimes called because they actually *do* things) include fiber-optic network switches, microgyroscopes and wind meters. In the laboratory, for example, valve setups that control the flow of gas to chromatographs to detect poisons can be replaced by microvalves of pure gold mounted on computer chips.

There are many uses for which micromachines are contraindicated. As with all new devices and technologies, applications must be chosen carefully. They cannot be used, for example, where friction, static electricity or surface tension is present because the proportional effect of any one of these is exaggerated, often too great for the tiny devices to overcome. However, the effect of gravity on a microdevice is negligible.

Currently, miniaturized machines and robotics are used as simple mechanical devices, sensors and control mechanisms. The smallest electromagnetic version has a diameter of 0.03 inch and spins as fast as 10,000 revolutions per minute. It has no practical use right now but will eventually be used in microsurgery and micromechanical factories.

Microdevices that are intelligent, self-powered and self-monitoring are being investigated — especially for medical purposes. Dwarfed even by dollhouse standards, these micromachines and micromotors are usually mounted on a silicon chip, which can also contain artificial-intelligence software, sensors, radio control units or computing capability. Among these are "smart" defibrillators that can detect and react to certain heart problems. Inserted by catheter and installed near the heart, these tiny, inexpensive devices are programmed to detect signs of irregularity and emit mild electrical stimuli to coax the heart back to normal. [Lubove91]

In factories and assembly plants, much of the old, bulky and unreliable equipment can be replaced by reliable, much cheaper micromachines. This greatly streamlines procedures and cuts rework charges. Remotely located equipment fitted with cameras allows off-site observation and telecontrol via virtual control centers, cutting many maintenance costs.

In space, micromachines are making a number of complex, intricate activities both possible and relatively inexpensive. Equipped with advanced video features and launched into space, micromachines serve as compact, reliable units for controlling space factories or manufacturing other micromachines. Also, in the near-total vacuum and the absence of corrosion or mechanical stresses in space, micromachines can be used for assembling experimental molecular modules. Microscopically tiny itself, each molecular module holds hundreds of thousands of electronic components — up to hundreds of millions per square inch. [Gannon89]

TELEMANIPULATED MICROSURGERY

Virtual reality and micromachine technologies combined with remote control are increasingly becoming part of what is called minimally invasive surgery (MIS) — i.e., with minimum incisions and probing, thereby sparing patients unnecessary trauma. Laparoscopic abdominal surgery was among the first successes of minimally invasive techniques, and it may well be among the first applications of virtual-reality telepresence in the operating theater.

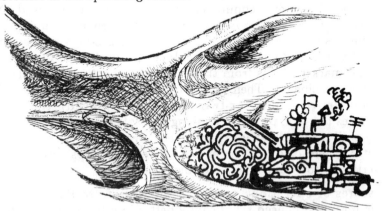

Surgeons and specialists, aided by VR displays, perform teleoperation of devices within human patients. Other applications may utilize tiny micromachines put into the body and bloodsteam as micromedical emissaries to clear obstructions, diagnose ailments or administer medication.

Body sites previously inaccessible or inhibiting to surgical or mechanical intervention, e.g., vascular systems, cell and gene levels, etc., are candidate areas for microsurgical or micromechanical intervention that is aided by enlarged virtual displays. A greatly enlarged virtual realization, one that parallels the real site, gives surgeons an added option of helping them better visualize the operating site, the micromachine and its working components. This, along with accurate telecontrol of the devices, helps surgeons perform delicate microsurgical procedures more confidently than if working to scale.

For a number of applications, size constraints were the only things that precluded machine intervention. Microsurgical techniques address those problems. However, many other problems that have nothing to do with size remain to be solved.

Notable among efforts to solve problems in VR surgical simulation are those being conducted at the Silas B. Hays Army hospital at Fort Ord in California. Its Chief of General Surgery, Col. Dr. Richard Satava, has collaborated with a Menlo Park think tank and VR product developers to add the virtual dimension to surgical techniques that already couple laparoscopy and video endoscopy. From off-the-shelf equipment and code, a relatively simple simulator was constructed for research and for training resident physicians. It hosts a virtual abdomen, complete with stomach, pancreas, liver, biliary tree and gallbladder, and a number of surgical manipulation devices. [Satava92]

A veterinarian is using telepresence to perform hip replacement surgery on dogs with osteoarthritis. The procedure requires that a surgeon custom-drill a socket in the animal's thighbone to accommodate the exact shape of whatever commercial replacement is being used. Now, computers facilitate precise measurement of the new piece and generate virtual images of the ideal cavity for it. Securing the dog's limb so that it does not move, the surgeon then places a number of pins in it as locational markers. It is from these that movements of the little robot driller are coordinated. Then, guided by the virtual images (either within an opaque environment or transparently displayed), the surgeon teleoperates the tool, progressing along a preplanned route, milling and drilling until the exact shape is pared out. Throughout the procedure, the computer system detects if the limb is moved and keeps precise track of the exertion of force and position of the cutting tip.

In scores of operations, veterinarian Dr. Howard Paul found that robotic milling produced significantly better interfacing cavities for hip replacements than hand-broached and reamed sockets. In every case, postoperative x-rays to assess placement accuracy confirmed that results were faithful to preoperative plans. [Paul92] Variations of this technique are being investigated for milling hard-to-reach replacement parts and sites for industrial equipment and commercial products.

Accentuating Features

Some virtual-reality environments allow a surgeon to accentuate his or her sense of feel or position. By facilitating a high degree of control over the actual surgical device and site, enlarged virtual scenarios allow surgeons not as dexterous to perform operations not possible with present systems. Other virtual environments provide additional feedback of various kinds to notify physicians of impediments, whether electrical or mechanical, that may interfere with the surgery.

Treatment of Aneurysms

An aneurysm is a blood-filled bubble that forms on the side of a vein — in the brain or anywhere else in the body. An aneurysm is often associated with arteriosclerosis and forms when pressure from the blood flow pushes against a weak spot in the wall of the vein. Then, as the blood circulates, it flows in and out of the cavity, as well. A fast flow past a further weakening wall can cause the aneurysm to burst, leading to hemorrhage — and the possible death of the patient.

To lessen the danger of this happening, a variety of challenging methods are used. The goal is to restrict new, fast flow into the cavity and allow the blood there to congeal. One solution is to narrow the neck of the aneurysm, thereby either slowing down the circulation within it or stopping it altogether.

Approaching the aneurysm from outside the vein involves clearing enough of the area surrounding the bubble so the surgeon can position a fiber-like tube from which a loop is extended. The aneurysm is then lassoed, its neck constricted or tied off. This approach is possible, however, only in cases where the doctor can push surrounding tissue away from the aneurysm without seriously harming the patient. Obviously, it is not indicated for aneurysms in the brain.

In brain surgery, invasive techniques must be kept to a minimum, and manipulation of surrounding tissue is usually precluded. Because of this, techniques that cope with aneurysms from within the vein itself are capturing physicians' interest. Until recently, though, the delicacy and microscale of the task have curtailed the number of instances in which it can be performed.

One approach from within the vein involves plugging up the mouth of the aneurysm with a coil of metal. But aneurysms in the brain pose a particular problem in that *any* intervention, even just maneuvering the cork into place, can cause the aneurysm to pop. Under traditional conditions, surgeons are unable to accurately gauge when this will happen.

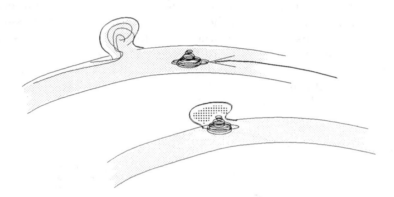

Here's where VR technology helps. An enlarged virtual scenario of both the devices and the site of the aneurysm gives a surgeon a high degree of control and allows close, real-time observation of the dynamics of the blood flow in and around the affected area. Methods are being developed to permit the surgeon to observe the blood flow patterns as the coil is actually being moved.

This approach may benefit from results of research on the behavior of steady and unsteady air flows as displayed in virtual windtunnels (described in Chapter 12). The techniques used there are applicable to studies of other types of fluid flows, as well, such as blood through our vascular systems. By real-time monitoring of changes in the virtual blood flow and examination of wall dilatation — all via displays corresponding to the operative process — surgeons are better able to weigh the probable risk of the aneurysm popping against the probable risks of action.

The techniques are also being incorporated into studies of the heart. Researchers in Germany are compiling all known data and function information of the heart to observe from within a virtual ventricle or artery what happens during an attack or fibrillation. They are well on their way to getting an inside look at the pump.

VR-IMPROVED COMMUNICATION

Between Patient & Physician

Patients aided by the technology are able to more actively participate with healers in determining the course of their treatment. Symptoms such as pain in a specific area or intensity of discomfort can be presented by the doctor in a realization that the patient adjusts to align with his or her perception of the same symptoms. Armed with this visual language, patients and doctors more effectively understand and communicate to each other what is going on. Decision making is infused with valuable feedback and an emotional aspect often overlooked in treatment.

Virtual scenarios will be effective in diffusing fears in patients when they are able to observe virtual procedures of operations or courses of treatment being considered. Virtually on-site with his or her physician, a patient "walks through" the process, perhaps taking a look at the ulcer that hurts so much, and can query the doctor along the way about how it is to be treated.

Among Specialists & in Therapy

It will be possible for colleagues to examine the same virtual anatomical model and confer right at the site of a virtual aneurysm, for instance, to arrive at an optimal plan of treatment. Networked facilities also provide access from remote sites to services and literature that might otherwise be unavailable.

Collaborative exercises can also be designed for specialists to transfer their expertise to interns. (Coinhabitants of a virtual space, however, will be cartoonlike renderings, not exact likenesses of the real participants.)

The heightened sense of control and safety that a person can feel in a virtual environment makes it a suitable venue for therapeutic role-playing. Because a person is engaged in the action and helps determine the course of events, he or she can safely explore issues that hurt or frighten under ordinary circumstances. A confidante or healer can accompany a client through visual scenarios, encouraging dialogue and behavior modification techniques along the way. Alternate perspectives can foster insight on the parts of both.

From local or remote sites, participants can connect to a shared virtual space for interpersonal group exchange or to practice social skills. Members of such groups may be real or may represent therapeutically contrived agents programmed specifically to address an individual client's needs. It is teleconferencing at a new level.

Certain psychoanalytic procedures stress a person's awareness of environmental demands and address the ways in which a person adjusts to them to meet instinctual needs. Exposure to the relevant principles of reality is, perhaps, better handled in safe, controlled and controllable environments specially designed to introduce such elements in measured doses. These virtual environments facilitate creative structuring of sessions. They also allow gradients of intensity and distance. As treatment progresses, the process is accelerated, slowed or repeated to accommodate the patient's needs. How successfully a patient adjusts determines the nature and pace of treatment.

The nonthreatening aspect and manipulative visual props of a well-designed environment accommodate subverbal cues and communication between participants. Together, in safe virtual scenarios, the patient and analyst visualize and explore underlying problems. There, the patient is provided with self-controllable, therapeutic opportunities in which to practice behavior modification and discover positive ways of dealing with situations.

The effectiveness of other therapeutic techniques may also be bolstered by the enhanced visual features of VR technology. Biofeedback is based first on a patient becoming aware of his or her involuntary bodily processes — e.g., heart rate, temperature or blood pressure. Then, variations of conscious, voluntary mental effort are used to control them. Immersion in a virtual environment or the use of transparent displays help a person visualize what is happening and can positively reinforce mental and behavioral techniques that work best for him or her.

Though these techniques will not supplant strict biomedical models now entrenched in western medicine, they are increasingly becoming adjuncts. Physicians are including what are termed biopsychosocial models into their practices and have found that the use of guided mental image paths often speeds up the healing process. Positive emotions, for example, affect immunity by enhancing a brain's signal to the thymus gland, which releases microphages — immune system cells. Negative emotions depress this response by the brain. By going through trial runs and viewing a virtual realization of the process (as it happens in his or her own body), a patient can learn how to stimulate or inhibit particular responses. Techniques for meditation and stress reduction can be reinforced when enhanced through visual stimuli in a properly designed virtual setting. [Barasch92]

Emotional/Cognitive Creatures

In the *Oz* project under way at Carnegie Mellon University (described in Chapter 8), researchers have created shallow but broadly capable virtual characters called Blobs. These are joined by emotional/cognitive creatures called Woggles and a simulated house cat named Lyotard. Through these, designers hope to integrate elements of perception, cognition, emotion, action and language into virtual environments.

A set of *emotions* such as fear, gratitude, anger or happiness and a list of *features* such as contentment, curiosity, energy or friendliness were assigned to Lyotard. Also written into the AI-based software were *behaviors* that might connote Lyotard's (or another cat creature's) underlying reasons for acting that way.

Computer-created and generated Woggles are programmed to act and respond in believable ways. They are positioned to interact with humans in a virtual environment. Applications like this read like scripts, and features, behaviors and choices are varied to broaden the scope of possible environments. This type of embedded capability for "intelligent" interactivity will not only form the basis for many game applications in the future but will allow more flexibility within therapeutic environments.

ENABLING THE DISABLED

Luckily, the same engine that drives products for entertainment is driving applications to *en*able the *dis*abled, as well. This area includes some of the most humane applications to date. If only temporarily, on a virtual diamond, kids who could only watch will now virtually feel what it's like to swing a bat, hear the crack as the ball connects and run around the bases. The bedridden can re-experience the joy of a bicycle ride in the neighborhood or, perhaps, stroll downhill through the Alps.

Reinforced by glorious audio renditions of a favorite piece of music, a music lover may take the baton and be transported into the virtual black tie and tails of a favorite conductor leading the Philharmonic. The only limitations will be those of the participant's imagination and the creativity of the designers of the virtual-environment programs.

Virtual experience will never be real experience. Unfortunately, even with all the technology in the world, a person who cannot walk still cannot walk. However, a carefully designed virtual experience can approximate participation in a person's mind, give the person a sense of control over the environment, albeit virtual, and greatly facilitate learning and training processes.

The virtual world can offer a safe, common ground of equal mobility to its population, and the psychological benefits of being able to interact free of the trappings of affliction are obvious. Aided by the technology and sensors that reinforce illusions of reality, a homebound individual can tap into a virtual office shared by other professionals and interact naturally and productively with them. Together they can "walk" down to another person's virtual office and include him in their discussions.

Scenarios will eventually be constructed to include environments as realistic as possible for many professions. Emancipated from his or her dependence on physical mobility, a user can access a virtual library, that looks and "feels" like a library and may even smell like a library, to pick up a virtual book and turn its pages. He or she may even query a virtual reference librarian about a topic.

Biocontrollers

Conceivably, the standard set of input devices such as gloves or steering bars will be augmented with eye-controlled or muscle-controlled signallers — whatever limited controls or movement a user has. Measurements are made of a person's possible range of motion, and motions within that range are converted into computer-readable signals to start the software and keep it running. [Pausch91]

These biocontrollers or biosensors, as they are called, can detect and process most bioelectrical signals, such as eye movement or the electrical activity of muscles or the brain. Collections of biocontroller signals can be programmed meaningfully as complex commands to the system, thus giving the person an enabling sense of control to manipulate his or her virtual environment in ways not directly possible in the real world. Biocontrol technology will affect the ways in which many of us interact with computers and exploit them for our good.

From among the many types of biocontrol, three types seem to be particularly suited for medical applications [Lusted&92]:

- eye controllers, which enlist horizontal and vertical eye movements as control signals;

- muscle controllers, which capture as signals and map various traces of electrical activity in muscles; and

- brainwave controllers, which don't yet exist but which hold the potential for detecting and transmitting brainwave signals representing subvocal (sometimes called subverbal) commands to systems. (See Chapter 14.)

Biocontrollers are being investigated in conjunction with MIDI, special code designed to accept many kinds of signals as commands, including those from eye, muscle and brainwave activity. MIDI then implements those commands to control electronic instruments.

Players of video games have used eye-control devices as substitutes for joysticks to control the movements of a game character with normal eye movement. Combinations of eye and muscle controllers have also been programmed to emulate computer-mouse commands — eye motion positions the cursor, and muscle movement clicks the mouse buttons.

Other applications route signals produced from muscle activity to robots or other mechanical devices. The intensity and duration of the muscle signal extend the range and accuracy of a user's control. Muscle controllers are particularly suitable for use by physically disabled persons, many of whom have residual electrical activity in their muscles that is functional but too weak to produce movement. Very often, this can be detected by computer and, with the proper biocontrol setup, captured in control code and used to run devices.

Muscle tension can be mapped to note number and volume on a music synthesizer, for instance, enabling different amounts of exertion to change pitches and sound levels. With the aid of a sequencer, tunes or even whole musical pieces can be performed with the user controlling emphasis through tempo and volume [Lusted&92] — in essence, playing music with muscles.

The software and the environment setup for each application are independent of the way the actual biocontroller works. So, with any one biocontroller setup, a user may "plug into" and activate different application modules.

For the many persons for whom real physical movement is increasingly impossible, and for those who cannot move at all, the combination of biocontrol and virtual-reality technologies could be the best thing that has happened for them in a long while. Through virtual imagery and feedback technologies, they can now occasionally shed their dependence, exercise control and navigate freely. Virtually moving through virtual worlds, they can experience what it is like to act unencumbered and interact as freely and expansively as their minds allow.

Virtual movement enables a person to transcend being stuck in a wheelchair or a bed, in other words, to temporarily "leave" it. He or she may not actually walk along the Great Wall of China but, after doing so virtually, would come close to knowing what it would be like. The psychological boost alone justifies some applications.

Brainwave controllers are being investigated as volitional control mechanisms in a number of areas. Pattern detection programs analyze and program different types of brainwave activity as commands to a system. Those connected with emotional intensity, anxiety, happiness, anger, etc. can possibly be channeled into control signals. To date, there is no controller that can interpret subvocal commands, but controllers are already used to modulate background noises or music. The emotional tension of the performer (user of the system) can influence the sound quality of a piece of music being played.

Fujitsu is developing a helmet to tap into brainwaves without the use of electrodes — initially, to discern only "yes" and "no" thoughts. However, much of their work is in an early experimental stage.

Barrier-Free Homes & Transportation

One very practical use of the technology was prompted by a federal law passed to provide wheelchair access to all forms of public transportation by 1996. [CNN92] In order to comply in time with the regulations and not incur high development costs that would have to be passed on in increased fares, transport authorities needed a way to develop and build prototypes of renovated mass transport quickly and cheaply.

Eclectic teams of program designers, architects, transport engineers and legions of wheelchair volunteers were brought together to come up with virtual solutions and test them in virtual scenarios. With input from all of them, for example, a new lift system is designed, then built as a virtual system and tested for ease of use.

The software contains collision detectors so that a user is aware of bumps and the virtual limits of the proposed design (including walls). If, when tested, something presents a problem or suggests a better solution, the design is adjusted on the spot.

Being able to refine the design like this, without having to rebuild a prototype, dramatically speeds up the timetable and keeps costs down. Work progresses on schedule and within budget.

In the same way, the Veteran's Administration has employed VR design teams to design and test customized living areas for residents and outpatients. On-site facilities are being upgraded to accommodate and encourage independence in persons with varying handicaps. Designs for off-site housing adaptations (e.g., widening doorways, making a stove's back burner reachable from a wheelchair, adjusting the heights and depths of bathroom fixtures and outlets, etc.) are tested first in a virtual mock-up by people who will actually use them. Only after the virtual designs have been thoroughly tested and approved does actual construction begin.

Living spaces for any group with specialized needs can be designed and tested by prospective dwellers or users before actual construction or renovation takes place. These might include retirement housing, nursery facilities or outpatient centers.

Helping the Blind "See"

For blind persons, getting familiar with new territory or activities (e.g., moving to a new house, using an escalator in an airport terminal, changing a dirty diaper, etc.) can be fraught with hazards. In one application, safe virtual reproductions of new territories, complete with haptic feedback, are constructed to allow blind persons to adapt to them and know what to expect before being exposed to the real thing.

In such a virtual setting, a user is alerted to physical obstacles such as raised door jambs but won't actually trip over them. A person bumping into a virtual kitchen cabinet "feels" the bump but does not get hurt.

Interaction between a nonseeing user and the machine is facilitated by tactile, raised-relief screens. More than just pictorial Braille, these convey information in a variety of nonvisual ways such as texture, vibrations, sounds or elevation. The same system could generate tactile, screen-size floor plans of areas or physical environments the user intends to explore, so that he or she could become familiar with points of interest (such as the check-in counters, restrooms, etc.) relative to the entrance before actually going there.

Nonhearing & Speech-Impaired Participants

One type of system is designed to accommodate nonhearing participants in multiparticipant scenarios. In effect, a cross-sensory substitution is made; the participant sees instead of hears. Whatever is said is not only heard but converted by a speech synthesizer and displayed simultaneously over the head of the speaker as a bubble caption for the nonhearer to read.

For participants unable to speak but able to provide some sort of communicative input to the system, signals such as gestures made via glove or other devices are translated into synthesized speech. Currently, a few hundred speech patterns can be programmed into a glove. These can be displayed simultaneously as bubble captions over his or her head for use in shared virtual environments.

VR TECHNOLOGY IN REHABILITATION

With the help of specially developed physiological monitoring software, researchers are producing aids for persons who are physically impaired. This kind of software produces flows of clinical data from individuals to a system. This, in turn, is analyzed and used to develop products for diagnosis and therapy.

Elements of virtual-reality technology allow individuals who have movement or communication difficulties to exercise greater degrees of control over their environment, whether at home, in the office or in society at large. They also allow specialists to monitor and measure critical motion thresholds, facilitating the review of patient progress throughout a course of treatment.

In cases where memory re-education is indicated, virtual technologies provide opportunities for the re-establishment and monitoring of lost functional patterns. The immersive nature of virtual stimulation can accelerate this type of memory re-education and pattern imprinting.

Industrial medicine practitioners and industries have also shown interest in the technologies to improve their facilities and provide their workers with tools designed to minimize the potential for work-related injuries. Settlement of worker compensation claims usually require extensive clinical assessment and progress reports, and the sensing technologies developing along with VR applications help ensure accuracy of diagnosis and appropriate corrective measures. Stressful, repetitive motions, such as those made by keyboard operators or assembly line workers, are being analyzed in order to extract patterns of behavior that aggravate or minimize the effects (e.g., carpal tunnel syndrome). When detected, virtual rehabilitation aids are designed so that individuals can practice optimal patterns of motion and receive feedback that reinforces that behavior.

Medical researchers use the DataGlove and DataSuit for studies of motion assessment for applications and products for rehabilitation training and preparation, e.g., helping victims handle objects in the everyday world. A system's ability to detect, measure and record changes in degrees of mobility alerts therapists to a patient's progress or regress during a course of treatment and enables the physician to alter or reinforce the program when needed.

Gesture-recognition systems provide an enabling input technology for the physically impaired, and one called the GloveTalker is being tested as an alternative communications device. [VPL91b] A gesture-recognizing device like the GloveTalker can be programmed to interface with a system so that hundreds of phrases can be evoked merely by gesturing.

Phrases can be displayed as text, rendered into synthesized speech or fed into equipment as commands — perhaps displayed simultaneously as a comicstrip-like bubble or electronic stream of words accompanied by the spoken rendition. With minimal exertion, physically challenged persons can make their wishes known and exercise some control over situations.

Ultimately, individuals can acquire device-resident (e.g., programmed glove) libraries of useful phrases unique to their lifestyle. If commands are programmed in standard code, they are portable to different systems, enabling users to plug into and control many devices or appliances. One such de-facto standard is the MIDI code interface to electronic music synthesizers. It is being adapted for use with other devices and appliances that can be made to respond to computer signals.

Architectural
Walk-Through

7

USING COMPUTERS FOR ARCHITECTURAL DESIGN

Computerized drafting aids and visualization techniques have been used by architects for close to two decades. Over the years, professionals in the fields of design engineering and architecture have been quick to appreciate the advances of graphics technology and to exploit them for savings in development costs and time.

First used merely to draw up simple plans and produce printouts, computer programs evolved to generate two-dimensional drawings or images on a video screen, allowing users to either zoom in on a particular spot for detail or zoom out for a look at the drawing as a whole. The majority of architectural design programs in use today are of this type.

Other computer packages adopted by architects include programs that generate elaborate, almost three-dimensional images that can be rotated, altered or combined by a user via computer commands. Designers who became skilled with these advanced tools felt empowered to challenge even their own creations and were encouraged to try out new ideas and more actively include their clients in the planning and design process.

However, even the best of these packages leaves the user an outsider, denied immersion in or direct interaction with the environment. And, because the design is relatively static, changes are costly and time-consuming, requiring regeneration of sequences of fixed frames to create the new images. The power and speed of the convergence of technologies that is virtual reality changes that. It provides architects with not only sophisticated mechanical and electronic means for producing designs but with a way of exploring them and expressing their talent at heightened levels of creativity.

Because most virtual architectural applications rely almost solely on visual exploration and do not require special effects such as sound or tactility, they are referred to as "walk-throughs" — the logical next step in the design and marketing of architectural ideas. Walk-throughs facilitate creative collaboration between designers, clients and subcontractors. Via remote access to a shared virtual space, pipefitters, decorators, consulting engineers and anyone who will ultimately be using the real spaces can be brought together to confer.

Blueprints & Elevations

Blueprints will always be necessary in some form or another, and their unique aesthetic qualities cannot be denied. But volumetric space is difficult to define on the flat drawings, and most people find thorough reading of them difficult.

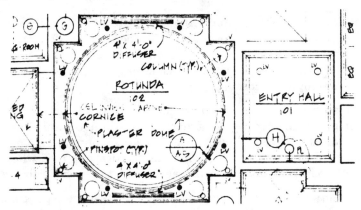

To accommodate this, architects include "elevations" in sets of blueprints. These two-dimensional line drawings of sections of the master plan help a client further visualize what the plans specify.

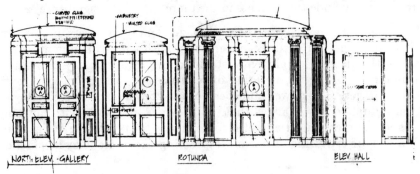

Elevations succeed in presenting a "picture" of a planned design. They fall short, however, of delivering a comprehensive view.

Virtual-reality techniques allow an architect to progress smoothly from blueprint through elevation through two- and three-dimensional renderings to — finally — an experiential realization of a finished product.

Walk-Throughs: Experiential Plans

Virtual constructions invite participants in. A virtual walk-through enables them to understand the plans another way — experientially. Now, even before a building is started, an architect and client can view and modify plans by walking, room to room, through a computer-generated, three-dimensional model of the space.

Initially, plans for a walk-through model must be entered into the computer, and a virtual building must be created. It sounds easy, but it often takes from 6 months to a year to create and debug an original model. Then, it is possible to introduce light, specifying its intensity, the direction of its source and its color, and it is also possible to simulate refraction, reflection and shadows. [Selkowitz&86] The application may be "smart." For example, doors can be programmed to open as a person nears or to close behind them.

Donning headsets and standing on a steerable treadmill, the architect and client get the sensation of stepping right into the design, where they can look at it — up, down and around — from the inside out, from any angle. By being completely surrounded by the created environment and able to walk through and manipulate the design, engineers, architects, cost estimators, maintenance personnel and safety specialists will react differently than they would if relying solely on flat, blueprint impressions. Oversights, mistakes in the design or necessary changes can be spotted quickly and rectified by their ability to "take a walk" inside and outside the facility under consideration, to see it in all its detail, to react to their observations and, if it is a shared system, to collaborate on and make modifications on the spot, in "real" time.

Because it is generally difficult for untrained people to read blueprints or verbalize design specifications, clients may not be able to convey their ideas clearly. However, in a virtual setting, a client could grab a virtual window with a virtual hand and move it or remove it. By consent, the attributes of each of the virtual components could be changed on the spot. For instance, a window could be replaced by French doors or a solarium. Tall, elegant doorways designed by an architect may make an inhabitant feel short, or washbasins may be too low for a tall occupant. By being able to experience the designs before construction, he or she can request adjustment. Knocking out a wall might look quite dramatic on paper, but experiencing the space might prompt a client to realize that he or she prefers more privacy. The created environment becomes a virtual testing ground for parties concerned.

Computer-Aided Creativity

The advantages of computerizing the design and revision processes are not only mechanical. The creativity of the designer is both enhanced and challenged by the power extended by the computer. Experimenting with novel techniques or designs is often precluded by time and cost factors, and the full potential of any design idea is seldom realized. Now, however, armed with the speed and power of computers able to generate the complex designs our minds dream up, architects are compelled, if not seduced, into exploring new options.

The possibility of rapid revision and iteration of designs promotes dramatic exploration and testing of new ideas during virtual construction. Designer and client can view and modify the virtual building and regenerate updated versions of it until they are satisfied. Revisions are far less time-consuming than original designs. Because specifications are kept up to date in the system, plans drawn from them are current and accurate, and subplans drawing specifications from the master plan — orders for materials, wiring specifications, cost projections, etc. — are automatically updated, as well. All this goes on before any actual construction is begun.

Short of actual wood and cement construction of the project, virtual-reality renderings are the best possible means of exploring what the final design will be like and are extremely cost-effective in troubleshooting before expensive physical construction is begun.

SYSTEM REQUIREMENTS

Architects invest a lot of time and effort in creating their designs and documenting them with currently available computer drafting programs like AutoCAD. This investment need not be completely lost if conversion to virtual-reality exposition is planned. Some systems designed for use with VR applications leverage this investment by providing ways to convert old files into files compatible with virtual worlds. [Zaliznyak91] With slight modifications, previously created, passive AutoCAD environments can be recycled into interactive virtual walk-throughs.

The graphics requirements of a virtual-reality architectural system often pose problems and force a trade-off between photorealism and real-time operation. Generated images are made up, mosaic-like, of many, many polygons, and the quality of the image depends on how densely the polygons compose the picture. The quality of image is directly proportional to the number of polygons used to create it.

The speed at which a system delivers images depends on how fast these polygons can be produced, and then how fast the frames they comprise are generated and displayed. To approach the realistic motion that is so much a part of virtual-reality scenes, the real-time graphics systems must generate at least 60 frames per second. The less expensive systems cannot do this, and the quality of image and the bid at realism of these systems suffer greatly.

Systems within most architects' affordable budgets sacrifice speed in favor of features needed to display the architect's designs. Whatever advantage is gained by buildings being made up mostly of rectangular planes, each of which can be represented by a single polygon, is more than offset by many other components that require polygon-intensive representation — such as renderings of light, reflection and texture. In such systems, computer power is not the issue; the display mechanism is. In most systems, the computation is done and messages are passed much faster than the images can be rendered.

One way designers deal with polygon intensity is by partitioning the entire model and concentrating resources on one good viewpoint at a time rather than maintaining a "live" image of the whole building. [Airey&91] The overall application is segmented into relatively independent cells. Depending on the viewpoint determined by where a user is located within the virtual environment, only potentially visible cells are called up to display. Thus, if a person were standing at a doorway looking into a sitting room, only those parts of the model that would be visible from that viewpoint are actually loaded for display — one room and parts of another, perhaps, rather than the whole house.

Another means of leveraging computing resources, "texture mapping," reduces the number of polygons needed to create an illusion of surface design. By filling in polygons with ready-made textured patterns instead of designing and generating the look from many individual polygons, the toll on computing resources is reduced. Mottling, woodgrain effects and construction material surface patterns are substituted for single colors within individual polygons.

System Savvy

In order to use the systems, architects must already know how to use one or more of the standard computer drafting packages. Also, since the needs and apparatus measurements of every user are different, someone working on the project must know how to maintain and manage the virtual-reality sensing gear and adjust it if necessary to custom-fit individuals wanting to interact with the virtual world. This would include the calibration of gloves or bodysuits or helmets.

An architect's investment in this technology is high. Even for a simple, one-person system, no fewer than three software packages and a lot of expensive hardware are necessary. For a two-person system, which is warranted for good designer/client collaboration, more expensive hardware is needed, and initial investment costs rise an average of 50 per cent, which is prohibitive for many users. [Zaliznyak91]

Hardware System Characteristics

The systems used for architectural environments consist of many rather expensive pieces of computer hardware. Deciding to use such a system entails a major investment of both time and effort on the architect's part.

For a start, a purchase order for the most notable piece of equipment, an advanced graphics workstation, must be doubled; one computer is needed for each eye of the user. If two users want to access the virtual environment simultaneously (which is usually the case with architect and client), four machines are needed. Some software exists to render images for both eyes with one computer, but it slows everything down, especially the rate at which frames are updated, and makes walk-throughs prohibitively unrealistic. It is not a viable option.

Cabling and networking facilities are required for the transmission of signals from the input devices (whether headgear, glove or remote manipulator) to the workstations and then, from there, to the displays. If a designer wants to add audio features to the virtual environment, the list of hardware grows. Audio components containing a real-time signal-processing subsystem are needed, as well as the means to provide a wearer with sounds simultaneously from as many as four sources.

Tracking devices are needed for both the headgear and the glove. If a treadmill or other device is specified, that and the peripheral hardware for it must be bought or built. If, instead of headgear viewing apparatus, a wall screen is preferred, an appropriate one must be installed and hooked up to the computer.

Software System Characteristics

Generally, for architectural purposes, three different types of software are needed to:

- design virtual objects;
- define the manner of behavior of the virtual objects;
- import data available in other formats for conversion and use in virtual models.

Software used to design virtual objects and virtual worlds is very similar to AutoCAD and other drafting packages. It allows a user to create the shapes, layout, hierarchical linkages, lighting, color, texture and motion constraints of three-dimensional objects. AutoCAD incorporates extrusion features; so, it is better than 2-D (about 2-and-a-half-dimensional) but not quite 3-D.

Once the objects have been designed, it is important to define how they appear to act in the virtual environment, what attributes they display and what control information they employ. For example, water flows, and it would be defined as an object that moves of its own accord.

Some objects will have to embody particular qualities of motion, density or radiosity — falling, floating, illuminating, etc., and these must also be defined through the software. The software contains algorithms for this purpose.

Other objects will appear to move or be transformed only in response to being "touched" or otherwise manipulated in the virtual environment, e.g., a kiss. When the system detects common coordinates between the two objects, in other words, a virtual "touch," it initiates the animation.

The third (usually optional) type of software, converts existing CAD/CAM data (such as AutoCAD files) into virtual-friendly code. It is, therefore, a tool for designers interested in minimizing the time and cost of switching from old computer-drafting systems to VR systems. Conversion software allows architects (or others) to salvage designs that represent substantial previous investments of designer time and money.

Separate software is also needed for the calibration of gloves, control of audio components or two-handed use. This type of software is usually included with the purchased equipment pieces.

METHOD OF UTILIZATION

After the hardware equipment is set up and the system is up and running, it is time for the architect and client to enter the virtual world. Seldom is an architectural system for virtual-reality design meant for use by the architect alone; most systems are used by two people, architect and client. Each participant dons a head-mounted device and an instrumented glove. Calibration for each device follows and usually takes several minutes.

Calibration

First, the distance between the eyes is measured for each user. The feeling of depth sensed by a user is due to images displayed to each eye as if being seen from slightly different angles. Eyepieces must be adjusted accordingly to optimize this depth perception and to avoid clue conflict and the occasional motion sickness it may cause. Nausea may also occur in so-called "barf" zones, i.e., when the display is updated too fast or too slowly.

Liquid-crystal displays (LCDs) were used in most early versions of the head-mounted displays and could not be placed very close to the eyes because of their low resolution. More and more, these are being replaced by little televisions, cathode-ray tube (CRT) screens that deliver brighter, higher-resolution results and can be placed closer to a user's eyes. This is because CRT display technology has evolved very quickly over the last decade, and light, flat, little (1″ square) CRTs are now available.

Glove calibration comes next — for each glove and for each participant. This is usually done by the user merely making a fist a few times after putting it on. Adjustments are sometimes warranted later on, but most problems are results of improper sequences of hand gestures rather than faulty calibration. [Zaliznyak91]

Navigation

Once the user has been outfitted and the gear properly calibrated, he or she prepares to navigate through the virtual world. Routes may be prearranged or free-form, and constraints are built into the system to prevent a user from doing such things as walking on water or going through walls.

Architect and client can step through the scenario using treadmill devices, in which case, each participant mounts one, or they can be "pulled" through, conveyor-belt-like, on a preset visual tour. Alternately, they can zoom through via hand commands.

By pointing an index finger toward the top of a stairway and flexing the thumb, a user indicates to the system that he or she wants to go upstairs. How quickly or slowly this command is executed is determined by how quickly or slowly the user moves the thumb. This is the indicator most often preferred for traversing large distances or for going upstairs, but other gestures or simple spoken commands can be programmed for navigation.

Communication

To communicate, participants usually go back to the basics — they actually speak to each other. Systems are being devised to accommodate other means of communication, especially for the purposes of virtual conferencing or shared virtual environments; however, most architectural applications in use today use no special speech or translation devices.

To some degree, while inside the design, the architect and client may create new components or alter those there. A specialized virtual-object-building "toolbox" can be invoked as part of the display. This may float around like a menu-driven paintbrush screen. Tools may be activated by virtual touch or by simple, prearranged spoken commands. A designer chooses from available toolbox options and works with them as if in the real environment.

A PRACTICAL FUTURE

Experiments with Reality Net aim to one day provide architects and clients, as well as many other classes of users, venues for common virtual spaces in which they can communicate and collaborate. Architects and clients will be able to hook up, separately and by long distance, to one virtual environment and walk through it together in virtual reality.

Using computer visualization and renderings for architectural walk-throughs not only saves time and money compared with production costs of 3-D models, but it also extends the creative resources of the people working on the project. A flat rendering of an intended design can only hint at the depth, texture and potential that a creative person imagines. A two-dimensional view is a poor representation of the final product. Being able to walk through the virtual model with the architect or others involved in the job also gives the client an opportunity to examine the design from a vantage point closer in spirit to the original ideas than is offered by conventional plans. The virtual design is closer in appearance to what the real product will look and feel like when built.

Together, "on site," a designer and client will communicate in a timesaving and cost-effective way, making changes as they go along. The immediate applicability of the use of virtual-reality technology for architectural purposes is seen in the numbers of systems already employed. (See "Enabling the Disabled" in Chapter 6.) However, the quality and speed of display of the images remain less than realistic.

ARCHITECTURE &
THE TRANSMISSION OF CULTURAL HERITAGE

Words and gestures have long served as effective input to oral-tradition systems. These natural, low-bandwidth means, shared by all cultures, stimulate powerful mental images to communicate the uniqueness of a people's history and heritage. Passed from generation to generation, poems, adages, ceremonies and folktales provide colorful storylines of identity and belonging. Honed over millennia to evoke vivid images in young and old alike, lyrical extracts of what a people are all about succeed where high-bandwidth technology often fails — in fully immersing listeners in a form of mental magic. This will not change.

What may change is the use of virtual architectural models to accurately reconstruct the brick and mortar details that also embody elements of a cultural heritage. Oral tradition guarantees transmission of a people's spiritual and personal lineage; architectural models can help preserve the historical.

As noted in Chapter 8, applications are already being written to recreate archaeological sites of global interest. *Virtual Ancient Egypt* is one such project. Visitors to a shared virtual space can wander through historically faithful renderings of classic buildings and archaeological sites. Similar virtual environments can be built at local, focused levels for indigenous and ethnic groups.

The World of Entertainment

8

> "Going to the feelies this evening, Henry?"
> BRAVE NEW WORLD

HOLLYWOOD FILMS & COMPUTER GRAPHICS

In the past, computer graphics and film production evolved along separate paths. There was little hope that computer-generated worlds would ever approach the photorealism of films. Little by little, though, computer technology found its way to Hollywood, where it was welcomed and used in that town's inimitable way.

Now, Hollywood's brand of creativity and animation techniques are being adopted in the world of computer applications. Between the previously divergent paths of films and computer graphics, numerous two-way collaborations and trades are going on. The arts and technologies are merging.

In particular, the push for futuristic film adventures has spurred creativity in computer-assisted animation. Cyborgs of recent Hollywood films, *Terminator 2*, *Lawnmower Man* and *Robocop 2*, are familiar examples of techniques that are precursors of virtual scenarios. Through the power of computers, spiritless characters are energized, and audiences are drawn into the action, as if mesmerized, cheering as the illusionary transformations escape annihilation.

Morphing

The pioneering work done in Hollywood will help us populate our virtual worlds. However, the slick images shown on television or in the movies are not easily created and are not typical of what a person would see in a virtual environment. That part of the process is still labor-intensive and time-intensive and requires powerful computing capacity.

One of the techniques developed has been coined "morphing," which is a computer-generated illusion of metamorphosis. Few moviegoers realize that morphed, cinema-robotic figures are modeled directly after a person. The first step of the process is to digitize photos taken of a real person, filmed from many angles, while he or she "models" whatever moves are needed for the story. The muscle-action images are digitized, fed into a computer, "studied" and then manipulated into a photorealistic graphic image — a cyborg.

Digitized information from more than 70 photos, for instance, was used to create the wire-frame synthetic actor in *Lawnmower Man*. The cyborg is then enlivened with animatronic effects. Combinations of static facial expressions are animated to accurately depict lip-synching, for example.

Morphing is not only being used for television product advertisements, but it is also being adopted as an effective business tool. In industrial manufacturing, if morphing capability is incorporated into the design process, new virtual components can be made to fit existing or revised designs. Visualization and realization techniques described in Chapters 1 and 2 allow designers of manufactured components to immediately assess the impact of new ideas or changes via their screens or virtual design environments.

Computer Animation

The entire animation process has been simplified and streamlined by computer technologies. Programs assist the animator in creating frames that project the illusion of movement. Movement may consist of the camera scanning across a scene, an actor walking in a scene or some combination of the two.

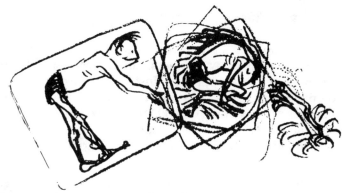

With computer programs, the animator and artist no longer have to predict how a character will walk or how a ball will follow gravity as it bounces; these things can be programmed into the computer to generate frames accordingly.

Enhanced Creativity

So far, computer capabilities have not caged individual creative spirit or the energies of the professionals; rather, they have extended their human capabilities and have helped them increase their productivity. Animated modules created with computer help are usually fluid and of high quality and exhibit photorealistic, believable animation.

As the imaginations of the film animators soar wildly, they continually challenge technology to keep up with them. Their work has provided an important platform for the advancement of virtual-reality techniques in many areas.

Designing sets, for example, is very much like designing a scene for a virtual environment. A simulation by computer of the destruction of city buildings is a more useful, cost-effective and time-saving tool for fabricating and redesigning images than are physical, scaled models that have to be completely rebuilt after each trial-run destruction.

The sophisticated graphics programs originally intended for use by engineers and architects had the very features that Hollywood animators wanted for their work; however, they required advanced computer skills. This precluded their use by most designers. Only recently, when the software industry simplified the interfaces of its graphics programs, was the world of computer graphics and animation opened up to the multimedia artists of Hollywood. Today, the expertise gained by movie-makers in animatronics and computer graphics as they exploit their new-found computer power extends well beyond illusions of metamorphosis and is being transferred to other media, as well.

Computer-Assisted Cinematography

The difficult task of creating a photorealistic image for films or computer screens is made a lot easier by scanners, small devices similar to copy machines but connected to a computer. Instead of reproducing an image with toner on paper, as copiers do, scanners use a finely focused beam of light or electrons to optically or electronically sense the image or recorded material and convert it into digitized form, which can then be cleaned up and modified with a computer paint program.

The transformation or animation of one character to another form was first advanced in motion pictures in two dimensions. The current technology provides scanners that can digitize 2- and 3-dimensional images from photos, books, magazines, oil paintings and relatively flat objects such as pressed flowers. Scanners analyze the image (actually, record how the dots making up the image are arranged) and send the data to the computer. The amount of data provided is determined in part by the resolution set by the scanner; the better the resolution (in other words, the more dots per inch), the more information the computer has to work with when regenerating the image.

The quality of the computer image is also affected by the optics unit on the scanner. The caliber of the focus of light reaching the scanner sensors through a lens also affects how well the image can be reproduced. Colors are often ill-defined as errors are introduced through lens manufacturing or asynchronization. To separate colors or shades of gray, scanners make several passes over the material, each sensitive to one color or shade. All information must then be integrated. Scanning is also time-consuming; it can take up to 2 minutes to scan an image for one frame of a sequence.

So, scanners are very useful, but they do only part of the job. Much more work is needed to create realistic characters and scenarios for virtual-reality use.

Various other scanner devices and image-processing programs are available to digitize images, and printers attached to the computers for other purposes can be used to produce hard copies. Image-editor programs are also available to enhance, modify or embellish the computer images.

Transfer of 3-D Data from Video to Computer

The transfer of 3-D data from video to computer is a highly sophisticated process. Video productions are synchronized, time-based interactions of visual images, animations and sound. Multimedia design tools convert this kind of time-based data into computer-storable data. Then it can be accessed by programs and attached, for instance, to documents.

Previously, conversion of the data was not enough. Specialized hardware was required to combine computer programs with any type of video presentation. Usually, a person could not attach a video segment to an electronic document without first having installed a video disk player, a CD-ROM reader, a video monitor or a video window board in the computer. This is because video presentations are made up of so many bits of data, they need to be compressed for storage and decompressed as they are accessed and used.

Now, some programs and machines can include movie segments in computer programs without additional peripheral equipment. Some can synchronize time-related data without regard to the speed of the system being used. Some even control the compression and decompression of the video signals.

Editing options for improving the quality of images that have been transferred from video into computer storage include programs to convert the signals to particular standards (such as NTSC for U.S. sets or PAL for European viewing), control flickers, sharpness, alignment and gamma correction. Many video-editing programs can be run on ordinary personal computers, particularly the Macintosh. With the aid of such machines and programs, video and audio segments from camcorders, VCRs and other sources are digitized and compressed.

The reverse process can also take place. Once the movie is created through some computer program, it can be transferred back to videotape or other television-compatible medium. As standards are established within the industry for the organization, storage and exchange of time-related data, this process will be greatly simplified.

Enhancing Digitized Images

Images that have been digitized and computer processed usually need some editing and touching up. Scanned-in colors are often distorted, producing, for example, too much red or too much green.

Image-editing programs allow a viewer to edit images. They also give a programmer or user the option of "masking" or protecting an image or part of an image. A stencil-like mat is superimposed on the image, allowing users to change only what is displayed in cut-out areas. Sharply defined edges or fading edges are also options. Most tools used for altering or enhancing images require a great deal of expertise and experience. Many designers have opted to invest the time and effort needed to obtain the flexibility and power that these programs give them over images they wish to use.

Rendering an Application

Virtual-reality applications require that information be translated from the digitized form into another form that is realistic and understandable. The computer uses mathematical formulae to do calculations on the data to arrange pixels on the screen into images that reflect what is being communicated. Reducing data to a pictorial state or interpretation often aids communication in that visual interpretations are more easily and quickly understood than other forms of representation.

One step that brings display technology closer to what is needed to create virtual-reality beings is visualization, a display technique not particularly suited to Hollywood's products. Visualization is used primarily for physics, chemistry and medical applications that need to communicate expert interpretation and analysis to a user but do not necessarily benefit from the user's interaction. Its benefit to the entertainment field has been primarily to spur on the development of dedicated, user-friendly machines that combine high-speed and high-power computing with elegant graphics capabilities.

Visualizations are generally a preliminary step in the creation of animated figures. After the image is created, it is given dimension, shading and coloring. Then, a graphics program modeler is used to render it into three dimensions. A modeler is special software that allows a user to create unique-being shapes or put them together from a collection provided. Other software is usually used for backgrounds, surroundings or objects. From the basic shapes, an animator may choose to alter specific shapes to create his or her own objects. These may be resized, distorted, rotated, smashed or stretched to suit the user's fancy.

Other software useful for animation purposes are the extrusion editor and the lathe. Images from other files can be imported to the file the animator wants to use. The line that appears around the edges of the shape (around things sticking out, its extrusions) can be traced over for use in the new file. The extrusion editor is used to do this. The lathe is used to create a solid, three-dimensional object out of the outline — as if it were rotated on its vertical axis.

Characters can also be created from different objects or parts of the body linked together. In animation, the character's parts may move around flexibly, separate from each other. For example, the creation of a cyborg from complex, linked parts can be accomplished in several steps. First, each body part is created separately to allow for detailed drawings of the arms, legs, head and body. These parts are then linked using the option of pivot locks, part of the software. Pivot locks allow two jointed pieces to move uniquely simultaneously. This feature helps the artist create realistic moving images, such as a cyborg walking. It is also used to animate objects that are usually inanimate, e.g., a walking chair.

The creator works on the characters in three dimensions and can view the image from any perspective and play with focal points within that perspective. Combining these and other options, the animator can produce very realistic-looking images.

Animated Sequences

Parameters are stored in the computer for each of the images created. These can be programmed to change. The image can be rotated, scaled up or down or translated into another form. The rate of change and timing is controlled by the program, as well. Basically, animation works as a series of parameter changes within a set period of time.

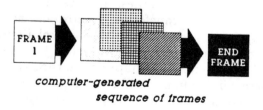

computer-generated
sequence of frames

Animation is the last phase of the image processing. To create the illusion of motion, the program starts with two frames of the envisioned sequence, the first (of the current position of the object) and the last (of the desired position of the object after movement). The sequence of frames in between is generated by computer program.

Then, to the first frame, the program applies a formula for type of change and rate of change. It is incrementally changed to reflect that bit of motion, and a new frame is generated — becoming the second frame (the first of the in-betweens). The formula is then applied to that frame to produce the next frame, and so on, until the image matches the one in the last frame, the destination frame.

Thus, the object changing from its start position to its goal position creates the effect of movement. The creator does not have to draw each and every frame; he or she needs to provide only key frames. The program itself fills in the steps between and creates the frames necessary for animation.

Basically the same procedure is followed for the metamorphosis of one object into another. As used in motion pictures, two snapshots are taken of two different objects. Increments of movement include the change of shape and surface of the beginning object. A few changes are made in each frame, and a sequence consists of many frames. When the sequence is played, it appears as if the object has transformed from the first object to the second.

In the same way, environments, backgrounds or special effects (e.g., lighting, colors) can be made to appear to change. Some programs include a gravity tool or a registered-path tool. With the gravity tool, for instance, an artist can specify the strength and direction of pull. A registered-path tool allows the artist to predetermine responses to certain actions, such as the kind of path an object will take if it hits the wall. How realistic the movement appears depends on the number of frames and the range of movements, which are usually set by the programmer.

Transfer to Videotape

Indeed, it would be nice if virtual environments could be created with the photorealistic effects we see in movies. However, the advances made in cinematography cannot be transferred directly, and adapting existing media to VR applications is a major research challenge. The high resolution of film photography is not matched by computer display technologies. In essence, what happens is that the film and the movements of actors in the film must be decomposed into digital signals and then recomposed as less resolute computer-displayed images.

There are ways and means available for capturing on a computer screen things that have been filmed or recorded in other media. There are also ways to capture in real time (on film or videotape) anything that has appeared on a computer screen. Artists and developers grab from both to create the effects they need.

These digitized versions can be then analyzed, reworked, amended and retaped. A programmer can view them in a continuous manner or in a frame-by-frame manner, stopping the generation of images whenever he or she wishes.

Storage of such signals requires a lot of file space on the computer; so, some animators use programs to analyze the digitized "film" frame by frame and record only what is different from one to the next. Then, they store a record of only the changes detected between frames.

The animator can alter the digitized versions of film material and then transfer the material to other media, including videotape. If the computer files are viewed at at least 30 frames per second, a viewer cannot see the movement of the frames, and there is an illusion of smooth transition in movements. This is one method being explored in the creation of realistic virtual-reality scenes.

System Requirements

Generally, what are needed for such animation applications are a fast computing machine, a lot of space on the hard drive of the computer and a lot of accessible computer memory. Good quality video monitors are recommended but not vital; they affect only how the artist or animator sees the image on the screen.

Problems & Necessary Improvements

In creating realistic animations, there are still many problems. When an animator or artist wants to do something, each step might require different hardware and software. For instance, transfer from video to computer file is simple through one kind of purchased software, but transfer from computer file to video requires different software and sometimes different hardware. Many modules are necessary to put together the kinds of environments envisaged for VR applications. Many of them are incompatible with each other. However, software is becoming available that combines many of the features needed, lessening the developer's need to improvise.

Among the separate problems encountered in the task of animation is that of video compression. Video compression technology is improving, but many programs cannot read entire screens from video, or frame rates are not compatible between the video and the computer display systems. Also, formats differ among programs, and there is often a need to convert one type of digital format to another in order for the modules to work together.

Another problem is the inability to easily represent animation within animation, e.g., animated characters watching animation on their television set. Currently, it can only be done if both animations are created and reside within the same file. Programmers would like to be able to create each separately and then combine them at will. [Biedny91]

Reproducing the movement of lights is difficult. As an example, headlights quickly heading down a freeway, when captured on film, spread across the image in a blurred fashion, an effect that cannot be recreated in computer images. The simulation of light effects, called ray tracing, is one of the most time-consuming portions of rendering, especially for complex objects. It often requires a machine that allows multitasking, that is, lets the programmer work on one thing while computations and renderings are being done in the background.

Speed is also sacrificed in animation. Digital photorealism is a slow process with trade-offs. To enhance speed, the standards for different things can be lowered, for instance, compromising high resolution for lower resolution and a bit of added speed or adjusting the rate of shading in parts of the image. Developers want programs that produce quality and high resolution at a reasonable speed.

Another important area for improvement lies in rendering text or the editing of text through image-editing programs. Although most programs allow for the animation of text, they do not allow editing of text.

ARCADES

"It's madness.
Nowadays the Controllers won't approve of any new game
unless it can be shown that it requires at least
as much apparatus as the most complicated of existing games."
BRAVE NEW WORLD

Arcade games can now contain computer graphics boards capable of rendering more than 180,000 kinds of graphic shapes per second. [Dunn92] Thus, the game can respond to a user's quick reactions with almost-real-time displays. Existing two-dimensional (2-D) arcade games are being upgraded to three-dimensional (3-D) booth versions, and a number of these are being extended to include aspects of virtual reality. Game releases have short lives and are replaced regularly by increasingly interactive versions. This is because players are willing to pay more per play for increased levels of interactivity — from about 50 cents to 1 dollar per minute.

Most users either don headgear or put their faces up against boxlike or periscopelike devices and view the three-dimensional images via small CRTs. Special optics reinforce the playing drama, and some arcade game boards produce stereo sound effects. A few commercial games have developed displays that appear 3-D to the naked eye.

3-D to Virtually-Real

Virtuality, *BattleTech* and the *CyberTron* are among the more visible of location-based VR attractions at sites around the United States. The general public is also gaining exposure to them through demonstrations staged by high-profile shops to draw customers.

W-Industries' *Virtuality* is installed in about 20 locations around the United States, with 100 to 150 more planned. A U.K. product, this game typifies an exploratory or puzzle-solving scenario, in which a player flies or zooms through fantasy territory, dodging and shooting at perceived opponents. Many home systems are evolving in this direction.

BattleTech, a networked simulation that typifies a popular jet-fighter theme, is based on U.S. Air Force simulation efforts. Each player on a shared network sits in a fixed-based capsule or cockpitlike "pod" to act out the role of pilot or soldier. Other players may be real or simulated players provided by the program. Virtual World Entertainment licensed a 30+ cockpit installation in Yokohama to a consortium of five Japanese corporations. It was the first of its kind in Japan. In *Mirage*, a "Star Wars" scenario based on Hughes Aircraft training technology, two players per pod share a wide-field display. Networked variations of science-fiction themes are planned.

StrayLight's *CyberTron* subjects a user to physical, as well as mental immersion by strapping a player into a gyroscopic mechanism that pivots and tilts 45 degrees on three axes as a user shifts his or her weight. Like other programmed games, a visual storyline takes a player over obstacles, through tunnels and into spins; however, a different sequence of user motions each session has the effect of varying the experience.

Carnival adventures incorporating VR technologies are being planned to feature interactive virtual spooks and virtual fun-house mirrors that users walk through, becoming the characters they choose to see. The effects will be combined with motion-platform rides. City fly-throughs and biking tours will attract the more mature visitors to the carnivals and parks. Less adventuresome is body painting. Within a virtual environment and armed with virtual paintbrushes and tools, users adorn themselves with colors and effects created at whim. Variations of this theme are also suitable for fashion and cosmetic-industry applications and may be offered for home systems.

The physical setups for some arcade experiences look awkward and are, indeed, awkward to use, but players usually learn quickly how to make adjustments for the equipment, and performance improves dramatically with exposure. In many games, the view of the real world is blocked out, and means have to be concocted to keep people from hurting themselves or wandering off. One contraption looks like a giant baby walker.

Formula Scripting

Game creators seem to rely less on good storylines than do Hollywood's animators. In film and theater, originality and content contribute to how "good" a storyline is and how well the creation as a whole is received. Being uniquely interesting is important to the success of a production.

In gaming priorities, originality sits much lower on the list. The production process is not unlike one used for romance novels sold at supermarket checkout stands. In what appears to be a basic formula for the commercial success of an animated game, there is conspicuous absence of unique storyline. For example, if you want to create a scenario, just make sure certain things are present:

$$ACTION + ENEMY + REWARDS + LOCALE + FANTASY = GAME$$

Plug in different variables for each of the necessary components — blond becomes raven, galaxies become dungeons, points earned become medals, and so on, and a new game emerges. The package is then massaged into coherency and marketed.

It seems to be enough. The reward for the player (or the reader) is the excitement along the journey and the player's level of participation — something not challenged, apparently, by repetitive structure. The rewarding aspects of excitement and participation are only heightened when users are able to make the journey through virtual environments, and the familiarity bred through similar presentations may actually be looked upon by the user as a favor because energy and attention need not be wasted on the interface.

Direction & Evolution

Game technologies are driven by a booming marketplace, and whatever makes money is top priority. Game vendors' plans are kept as closely guarded, in-house secrets. Game designers are in fierce competition to predict and develop features people will pay to get their hands on. Often, by providing companies with steady cash flows, short-term game projects support long-term, more basic research efforts.

Installations planned for museums, hospitals and schools differ from those targeted for parks and shopping mall arcades, but all incorporate elements of multimedia and varying levels of immersion. These include video projections of a player's image onto a screen, holographic images seeming to float in mid-air and highly immersive simulations such as those developed for battleground action or medical endoscopy.

Game Chairs

Comfortable chairs equipped with head-mounted display units will become standard attractions at many video entertainment centers. These may be recliner-like, in which a person rests with feet slightly elevated and swings a BOOM in front of his or her face for viewing, or they may resemble a doctor's examination table, in which case the player would lie on his or her stomach and look down into an adjustable viewbox. Other arrangements place individual players in little, closed-in booths or "pods," sometimes arranged in groups. All of these will display high-resolution, three-dimensional video images that are accompanied by multitracked, omnidirectional sound fed into the headgear.

A number of users may hook into the same system; chairs can be networked locally, or users of like systems can link into the same virtual environment via external transmission facilities to take part in multiplayer scenarios. Players will select the characters they wish to "be," and intelligent features will keep track of each player's record and skill levels.

Game-chair systems for two persons will probably cost about $100,000. An eight-person setup will cost about $300,000.

Amusement Parks

Many theme parks and shopping malls in the United States already feature attractions called simulators, which combine an actual ride with visual and audio effects. Combining fancy visual tricks and moving theaters, simulators come very close to fooling people into thinking they are, indeed, racing a car or hurtling through space.

StarTours of Disneyland and rides through the human body at the EPCOT Center in Florida are only the beginning. Simulators of the amusement-park variety are not yet interactive, but it is only a matter of time before a limited choice of scenarios is presented to the rider so that he or she has some influence over how the ride proceeds. The next logical step after that will be amusement park rides that enable people wearing special goggles and gloves to enter virtual environments and influence them through their actions. [Forbes92]

VIRTUAL THEATER

The flat, silver screen of films never quite captures the intimacy and near-reality of stage productions. Theater incorporating the interactivity of virtual reality promises to enhance the experience even further. To its proponents, virtual theater is an arena full of potential; to others, it's "vaporware." Indeed, it may go up in smoke because the development of a virtual theatric arena calls for an intense concentration of emotion, cognition and creativity not usually incorporated into other applications.

Real-World Deals

Collaborative deals are being struck between researchers and movie makers. University groups are being funded — by Matsushita and Fujitsu, among others — to hasten the development of commercial theatrical experiences. Current commercial film ventures allow audiences to collectively vote among subsequent scene possibilities and choices of character — pushing buttons, much like game show audiences do.

Presumably, in the next stage, all members of the audience will be fitted with lightweight shutter glasses or head-mounted viewers. A 270- or 360-degree cylindrical, 3-D screen wraps around the seating area, and spatial sound is coordinated with the visual displays to complete the effect of immersion. The direction from which a user senses the sound cues him or her to where the action is on the screen. Seats may be specially equipped for users to relay or receive signals via the system.

User enjoyment of virtual theater will undoubtedly derive more from active participation than from intellectual gratification. Even these experiences are fulfilling from a user's personal view since he or she is engaged in the action and helps determine the course of events. The sense of user-perceived control over the course of events suits it for therapeutic role playing. (See "Among Specialists & in Therapy" in Chapter 6.)

Although current plans seem to be directed toward providing venues more like group games than truly theatrical experiences, proponents of virtual theater arts hope to see the development of dramatic virtual theater. Among future possibilities are:

- computer-enhanced stage sets, in which performers interact or are embellished in real time with 3-D computer graphics;

- partially interactive performances by live actors amidst the audience in shared virtual spaces;

- performances by animatronic figures amidst audience actors in partially interactive, shared virtual spaces;

- partially interactive teleconference productions, where roundtable discussions are augmented with segments of relevant audio, text, graphics and video;

- interactive classical drama.

This last item, rendering classical drama, will remain difficult if not impossible. There are a number of very complex issues that must be addressed before it can happen. Some of them are discussed below.

Feeding the System with Emotion & Response

Giving a person the feeling of being transported into "another" world is only the first step of a complex trip, especially when the aim is dramatic interplay once a user is "there." In most VR applications, the initial, outermost computer interface plays the major role in drawing a person into a virtual world.

A virtual theatric arena, however, does not stop there. It has to continue and heighten the illusion through many subsequent interface systems that succeed in immersing a user ever more deeply. These must entwine that person in intricate, responsive human behavior and allow something of consequence to happen.

Ultimately, the success or failure of virtual theater will be played out in these substrata of plots and subplots; therefore, specialists must qualitatively enrich the behind-the-scenes databases that feed the system. Directors and dramatists need to experiment and establish ways of invoking effective techniques within the virtual stage environment, and domain experts need to define the particulars of human-inhabitant behavior. Not providing such depth and breadth is like introducing you to a person who speaks five languages but has nothing to say.

Things like patterns of human behavior and emotional reactions must be defined according to professional standards to ensure continuity and consistency across disciplines. In the theater arts, especially, doing so will help establish "givens" to underlie all productions. These will provide a basis for understanding, evaluating and comparing different creative works, as well as set down guidelines for ensuing work. For example, effective approaches to the works of particular authors can be kept in electronic repositories of directorial aids so that anyone working in the area or exploring particular styles can tap into it as a resource. This requirement of professional consensus also applies to applications developed for medical consultation or therapy, where the potential consequences of inconsistency are greater.

All the Stage a Virtual World

What the blank page of the playwright, the empty stage of the play and an empty virtual world all have in common is that, as long as nothing happens, everything is possible! Just as a playwright constructs a plot, defines the scenarios and populates his or her world, so do the creators of a virtual dramatic world design its components and inhabitants.

Then, the virtual population must be imbued with a number of characteristics, human or otherwise, and invigorated through animatronic effect. Enough must be going on in the virtual environment to engage the audience, whether one individual or many, and encourage participation.

Virtual inhabitants are called "agents" and are usually assigned attributes and goal-directed behavior. That is, qualities and a semblance of directed action are attached to them. Researchers have found, however, that it does not take too much to preserve a user's suspension of belief. Virtual agents need not even look particularly "intelligent" or be particularly active. Only when the virtual agents appear remarkably stupid, it seems, is the illusion jeopardized. [Bates92b]

The virtual stage designer is not, however, the creator of the original piece and faces a unique challenge. Within the constraints of the computer system and his or her imagination, the virtual stage designer must create an environment that closely relays the author's original intentions to the audience. The scene designer must juggle system resources to not only achieve a high level of data efficiency within system bounds but to also effectively present the original nuances of the author.

The virtual scenes created must accommodate the flow of storyline throughout and exhibit a continuity the participants (the audience) understand. Also, because of limitations on resources, assigning weight to the ways dramatic points are made is necessary to ensure consistency across the application as a whole. For example, if a surrounding display is rather complex, a designer is left with only minimal resources to convey expression, motion or connotative effects. If the surrounding display is relatively simple, consuming only a small portion of the resources, the designer may be tempted to overdo nuances. Jarring a user into noticing inconsistencies jeopardizes the believability of the whole.

A Key to a Larger Cage

By providing the audience (the user) with entry points and things to work with, the designer of a virtual world allows the user entrance to the virtual world but also limits the possibilities within that world — to what has been written, or programmed, into the system. Thus, for a user, the resulting framework is both liberating and confining.

Because each part (component) must be included (defined) and described (assigned attributes), and its particulars measured (specified), it is possible to imagine alternatives along most storylines. At any one of these points, VR technology can be merged into the linear production to offer users a chance to interact with the VR stage set or characters.

By circumventing or interfering with a standard presentation, a person in the audience can, conceivably, play a role in changing the course of action perceived on the stage — provided, of course, that the alternatives have been anticipated during the design phase and are built into the system.

From Passive Observation to Designed Drama

Interacting with virtual characters in a virtual theatrical production is not as straightforward an experience as scientifically examining a virtual molecule, for instance. The latter has specific, known properties and a relatively limited range of variance.

However, dealing with characters in a theatrical setting is more akin to submergence in a dynamic flux of characters and plots and emotions — complex variables dependent on other complex variables that are dependent, yet, on other complex variables. As we link into their relevant databases, which are continually growing to include myriad nuances of human foibles, the possibilities for altering the storyline become infinite — and unwieldy. Introducing the technology into the art form in the right doses at the proper times, is critical.

Roles

For a virtual production, the role of the creator of the original, linear production is to provide enough information so that most plausible variations of the intended story can be anticipated. This immediately precludes valid virtual renderings of works by dead authors. Experts, at best, can only guess what their subject authors would do.

The many variations are later built into the application and managed by virtual theater's equivalent of a real stage director — actually a computational theory of interactive drama [Bates92a] that also takes into account data obtained from relevant databases. The designer may also serve as a real-time director and intervene to influence the virtual environment. For example, he or she may change background scene elements, move virtual objects or communicate with individual actors as the production progresses.

Basically, during the "show," the user and the program take turns, the user opting at each junction of choice for whatever promises the most interesting experience and the program ("director") responding with a scenario that continues the challenge. Opponent moves are anticipated, and the possible consequences of one's own moves are factored in. It can be likened to a friendly game of chess, except that winning is not the goal. The response in each case must respect the story line and provide additional options — again, within story bounds.

Then, to some degree, the participants and director become creators as they exercise free will within the options presented. An observation by researchers at Carnegie Mellon University suggests that a participant submerged in the program is often overly tolerant of manipulative or aberrant "behavior" on the part of other inhabitants of the space. [Kelso&91] Wanting to believe so badly seems to blind users to subtle excesses of power over them — something equally observable in real life.

The Virtual Brick Road to Oz

In theater as we know it, the storyline is predestined by the creator; in virtual theater, it becomes prey to the free will of the audience — or the petulance of a single user. Not all works of art allow such theatrical detour, and its discourse is analogous to theological musings of free will vs. predestination. Suffice it to say that this underlines once more how important it is to carefully select applications for virtual venues.

Oz is a project under way at Carnegie Mellon University (CMU). It was begun by a diverse group of researchers primarily from the disciplines of fine arts and computer science to help artists build dramatic simulated worlds that include simulated people.

The aim of the *Oz* project is to explore how, with artificial-intelligence techniques, ideas and insight from traditional theater arts can become an integral part of virtual productions. [Bates92a] Current research focuses on the development of:

- shallow but broadly capable virtual characters (nicknamed blobs) that integrate elements of perception, cognition, emotion, action and language;

- a computational theory of interactive drama to shape the user's overall experience;

- computational methods for varying the presentation style of the experience. [Bates92b]

The system is basically a text-based narrative in which observers may witness and explore how personality is assigned to artificial characters. With the help of a scene designer, director, videographer, actors and a token participant, different ways are being investigated to endow animated characters with mimetic action. Researchers are also beginning to observe and document what is required to synthesize plots interactively and how users are drawn into a performance.

There is great impetus to merge these techniques with the spectacular animation effects of Hollywood. Japanese companies have supported much of the basic research in this area in the United States, and international collaborators hope to produce games and dramatic, interactive experiences that address what is a conspicuous dearth of emotion in applications today.

MTV & MVR

Musical performance incorporating the audio-visual effects of virtual immersion is now possible. With basic equipment or goggles, audiences participate in how the performance proceeds. Total escape into the music is made easier as virtual displays and enhanced sound effects surround each user, blocking out distractions from the real world.

As sophisticated home products become more available and affordable, Music TV (MTV) will be challenged to provide interactive viewing and listening. That is still a long way away, but live performances lend themselves well to the medium, and it will not be long before we are able to enjoy immersive music that is 3-D in both sight and sound, a type of musical virtual reality (MVR).

Shared virtual spaces can be sites for virtual musical concerts, talent assessment or practice sessions. Biocontrollers are already being used in demonstration shows of spontaneous musical composition accompanied by virtual visual effects.

VIRTUAL ART MUSEUM

Carnegie Mellon University is the host site of an evolving virtual art museum that will be accessible to outsiders via modem-to-modem connections and networking. U.S. vendors of VR equipment and software are collaborating with researchers at the university to develop the system, described as a multinational art museum in immersion-based virtual reality. A Japanese management association is currently developing the first virtual wing.

Configuration & Connections

The initial setup consists of a 486 personal computer, a specialized software program and a number of head-mounted displays. This allows a visitor to browse through a few wings of the virtual museum and be exposed to creations of virtual art as though he or she were actually present. These are not Rembrandts or Picassos, mind you, but examples of the new, experiential expressionism being made possible through the technologies of virtual reality.

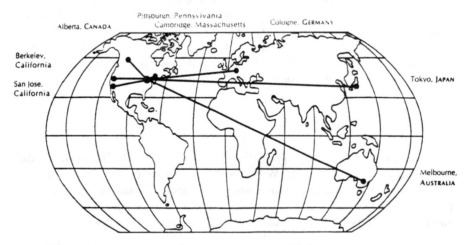

Modem connection is now possible from two places, one on the CMU campus in Pittsburgh and the second in Japan. Additional nodes in the United States, Australia, Canada and Germany are being added, and it is expected that each newcomer to the system will provide at least one additional wing to the model. Each node installed has access to all the virtual environments, and each is equipped with a local "toolbox" for construction of new virtual objects or modification of existing ones. Plans include a "server" model, in which one node will act as controller, enabling many users to share one immersive environment simultaneously.

The system is designed to be portable, i.e., pluggable via modem from almost anywhere. The mere establishment of such a network will provide a testbed for the many problems of connectivity and protocol that will arise among immersion environments. It will also provide a venue for the investigation of how people interact with and perceive things over networked sites.

All nodes on the network contribute to the museum, but the "galleries" themselves are being constructed at CMU. Museum wings and galleries shoot off from a central lobby, and there is also accommodation for temporary displays. Shared, central space will host tele-visiting curators of virtual art for conferences addressing VR as a means of cultural expression.

Current Projects

Currently, four projects are under way:

- *Virtual Ancient Egypt*, where Egyptologists lead "tourists" through realizations of classic temples and sites;

- *Archaeopteryx*, a flying machine based on Leonardo da Vinci's model;

- *Model, Car & Design*, a hands-on exhibition about cars and how they are modeled within a virtual design shop;

- the *Fun House*, a virtual adaptation of illusions and tricks from amusement-park attractions.

In this last application, the Fun House, a user can assume the image of any character from a roster including Dracula and can interact with other players or artificial characters. A player may grab on to a musical merry-go-round or drive a whizzing flying saucer into space. [Loeffler92] The effects of velocity, gravity and friction are simulated according to standard laws of physics, but it is conceivable that they be played with, as well, in future versions. In test runs of the Fun House between Pittsburgh and Munich, researchers recorded a relatively inobtrusive lag time of 22 milliseconds.

VR-Aided Study of Classical Art

Brenda Laurel has described art in the context of "time travel," able to transmit understanding across time and space. Like telepresence, the experience of the art remains with the observer, the operator in the here and now, the importance of improving all the tools by which this understanding is communicated is underlined. [Laurel91]

It is possible that advanced imaging techniques being developed for virtual-reality purposes be applied to the study of classical art. Medical imaging that allows differentiation based on tissue density can lend itself to the peeling away of layers of paint, as well, uncovering for the specialist an image of what lies beneath. Finished pieces may be studied as evolving designs, each stage computer-revealed and -enhanced.

The expertise of art restorers, educators, radiologists, historians and technicians may be brought together for nondestructive exploratory "surgery" on masterpieces of art. The ability of powerful computer systems to process large volumes of information may be enlisted to record, verify and compare data obtained from examinations of paintings and works of art in order to increase our understanding and to code pieces for authenticity.

In an Army repair application, a high-resolution, head-mounted CRT displays 640x480-pixel VGA screens generated by a miniature, belt-mounted, PC-compatible computer. This battery-powered system houses a variety of electronic technical manuals intended for reference by military and industrial maintenance personnel in the field. *(Photo: Frank Borkowski; Devices: InterVision Systems/Imaging & Sensing Technology Corp.)*

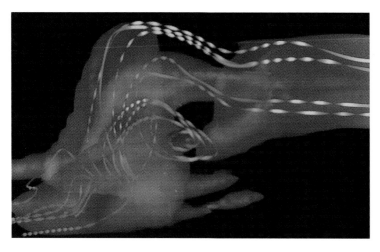

Scientists visualize the dynamics of severe thunderstorms by using solutions of many time-dependent equations to create a computer model of each simulated storm. Using a meteorological database, this image combines data on cloud water density (translucent isosurface) with wind direction and magnitude (colored streamlines from each point). *(Data: U.K. Meteorological Service; Image: IBM Visualization Data Explorer)*

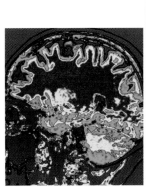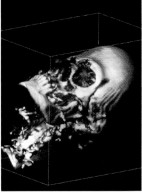

For medical purposes, images are computed from data gathered from many different sources—magnetic resonance, x-ray, thermography, etc. Three examples of computer-generated medical images are shown above. *(Image: IBM Visualization Power Series)*

Shown here is one frame from an architectural walk-through of the Romanesque basilica of the Benedictine Abbey of Cluny, France. This image is part of a video realization of the church. *(Data: IBM France; Image: IBM Visualization Power Series)*

For training purposes or group decision making, information can be projected off screens as 3-D images. Wireless stereoscopic eyewear is worn by meeting participants to view the displays. Output from PCs, workstations, videos and VCRs can be used. *(Photo: StereoGraphics Corporation)*

The Lawnmower Man, Stephen King's film starring Pierce Brosnan, evolves around an exploration of virtual-reality technology and experimentation on a human subject. A suspended Flogiston chair is featured. The minimal stress posture chair incorporates heat-sensitive padding and control panels. *(Photo: Suzanne Tenner)*

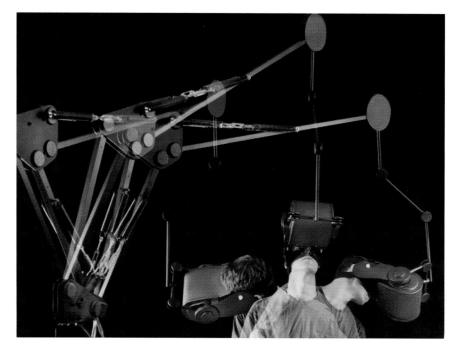

Used primarily for development of VR applications, this workstation configuration makes use of boom mountings, mechanical arms, tracking devices, Cyberface masks and stereoptic displays. Other options, such as binaural sound, can be added on. *(Photo: LEEP Systems)*

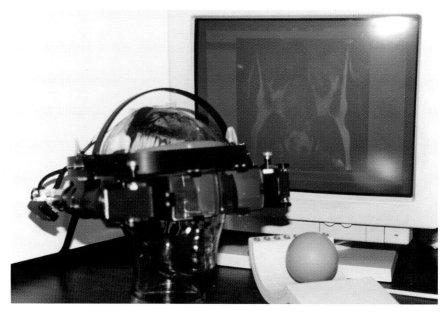

A single desktop virtual-reality system consisting of head-mounted display unit, force ball input device and workstation (screen only shown). *(Photo: Virtual Reality, Inc.)*

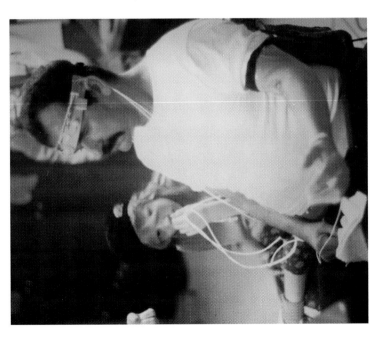

Computer-readable signals produced from residual electrical activity in a disabled person's muscles are used to run devices. Here, muscle tension is mapped to note number and volume on a music synthesizer, enabling this musician to serenade his daughter. Using different amounts of exertion, he can change pitches and sound levels; using a sequencer, he can compose whole pieces. This patient has also tried brain-wave controller functions. *(Photo: Loma Linda Medical Center, Dr. Dave Warner; Device: BioControl Systems, Inc., Dr. Hugh Lusted)*

Due to an accident, Crystal's movement is limited to her head. When first fitted with the biocontroller, she immediately realized that her eye movements controlled the external display. With little prompting, she used it to move a smiling face around on a video screen and was soon communicating via the device. *(Photo: Loma Linda Medical Center)*

Virtual little creatures like these are being created to inhabit such environments as the "Gas Planet." This is one example of state-of-the-art computer animation techniques. *(Image: Pacific Data Images)*

Dr. Scratch is an example of motion-data animation for *Dragonspeak*, a cartoon series designed to teach children ecology. A "bad guy," he uses his fireball to create deserts and destroy life. The automated choreography is produced by sophisticated use of tracking techniques, animator creativity and computer-generated imaging. *(Image: Mr. Film)*

To achieve the effect of "morphing," the first image (the car) is incrementally infused with data from the last image (the tiger). As the exchange of data progresses, interim frames are generated, and the process is continued until all data of the first image have been supplanted by data of the last. When the sequence is animated, the images appear to merge. This example is from Exxon advertising campaigns. *(Photo: Pacific Data Images)*

Typically, unless realism is vital to specific goals of an application, virtual inhabitants of computer-generated worlds are represented by cartoon-like renderings. A control panel can be seen at the bottom of this screen. *(Image: Dimension International, U.K.)*

Architectural models rendered for city planning or reconstruction may appear simple but are generated from detailed specifications. A virtual realization of the Newcastle Quayside development project in the U.K. was prepared as a sales aid, and this frame typifies the image quality of such applications. *(Image: Dimension International, U.K.)*

Virtual Reality in Education

9

To the ancient Greeks, true scholarship was defined as a life of leisure devoted to learning. The search for knowledge assumed an individual's total sensory and intellective immersion in life itself, and educators were challenged to nurture enthusiasm along the way and provide the young mind with tools it could use. In that spirit, schools served only to provide momentum to the pursuit of knowledge outside their walls, not replace it.

Today, things are different. Too often, the real world and excitement of the Information Age are left outside the doors of our schoolrooms. Innovative teachers arrange for them to occasionally sneak inside through the wiring — via electronic hook-ups to educational networks or through the use of other educational technology. As these chinks in the armor of the classroom are widened, freer integration of the school and world environments will occur.

LEARNING TANKS

The immersion technique is recognized as a focusing tool in programs from learning to turn phrases in foreign languages to grasping abstract concepts, and virtual environments are, basically, "immersion tanks" for learning. In virtual scenarios, clue conflict from the outside world is minimized or eliminated. Learning patterns are established quickly and easily reinforced by repetition or graduated exercises.

Virtual-reality environments extend the horizons of the learning arena beyond the classroom walls, providing students and teachers with yet another, powerful set of mind tools. Training modules can exploit the game-loving mentality of active minds and the heightened interest levels indicative of virtual environments to provide ideal venues for discovery and learning. The ability to interact with the environment and its displays allows a person to try courses of action not possible in a real setting. The increased number of "what if" choices available in a virtual environment encourages curiosity and stimulates the flights of thought so necessary to creative work. Discriminate selection of applications for the class use will provoke new ways of thinking and act as a catalyst for expanded learning opportunities.

Initial investments in VR seed programs for education are high, but they are nondepletive resources that evolve and grow richer as users add to them. As we are increasingly pressured by global competition, technologies promoting more global perspective and integration of disciplines are wise investments, indeed.

But the call for change couldn't come at a worse time. Providing the means for immersive learning is too difficult and costly for most school budgets.

QUALITY TEACHERS

The quality of educational facilities and availability of quality teaching personnel are often determined by a particular school district's resources; not all communities and citizens receive equal or timely privilege. Gifted teachers able to exploit the virtual extensions that technology affords will be given new spheres of influence and an arena for creative collaboration with other teachers on the network.

Learning circles of shared interest will be as valuable to teachers as to students, and teleconferencing will provide the platform for an array of guest lecturers, moderators or experts. Interactive debates and theme projects involving participants and instructors from many districts can be held and recorded, leveraging the talent already present in our schools.

ELECTRONIC OUTREACH CLASSROOMS

Long-distance education will benefit greatly from immersion environments that can be networked and shared among many people and institutions. Nodes on educational networks could host shared learning spaces for educational and training projects, seminars and social interactions.

Currently, one-way courses are delivered to remote areas via instructional television services, fiber optics and satellites; however, control and interaction with programs and teachers via these systems are severely limited. Two-way systems delivered via telephone lines, fiber optics or microwave signals allow more local control and computer-aided interaction but require long-term commitment and relatively high initial investments in equipment.

Some schools begin with a low-cost alternative to the above — a PC-based audiographics system that uses telephone lines and incorporates computer-generated graphics in ways that mimic electronic chalkboards. Still slides are transmitted in real time from one host machine to any number of members of loosely formed cooperatives. Facsimile machines are used for hard-copy notes or student written work. Software providing both transmit and receive modes costs about $1000 per site, and operating costs are limited to telephone charges. [Barker&92]

Computer-Based Systems

Ideally, each linkage in a computer-based system is to a more extensive network than before; so, a high-school student in Idaho may link (locally) to a county net, which has a port to a state net, which connects to a nationwide network that, ultimately, gives him or her access to one or more global networks. At each junction, various connections to available networks are presented. A user may elect to target in to a specialty, e.g., dedicated scientific databases, or broaden his or her field of search to more general, public connections and databases. Thus, students and teachers need not feel isolated or removed from information and expertise available to others.

At the Community Level

More and more community colleges in the United States are investing in microwave systems that support hundreds of virtual classrooms as an option to the construction of physical facilities. Many have found that setting up distance-education programs enables them to enroll far more learners in far more communities for the same initial investment and subsequent lower plant costs as perhaps only one additional building. Making computer-based training available through these systems will also encourage adult learning beyond formal schooling.

Active in providing this capability in the United States are telephone companies. Some private businesses improve their public image by offering select access to their corporate (often worldwide) networks to schools and communities in which they are located.

What is available from these final destination networks may range from stripped data to whole VR environments. What is shared depends on facilities at both ends and bandwidth capabilities between.

Stretching Resources

The dissemination and sharing of knowledge among educational systems are still basically labor-intensive, paper-intensive processes. If driven only by sheer volume, over the next few decades, state and federal governments will be pressed to pool resources and integrate learning systems. Those that take advantage of advances in technology, especially those linking their schools to powerful networks, rich databases, instructional equipment and teacher support systems, will be able to provide many more quality educational opportunities on limited budgets.

Too often, state and federal mandates reach farther down than resources and pools of qualified teachers. For example, orders to provide advanced courses or home-language instruction for non-English-speaking students hit some target schools in Mississippi hard. [Graham92] Despite good intentions, many cannot comply. Distance learning allows one qualified teacher to reach many more students, very often interactively.

Some efforts are showing results. Via Educom and similar educational associations, networking activity is turning from random trickles to flows of information that can be tapped by anyone with the technology — sometimes no more than a phone line, modem and personal computer.

NOT ONLY IMMERSION

Because VR technology accommodates nonlinear storage and retrieval of information, these systems can correspond more closely to human cognitive processes. As teaching aids, they may be enlisted to facilitate students' understanding at higher conceptual levels, encouraging students to question and correlate ideas much more freely than is possible with paper-based, linear educational models.

Through virtual experiences, learners from kindergarten through graduate school can enjoy at least representative exposure to many aspects of life that are or were not available to them in real life. Like a perennial "Head Start" program, experiential enrichment, such as that available through well-structured virtual scenarios, helps people prepare for independent, productive lifestyles. Shared virtual environments extend the personal world of an individual by making accessible places and experiences previously beyond his or her reach.

LEARNING SYSTEMS

Physics for Poets

Grasping and visualizing mathematically based concepts of physical phenomena are, for most people, extremely difficult. Course offerings such as *Physics for Poets* and *Cosmology & You* attest to the lengths instructors are willing to go to get their points across. Under many guises and from all directions, instructors undertake what, in private, they deem virtually impossible — to implant or evoke visual images in their charges that help them understand abstract concepts.

As early as next year, perhaps, high-school and college physics students will be given a chance to learn in virtual physics laboratories. [Dunn92] They will be given the chance to set controls for and manipulate virtual objects to observe their behavior. Paths of trajectories can be traced, and time can be frozen or run backward so that students can observe time-based phenomena. One such laboratory has been set up in conjunction with NASA at the University of Houston. Plans include facilities for macroscopic and microscopic domains.

Virtual physics laboratories now under development will evolve into the ultimate visual aids for the teaching of physical sciences, i.e., physics and chemistry. A virtual laboratory provides researchers and students with a flexible, visual environment in which they can, through spatial interaction, examine and attempt to control collisions between particles or bodies, friction and gravity (though model simulation of gravity has proven extremely difficult). Initial trials, collectively dubbed the Molecular Simulation System, were conducted at the University of North Carolina at Chapel Hill.

The sophisticated visualization tools that are part of a virtual physics-laboratory setup incite understanding by facilitating a learner's subverbal curiosity about physical concepts. Physics is full of "what if ..." hypotheses, and students can now represent physical phenomena as virtual objects and induce varying conditions affecting them. Instead of manipulating formulae, calculators and slide rules, students manipulate the objects representing the concepts and visually observe the projected effects.

Music

A virtual object can be created to represent a particular sound as produced by a musical synthesizer, and a user interacting with the object can cause the sound to be generated. Various parameters can be set for each sound, and different sounds can be combined.

Objects need not resemble traditional instruments, and any tetrahedal object can be defined as a sound producer. Virtual violas may be constructed from grids of crossed strings, and one virtual trumpet may blare simultaneously from multibranching flared bells. Indeed, in a virtual world, users can create and march to very different drummers and very different drums.

Movement through the virtual space and collisions with the objects can be programmed to control a musical synthesizer. A commercial version of this has been installed at the EPCOT Center. By moving and colliding or by causing objects to collide into each other, a user can create unique combinations of sounds. For instance, a "drum" object hurled at a "tambourine" would result in a cacophony of their assigned sounds.

Virtual reconstructions of real music by musicians can prove quite useful to the artists themselves. By digitizing and reconstructing his own finger movements on the cello, Yo-Yo Ma worked with researchers at M.I.T. to be able to examine and reinforce in real life the positionings that result in tones that most sensitively convey the feeling of the piece.

This same technique can be transferred to others via shared virtual environments. Students can be alerted to faults and, hooked up to a master system, can be prompted through tactile feedback of a master's patterns to adapt their own playing styles.

Chemistry

"Flying through Protein Molecules" is the name of a project at the University of North Carolina. This application allows users to interact with huge molecules and "fly" through their structures in an immersive setting. Scaling features allow users to scale themselves up or down, as well.

Eventually, school laboratory facilities that have not changed for decades will change. Physical experimentation of chemical reactions will be reinforced or replaced by advanced simulations and virtual realizations. "What if" scenarios will be staged in the safety of virtual desktop counters. On smaller computers, individual students may design virtual components of molecules and create their own models, viewing them via shuttered goggles and handling the virtual object that seems to float in front of them.

Biological Sciences

With the help of visualization systems developed for medical applications, students working with virtual anatomical bodies and parts will study human and animal bodies inward from the surface, as though peeling off layers to examine what is underneath, and outward toward the surface, e.g., displaying the layering around a vital organ. With tricky image enhancement or suppression techniques, levels of these three-dimensional displays may be rendered transparent, allowing students to look inside. Textbook study of anatomy, physiology, kinesiology and biology will be geared to exploiting the new media.

Sensorial immersion in a virtual anatomy laboratory, for instance, blocks out everything but the topic being studied. Therefore, a student exercises intense concentration, and an instructor can exercise control over the intensity and pace of the experience. Off-the-shelf software "body parts" such as those described in Chapter 6 can be used as learning aids. A student can examine a virtual object (such as a muscle or joint) from many angles and manipulate it or put strains on it to effectively learn how it works and how it breaks down. Students may be able to "infect" bodies with agents and observe the consequences in real or accelerated time as they spread throughout the body.

Mathematics

Although visualization techniques are used primarily for physics, chemistry and medical applications that need expert interpretation and analysis, they are currently being recognized as indispensable teaching and learning tools for the curricula for applied mathematics, as well, promoting new ways of mathematical thinking. Visualization systems enable teachers to work visually with the forms and relationships of geometry, the calculus, differential equations, linear algebra and complex mathematical analyses. Such systems enable users to interpret statistics, stochastic processes, fractal geometry and chaos and to present their underlying order effectively and colorfully.

By working with a concept as a virtual object, a learner becomes familiar with it in much the same way he or she learns to deal with things in the real world. Harmonic motion, for example, and changes in vector fields are more easily understood when observed through dynamic visualization. The cones, blocks, cylinders and spheres of solid geometry are created and positioned and rotated by the user at will. Unions and intersections can be viewed up close, in real time. Through interpretive visual images, both teachers and students alike are better able to appreciate the intrinsic beauty of the mathematics that inspired them.

Social Studies

Our world's store of information is growing exponentially. By 1850, the amount was double that of 1800, only 50 years later. By 1950, it took 10 years to double and, by the year 2000, will double every 3 years or sooner — an astounding projection. [PTel87]

The area covered by social studies programs challenges instructors to select from the deluge those data relevant to their curricula. Computer technologies help, and networking via telecommunications systems adds value to program activities. Access to large databases and electronic message-conveying services have made instructors' tasks easier and students' tasks more realistic. However, these are passive systems that allow little real-time communication or interactivity. As full of potential as they may be, existing technologies are no more than adjuncts to good, human teachers.

How will VR technologies help? Essential social studies skills generally fit into one of three main categories [Carpenter92]:

- acquiring information;
- organizing and using the information; and
- interpersonal relationships and social participation.

Well-designed virtual scenarios offer unique opportunities for students and instructors to exercise levels of efficiency and creativity in all these areas. Preparation for virtual scenarios hosting realistic confrontations, social concerns, recreational activities and adventures involves using available databases and information channels, discerning which data are useful and organizing the relevant data. Later, after participation in the virtual activity, the experience can be discussed in real classroom settings.

Re-enactments of historical or social importance can be staged in virtual settings and populated with real or imaginary figures. Roles can be rotated and perspectives changed. Instructors may either participate alongside the students in the virtual space or may direct the production to reinforce particular learning patterns.

Cultural exchanges could take place across districts, states and countries — with participants joining in from wherever a virtual space can be accessed. Translation and cross-sensory substitution facilities (such as those described in Chapter 6) would be enlisted to help dissolve differences and borders. This type of exchange will never take the place of or convey the warmth of true interactions but does provide students opportunities for practicing interpersonal communication skills under controllable circumstances.

Astronomy

Data collected over the years and stored in databases are being fed into supercomputers to reconstruct three-dimensional simulations of the whirls, ribbons and voids that portray our galaxies. These, in turn, will be the basis for virtual galactic realizations through which students and researchers may fly, viewing the universe from unique perspectives in space. Initial visualizations of the data have already provided scientists with insight into how the universe is structured.

Animated sequences of astral spectacles and phenomena are calculated at very high resolutions and transferred to motion picture film. Dual-projection techniques enable viewers to become virtual adventurers on fly-throughs within 3-D virtual renditions of the Big Bang or solar flares. Learning about the universe becomes exploration of the universe.

Arts

Within a virtual environment, any object can be made to resemble almost anything, and wand devices are often changed to paintbrushes, spray cans or bubblers to create colorful shapes. Children left to these and their own devices create original designs and virtual objects or "paint" surreal landscapes. Art becomes a creative, interactive experience of expression rather than just a medium. For theater arts, virtual sets and scenery designs can be realized in virtual spaces, and techniques being developed by research groups today can be tested and adapted for instructional use. (See "Virtual Theater" in Chapter 8.) Interactive plots can be constructed and tested with real or virtual participants.

Architectural tools for creating virtual designs can be installed on low-end desktop equipment. If adequate resources are available, navigation equipment can be used so that, together, student and instructor can explore the virtual space. There, from within the design, they can exchange ideas and change the design to better meet specifications. This type of on-site, hands-on interaction supports the creative process in a very practical way.

Driver Education & Industrial Arts

Any instruction that benefits from "hands-on" experience or is visually based lends itself to the immersion capabilities of a virtual environment. On virtual highways, student drivers can be challenged by road conditions and unexpected situations not available on command when practicing in a real automobile. Visually confronted by "what if" scenarios allows learners to gauge how they would react in real situations. Instructors can tailor an individual's practice sessions to reinforce specific skills. Arcade-type game pods already challenge players on race courses. Contextual road realizations can replace much of the content of text-based testing in driver education courses.

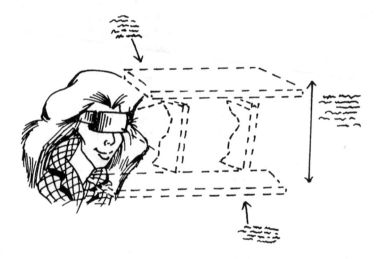

Workbench aids for industrial and domestic arts can provide learners with practical, self-paced guides. Superimposed patterns and step-by-step instructions discourage errors often caused by inaccurate transfer of visual clues and reinforce efficient completion of projects.

Environmental Studies

In our environment, relatively small qualitative changes are reflected in adaptive changes by living things within that environment. Living matter adapts to conform with atmospheric variations. When the ecological balance is challenged — as is happening, for example, with global warming and ozone-layer depletion, many of the changes may fall within ranges that environmental processes can assimilate. If so, these assimilative environmental processes will probably, over time, provide an acceptable ecological equilibrium.

Many other changes, however, will exceed what living matter as a whole can accommodate. To be better able to visualize the processes would advance our knowledge of critical thresholds for things that may disrupt the ecological balance irreversibly. Dramatic virtual realizations of variable "what-if" environments, if based on complex mathematical models, can prove effective tools for understanding the complexities governing our real environment.

Special Programs

Customized programs in which varying degrees of immersion via virtual learning environments may be useful include those aimed at:

- strengthening academic performance skills of the learning disabled or low achievers;

- imprinting or reinforcing patterning through repetition;

- improving socialization skills in children with behavior disorders;

- behavior modification;

- providing venues of self-paced instruction and immediate feedback for challenged students;

- providing practice test facilities for all students;

- providing shared "on-site" spaces for collaborative design and construction;

- raising awareness of hostile environments and handling hazardous materials.

Indeed, evidence is mounting that topics presented in responsive formats such as those offered by virtual environments engage learners in a higher degree of mind-body kinesthetic participation, providing them with more opportunities to combine cognitive, affective and psychomotor skills. Learners pursuing their own learning strategies through constructionist activities within virtual environments may more effectively interrelate and integrate educational content and experience. [Walter90]

CURRENT CONCERNS

Educators are no longer just challenged to keep alive the spirit of whole-life learning — they are dared to do so. In a climate of overbearing administrative requirements and short funding, there is a pervasive resignation among teachers that their efforts are underappreciated.

The introduction of multisensory learning experiences into school curricula raises a number of issues other than those of cost. These are added to the list of things a strapped-for-energy teacher has to deal with. Not many evaluations of the effectiveness of particular technologies on the learning process have been made. There is, however, general consensus that retention levels improve progressively along platforms of reading, writing, hearing and saying. They are usually at their highest after experiential learning, i.e., doing.

Educators have expressed concern about the differences between learning in a VR environment and learning in a traditional classroom environment. Discussion centers around the comparative long- and short-term benefits of each, the necessary instructor training and the need for specialized equipment and plant facilities for VR learning environments. Some educators express a fear that students will fail to appreciate the importance of discipline as stressed over the years by traditional methods.

Add to these other concerns the general difficulty of introducing any kind of change into the curricula. Often, it is simply because the reasons for change are misunderstood. Explanation and justification alone don't work; nor does change by mandate. There is a clear need for strategies based on what has been known to effect change and what won't. The acceptance of dramatic shifts in paradigm, especially those involving new technologies, is an evolutionary process, the success of which is tied directly to the levels of participation of the people involved. [Louis&90]

For example, innovative space and computer equipment must be made available in such a way that, after an initial period of training or hand-holding, those expected to be advocates can freely experiment and try the new approaches. During this period, uncertainties and personal insecurity about the technologies can be worked through. Thus, an understanding of the significance of the technology can grow incrementally, allowing comfortable acceptance or modification of the goals of the proposed changes. If either no tutelage is provided or if rigidity is imposed upon access to or use of the materials, teachers will never acquire a strong sense of "ownership," in which case, efforts to introduce change may prove counterproductive.

VR at Home & in the Office

10

MENAGE OF ANOTHER KIND

The previously separate industries of publishing, entertainment, computer technologies and telecommunications can no longer lock each other out. Each needs to tap into the strength of the others to stay competitive, and interesting alliances are forming to ensure they get what they need.

PUBLISHING COMPUTERS

ENTERTAINMENT TELECOMMUNICATIONS

Cable companies are hooking up with telecommunications networks, telephone companies are revising their images, and movie producers are taking computer experts to lunch. Few companies will remain dedicated to the types of services they were formed to provide.

As a result, a new variety of multimedia entertainment, learning and shopping facilities is already finding its way into our living rooms. As broadband facilities are linked into homes, varying degrees of "virtually realistic" services will become available. Eventually, home centers will evolve toward wraparound, room-sized displays and sound equipment.

Compressed digital signals will yield these completely new effects, and game-like control devices will facilitate interaction with programs. Initially, depth enhancers will be available as low-cost clip-ons for existing television sets, or viewing will be done with specialized equipment such as stereoscopic headpieces and audiophones. Voice-recognition features will work in conjunction with control and input devices.

TRENDS: RIDING HOME ON A BANDWIDTH

Advances made in imaging, combined with intelligent database retrieval services, will be incorporated into many different types of multimedia virtual applications. A home setting may, conceivably, be enhanced by natural input to systems — gentle breezes triggering complementary musical sounds or lighting patterns programmed to dramatize nature's reflections.

Other applications of the technologies ushered in by research in virtual reality will involve libraries, businesses, entertainment arcades, home video and resource centers, information centers and other services. In addition, automated library and archive services will offer improved efficiency via electronic search and retrieval facilities enhanced by virtual interfaces.

Virtual music can be produced or replicated in the home as it is done in school settings, and virtual instruments may be custom-programmed to encourage amateurs to improve their skills and repertoire. Creative visual patterns and combinations of sounds that reflect a lifestyle or portray a mood may be built in as parts of a household's atmosphere-enhancing features, much as today's recessed lighting fixtures. (See Chapter 9.)

CARTRIDGE & CD-ROM GAMES

"Imagine the folly of allowing people to play
elaborate games which do nothing to increase consumption."
BRAVE NEW WORLD

Growth projections for the home game market are very optimistic, and vendor announcements of annual sales increases between 20 per cent and 50 per cent are not uncommon. More than half the households in Japan, for instance, own at least one video game.

The beginnings of virtual games for the home were evident a few years ago in the first PowerGlove versions of Nintendo. A gloved player pointed a finger at the screen to direct imaginary laser bullets at a target or character. This was surpassed by an ambitious multiplayer game in which participants stalk each other through virtual checkerboard spaces, ducking prehistoric monsters and shooting virtual rays at each other. Current computer game systems do not display 3-D images, but add-on kits are being developed to provide home users with a level of immersion.

Today, videotape-based cartridge systems are being challenged by disk-based CD-ROM versions. These require different equipment (called CD-readers or players) but have more than 100 times the storage capacity of better cartridge systems. The storage capacity, however, does not speed up the action, and critics of the CD-based system maintain that its 16-bit processor does no more than the 16-bit processors of tape systems.

Vendors hope that a line of virtual-reality games and helmet interfaces being developed to plug into existing cartridge systems will convince users to stay with cartridge systems and stem the migration to 16-bit CDs. In the meantime, everyone seems to be headed toward high-bit CD game systems better than both. At the time of writing, the one 32-bit CD version introduced is rather expensive. The planned price tag for the cartridge-system helmet is much lower — more apt to appeal to the under-15 crowd that accounts for 70 per cent of software game sales.

Any attempt to track the home game market over the next few years will be difficult. The market is continuously being turned over with improved versions of existing games and completely new game kits, and these will be accompanied by more and more paraphernalia.

COMPUTER-CREATED DIVERSIONS

Immersion Sports

Adult products driven by powerful PCs already hook up to stationary bicycles, rowing machines, stepmasters and treadmills to provide visual stimulation to people using them. Viewing the computer-generated images either on screen or surrounded by a projected scene, a user rows or cycles or runs in simulated races or athletic meets. Ergometers and physiological data sensors can be added to provide feedback to a user. Generally, how real the graphics are and how much immersion is experienced are determined by how much is spent on the setup. Quotations for single-user products range from $1000 to over $5000. A major drawback is the inability to provide realism within the limited resources of most personal systems.

Applications are being developed for other sports, as well, and commercial versions of virtual racquet ball, downhill skiing, golf and skeet shooting are emerging from laboratory prototypes. For many of these, PCs would not be enough. Higher-end image-generating, tracking and monitoring systems would be needed.

One ski training system being tested in Japan and scheduled for a U.S. debut in 1995 provides levels of difficulty ranging from bunny to daredevil. Securely booted and standing on two movable steel plates of a slope simulation machine, a learner dons a head-mounted display with tracker. When the simulation is started, ski poles, fitted with stress detectors, serve as control devices. The system continually monitors the signals and adjusts the course to one that is comfortable for the user. Prepared routes include hills, tracks through woods and downhill pistes.

Motion-assessment tools may be used to analyze a user's performance and provide tips for improvement. Potential sites for this type of system include ski facilities, sports clubs, schools and rehabilitation centers.

Stereo viewing of contact sports such as football, boxing, hockey, etc. will be available through special broadcasting to homes, clubs and bars. To watch the programs, filmed with special cameras, viewers will wear battery-operated 3-D glasses. Stereo audio can be provided, as well.

Close-up action being recorded from a goalee's point of view may be shared with participants. Pre-recorded action scenes (from a stereo camera mounted on the helmet of the featured goalee) provide a site of immersion for a user to experience the game, heading off attacks or tackles from that perspective, complete with sight and sound.

Two players may hook into a higher-end system that provides more realism and opportunity for feedback. Head-mounted devices enable users to tele-play from different positions in the same virtual game and interact with the action or each other. What the players in the helmets see can be shown on a monitor or screen for same-time viewing by others.

Motion Analysis for Athletic Training

Kinesiologists currently conduct many motion analysis studies with the help of digitized images. Individual frames can be frozen for detailed inspection of the angles and peculiar combinations of motions that contribute to a champion performance.

Patterns common to successful athletes of any particular sport can be used as a basis for instruction and training. They can be instrumental in speeding rehabilitation after injury. Patterns suspected of contributing to injuries or poor performance can be studied and remedied through feedback techniques provided via safe, controlled virtual models.

Training sessions can be conducted so that ergometric readouts, blood pressure, heart and aspiration rates can be projected onto an image of the person on a wide-angle screen. Thus, feedback techniques may be learned and reinforced, and new patterns of workout can be introduced at a controlled pace. Athletes can prepare for competition in virtual meets of increasing difficulty, pitting them against virtual opponents of increasing prowess.

The design of sports equipment will be subjected to detailed scrutiny and iterative revamping through the use of virtual realizations of equipment models. These can be tested, modified, improved and customized for individual athletes according to professional standards. Accommodation for personal style can be embedded in the design of a golf club, for instance. A user can try it out and request changes during its design, before it is actually manufactured. The precise, computer-generated specifications is then used to drive the manufacturing process itself, ensuring products that reliably and exactly meet design standards.

Armchair Tourism

The most advanced "tourist" application today is NASA's virtual trip to Mars (described in Chapter 12). Mundane offerings are still just that, but limited tours of national parks and canyons are being developed by independent research groups. Initial commercial packages will adapt current sightseeing videos to enable a person to virtually become a passenger, cyclist or driver and tour the countryside or bazaar — or a user may choose swimming motions for navigation to explore an underwater cave. Locational sound effects including, perhaps, conversation practice in local languages would heighten the illusion of presence. Guidebook commentary would be a toggle-switch option. As resources and designer imagination allow, facilities for interactive queries, tactile and thermal feedback and other sensory stimuli could be added to upgrade products.

Virtual Toys

The need for powerful computing resources to generate high-resolution graphics in real time discourages the development of virtual versions of "toys" as we know them. Despite their potential appeal of disappearing when playtime is over, in most cases, the gadgetry that would be required precludes the ease and fun of their use by children. Until costs fall dramatically and equipment becomes truly non-intrusive and compact, individual playthings will remain quite real.

NEW DAY AT THE OFFICE

Virtual Desktops

No matter how large a computer screen is, you run out of space. Squeezing in too many windows only creates a tenement of information mess, like the one on our desk, only worse because it's compacted into a much smaller space. Enter the virtual desktop — about the same size as the real thing — and replacing the real thing. Its large screen will really allow users to exploit the possibilities of an electronic information world.

The new office could conceivably be equipped with such desk surfaces, high-definition television (HDTV) screens 4 feet wide and over 2 feet in depth. With the 100-dot-per-inch resolution possible today, nearly 13 million pixels would be at your disposal; with that resolution, you wouldn't get eyestrain. Just as you parallel-process diverse projects and information at your real desktop, you could tap into and work on four or five projects simultaneously via your virtual windows.

Team design projects could be worked on concurrently and compared. Financial trends and figures could be linked real-time so that the flux of the market changes before your eyes, giving you a competitive edge for time-sensitive trades. Literature searches and video games would be possible through other access points, and windows could be expanded, filed away or rearranged more quickly than you could bury the papers on your real desk.

Using your virtual desktop, you could watch the nightly news or participate in a virtual brainstorming session with your boss and colleagues. Each of you may be sitting (or reclining in a "flogiston" chair [Park92]) in your own office but will also be telepresent in a virtual conference room with a wealth of information at your fingertips.

Our new offices would be arranged differently to accommodate new work styles. Even lighting would change dramatically to give the projection systems the contrast they need for the best display. The desk would actually become a peripheral element to the system and could be tilted so that specially designed recliner chairs could be used for long hours at hard work.

What's holding us back?

Since the mid-1930s, television's early days, there have been few real changes in television display technology. Large, flat, high-resolution displays are still evolving, and each involves a trade-off. For example, the main drawbacks of the three types of screens are:

- Cathode ray tubes (CRTs) are clear and can have very high resolution but are bulky and heavy and use more electricity than other displays.

- Liquid crystal display (LCD) technology provides a slim, flat panel that weighs very little and can work off a small battery, but its picture suffers from low contrast in bright light, obscuring some characters.

- Gas plasma displays are clear and flat but expensive and power-hungry.

The technology currently used for computer monitors is very bulky and is limited to a maximum of 36 to 38 inches. In addition, CRTs are too heavy and cumbersome to serve as desktop surfaces. It takes eight people to move the 38-inch Sony. Even if you could get it through the door, it would be tantamount to having a refrigerator on your desktop. These displays also require permanent installation and peripheral projectors and equipment.

The upper size limit of the next choice, liquid crystal displays (LCDs) with thin-film transistors, is 20 inches — flat but too small. Grouping smaller ones (e.g., as done, tile-like, for CRT wall screens at some exhibits) introduces seams. Even so, they are very expensive, not many are being manufactured, and some users say they are unpleasant to work with for long periods of time. The other technologies that are being developed could yield large panels; however, right now, they are not available, nor will they be affordable when they first come on the market. [Park92b]

There is also incompatibility between the old screen proportions of 4:3 and the aspect ratio of 16:9 that is required for the newer, high-definition screens; so, large, similarly proportioned images are needed. Alternative gas plasma displays use a lot of power and are still prohibitively expensive. Gas plasma screens are also heavy.

This leaves LCD-projection screens as the only viable choice for the large images needed for virtual desktops. LCD technology holds out a promise of big screens only a few inches in depth. In Japan, a three twin-panel LCD HDTV projector is available. Each panel displays 1.2 million pixels. Mass-market versions of the projector HDTVs are expected between 1995 and 1997. The only limitation to these might be your budget.

Other high-resolution projectors are available in Japan today, but plans do not include their being introduced to the U.S. market just yet. We have to wait. In the meantime, a stopgap measure might emerge in the form of feelable, virtual desktop-monitor displays for students and researchers.

CORPORATE TOOLS

The real business world often demands that judgments be passed and decisions be made in the face of many unknowns, but it is no longer feasible — nor is it advisable — to depend on data-processing specialists for time- or context-sensitive material. Decision-support computations should generally be done by persons actually using the information because they understand the business problem they are trying to solve.

Flattened Corporate Structures

From 1983 to 1988, 89 of the largest 100 U.S. companies reorganized into a flatter, leaner structure. [Drucker88] Mid-level management is disappearing, and the gap between executive decision makers and their customer base is closing. In these newly structured companies, the needs of customers are no longer clouded in circuitous journeys through middle management.

Consequently, everyone needs to be able to think at much higher levels of abstraction and act at higher levels of coordination. Specialists are needed at the top, and people at all levels will become part of the decision-making process.

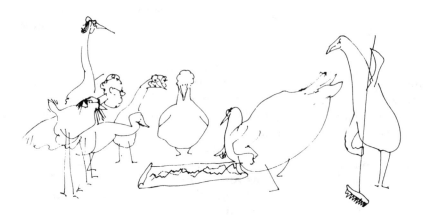

Visualization techniques that clarify all the multimedia information gathered, processed and shared by functions within a business enable personnel at all levels to make more informed decisions. This is one of the final stages of the migration of computer power and decision-making tools from the desks and back offices of information systems engineers to the desks of employees and previously immune executive suites.

Limitations of Decision-Support Systems

Computer-aided executive information systems (EISs) and decision-support systems (DSSs) are available to keep track of what is known about a corporation and present it in understandable terms. They are, however, only tools. Making decisions in the face of variables and unknowns is something that a human brain just naturally handles better than a computer. Compared to a savvy businessperson's acumen, a DSS is unsophisticated and can never replace a person's innate abilities.

The visualization and realization technologies developed for virtual environments are not designed to usurp a person's responsibility for decisions but rather to augment the ways he or she works with the information available. This will influence how corporate data are displayed and manipulated and how decision makers use corporate database resources.

Executive Knowledge & Models of the Corporation

Because the ultimate decisions necessary to achieve the goals of a company are made at the top, senior management — traditionally computer-phobic — is now being forced to understand the technology driving not only their organizations but also those of their competitors and customers. Trained to succeed in business, competent executives are aware of the impact on the corporation of new technologies or markets or capital investments. They usually possess well-honed personal skills for evaluating risk factors, but they need to have at their disposal tools and training that give them a competitive edge of information.

Knowledge-based facilities are usually available. However, the decision-making process is often influenced by the structure of the models used for analysis and simulation. Therefore, executives must be sure that the information system being used accurately represents the corporation — as *they* see it, not as the data-processing department sees it. Executive decision makers need facilities that allow them to visualize relevant information and use it quickly. They must be able to try out strategies in light of real-life challenges and to explore possible solutions and organizational reaction to them. Simulation models must include elements of corporate history and corporate culture, e.g., what works now and what has worked in the past and why, so that an executive is able to anticipate what might work in the future. This entails processing millions of pieces of data relevant to the company's position, harnessing the accumulated knowledge and learning capacity of the organization, integrating everything with the functions of the business and then displaying the information in ways that are meaningful. These are the areas in which VR interfacing and display techniques can be best applied.

The display must facilitate analysis of those factors most likely to affect business, and the support software must provide the executive with the means of manipulating and questioning the data. Notes and comments by a person's predecessors or field specialists may be made part of the presentation, to be reviewed as necessary. The system must allow decision makers to pose what-if questions in natural language and observe the impact of real-world effects on their business plans. Ease of use can be promoted by integrating semantic maps of human knowledge into the corporate knowledge base. This helps provide users with context-sensitive, visually meaningful detail.

By providing a tool for high-level conceptualization and a safe virtual environment in which manipulation of those ideas is made easy, VR technology supports insightful, informed decisions. For example, one window may be reserved for a round-the-clock fluctuating graphical representation of select stock prices or market trends, inventory, trading partners' interests, competitive moves by other organizations, etc. Select views of these, enhanced by the executive's acumen, can be made available to all the corporation's knowledge workers. Thus, all employees in the organization can share and absorb insight, and innovation can be spread.

The New Manager

Because, in most corporations, information is the resource upon which the rest of the company relies, an important function of managers is to encourage the enrichment of that resource. This is done through refinement of existing knowledge and expansion of that knowledge and expertise into new areas of the company. Another function of a manager in an information-based company is to shore up the learning process of everyone in the organization. This entails raising the capacity of personnel for high-level conceptualization of factors important to the company's well-being. [Zuboff88] Complex data and information that are deciphered and rendered into understandable, interpretive displays help executive managers visualize the ways information and resources must be allocated to add value to the corporation.

VR systems make it possible for decision makers themselves to define and create the environments or problems in clear, graphically explicit images. When creative investigation of numerical data is required, highly complex business "realizations" (models) can be generated and explored. Courses of action can be challenged before resources are committed. The technology will allow them to produce "what-if" scenarios in innovative, ad-hoc ways without stringent specifications. The dynamics of office operations and business functions will change as employees learn to use information as a strategic resource. As part of a proactive process, workers perceive themselves as having a stake in the business.

Project Management

The visualization systems developed for VR applications can be employed to help a manager better assess ongoing projects or enable him or her to implement contingency plans. Continuously evolving in synch with a project, pictorial visualizations of the actual progress being made can be matched with visualizations of planned schedules and can serve as early warning systems.

The state and activities of real corporate life may be tied in to displays of strategic plans and resources. Unfolding in fast-forward, slow motion or in reverse, project managers can watch a project develop — seeing it unfold as a flower does on speeded-up film. These visual reminders not only alert an executive to tangential or nonproductive efforts going on but spark insight, enabling him or her to influence the course of events.

Completion of a project depends on the successful completion of each of many tasks, often scheduled in sequence, each dependent on the one before. Others may be worked on in parallel and coordinated at a later point in the lifecycle. Resources (including money and manpower) assigned at the beginning of a project usually have to be reallocated as actual work progresses. Benefits or consequences of reshuffling or augmenting resources (such as putting more people on a task) are not always correctly anticipated. Many projects take twice as long when more people are added.

Considering all the variables connected with such changes, there are simply too many variables and too much input for most systems to handle and display interactively. The systems developed for VR are able to process and display these large amounts of data quickly and effectively. With VR display techniques, the state of the project is reflected by the system at all times in a dynamic model that can be run and examined at different speeds under varying circumstances. The fast generation of many points of view from the same base set of data facilitates mid-cycle observation and examination. Being able to clearly visualize and prioritize the amounts and kinds of data upon which a project is based gives a manager a distinct cost and time advantage. People assigned to projects will understand the dynamics of the activities by observing the dynamics of the model. All those involved can confer and pose solutions. Changes can be proposed and trials run to observe consequences before implementing.

Troubleshooting alarms may be embedded in the project program to alert a current project manager to potential slowdowns, and image enhancing and scaling features can be used to emphasize priorities. VR techniques afford a project manager the freedom to propose different solutions, to manipulate influencing factors and to observe quickly what results each may produce.

Histories of similar projects may be hooked into the system as adjunct resources and brought into the display area as comparable charts or patterns of spending, and track records of individual project managers may be linked into the system, as well, to automatically generate the types of visual displays preferred for each one's unique approach and style.

Virtual Teleconferencing

Enhanced business videoconferencing in the form of shared, virtual boardrooms can foster productive communication among executives determining courses of action. Knowledge and expertise can be shared, expanded upon and refined, and then presented to others at either a high conceptual level or in excruciating detail. Visualizations of complex situations would be rendered to illuminate or clarify the information. Group decision making, with the aim of solving complex problems through autonomous decisions, will be facilitated through the enhanced communication that virtual environments make possible.

Two-way imaging services provide enhanced video telephony for client/broker transactions and business videoconferencing. Training sessions conducted in virtual worlds allow trainees to interact harmlessly with others in safe scenarios. There, potential managers and salespersons may negotiate, sell or develop products and services in virtual scenarios constructed to challenge them under the constraints of stress or time.

Here, however, it must be acknowledged that there are some instances in which solving problems or focusing on training can best be done in isolation, away from the corporate environment. Off-site seminars and classes are often very productive. For most purposes, however, electronic outreach seminars, conducted via a shared virtual center, are more cost-effective and allow participants to take immediate advantage of feedback to and from their parent companies.

Enhanced Marketing

Corporate marketing will take advantage of VR technology for analyzing archived masses of business data (such as those gathered by insurance companies and banks) and displaying interpretive realizations of them. By being able to visualize the market, quantify its risks and manipulate it according to various marketing approaches, marketing personnel can better determine the most profitable strategy and achieve better results. Dynamic visualizations of marketing information and forecast systems can increase the odds of success for introducing new products.

Visualized spreadsheets connected to real-time databases encourage timely action by people responsible for financial decisions. Customized training programs for both management and technical subjects will provide users with believable situations in which they can be challenged in accordance with their own learning styles and levels of skill. Virtual on-the-job "experience" can be gained without the toll of faulty decisions or mistakes of procedure.

Eventually, all of the high-resolution image-processing computers for the above applications should be integrated with copying, facsimile and text-reading or scanning systems. This will affect a host of office applications and enhance the support of marketing efforts.

Bulls, Bears & Wind on Wall Street

The complex, chaotic mathematics behind meteorological phenomena are being tamed into comprehensible realizations in simulation models, and researchers have noticed a remarkable congruity between virtual meteorological environments, which mimic, measure and attempt to recreate unpredictable weather elements, and the nonlinear, dynamic climates of the world's financial arenas. Trend forecasting, market timing and price movements indicative of today's capital markets all depend on equally unpredictable, underlying fractal statistical structures.

The powerful systems developed for VR applications are particularly well suited for interpretive displays of information regarding changing financial markets. A difficult-to-predict flux of virtual air currents bears striking resemblance to the difficult-to-predict fluctuations associated with stock market transactions.

Models and patterns used to display and manipulate virtual weather are increasingly being borrowed or finding their way into financial institutions. Virtual meteorological models are adapted by financial scrutinizers as cross-purpose models for the display and analysis of virtual financial fluctuations. It is difficult for analysts to remember and continually adjust more than six or seven of these variables over any length of time. The visualization features of financial models help analysts track the variables both for real-time trends and for later analysis.

Within the safety of the model, the potential impact of a real transaction can first be explored and observed by effecting a virtual transaction and examining the evidence via a dynamic, "evergreen" visualization of the marketplace. By being able to "see" and "fly through" data, financial analysts will be able to spot areas of data overload and take steps to minimize or balance their effects. [Rheingold91]

Applications
for Manufacturing

11

Computer-aided manufacturing has been around for a long time, and all competitive industries have enlisted new techniques to some degree into their manufacturing processes. CAD (Computer-Aided Design) systems feed into CAM (Computer-Aided Manufacturing) systems that are driven by CAPP (Computer-Aided Process Planning) models. VR visualization techniques will be adopted wherever in the manufacturing process sophisticated image processing has proven helpful in the past. Their purpose will not be merely the generation of computerized drawings but provision for a wider array of conceptual product design and engineering analysis options.

MARRIAGE OF 3-D & VIRTUAL REALITY

What is making this possible is the migration of solid-modeling (3-D) capabilities to individual workers' desktops, ensuring their involvement through all phases of a product's lifecycle — from planning and design through shipment to the customer. Powerful workstations will provide all those responsible for the design, engineering and implementation of a product's manufacture with an integrated, consistent operating and communications base.

Simulation and virtual-reality programs already in use today will be integrated with databases used for production. The combination will replicate, in a few minutes, conditions that, previous to the convergence of high-speed computational technologies and high-resolution graphics technologies, would require hours or days of separate processing tasks.

In-House Expertise

Throughout the manufacturing cycle, from inception to final product, designers embed their ideas and comments into ever-growing product databases, which become available as valuable internal resources. In addition, corporate justification for particular design choices or reasons for eliminating products or features become part of the program itself, available to all subsequent designers. Customer complaints and comments may comprise a "hit list" for future designs.

A confidential, in-house expertise is thus built up and passed on from original designers to those working on new systems. If the system is well planned and implemented, people working on current projects can learn from the experience of designers before them. By querying the system about a certain design aspect or decision, a user is, in effect, consulting with colleagues from the past and can leave notes for future users of the facilities.

In addition to the qualitative benefits of expertise passed on, systems supported by high-speed facilities of the type being developed for virtual worlds promote quantifiable benefits such as just-in-time scheduling, reduced inventories and low maintenance costs. Planning efforts proceed quickly and effectively, and potential bottlenecks of the system are identified before expensive equipment is ordered and installed.

Aircraft Manufacture

Commercial aircraft companies and military acquisition units already use simulators and shared VR environments for designing and developing aircraft models. In most cases, the savings realized through use of VR technology and techniques have more than justified high initial costs. By eliminating the need for building and testing actual working systems as prototypes, for instance, the U.S. Army saved close to a billion dollars in development costs for one new helicopter design. [SCS92]

Commercial manufacturers are realizing similar returns on their investments. Boeing has created a virtual "protospace" for building airplanes, and plans are in place for computer-generated and computer-controlled manufacture of the 777 aircraft.

Virtual prototypes allow designers and pilots to test how well new components work. Prototyping also allows them to move gauges, control panels or fittings, as necessary, to streamline the model and make it more comfortable. Often, a small detail — such as a dial that cannot be read or a frequently used control switch placed farther away from the pilot than a rarely used one — go unnoticed until an expensive clay mock-up or an actual aircraft is built.

Not only will collaborative virtual spaces be used for almost-paperless design and prototyping, but VR will be taken into the production line of manufacturing, as well. The superimposition of control displays onto real parts and pieces ensures precision and speeds up assembly and production processes. In the aircraft industry, applications range from affixing wing bolts and nuts, to laying wiring according to exact specifications or preparing composite layouts for wings.

Checking for weaknesses in the shell of the aircraft is now done painstakingly by human examiner, and the trained eye and expertise of technicians will never be replaced by instruments. However, little armies of teleoperated robots can be set loose to scour the body of the plane, testing and recording every centimeter. When their highly precise instrumentation detects anything less than a perfect reading, a central control unit is alerted, and the area is automatically marked. Skilled technicians then see to the problem personally. The process continues until all trouble spots are resolved. The tireless little robots are then let loose to scurry all over the next plane in line.

MACHINE-VISION APPLICATIONS

This convergence of technologies — from artificial intelligence and computer vision to machine learning, neural networks, pattern recognition, parallel architectures and signal processing — will accelerate the use of machine-vision applications in manufacturing. Telepresent robots installed at sites even hundreds or thousands of miles away can perform round-the-clock inspection and preventive maintenance tasks. Optical neurocomputers, used in conjunction with tiny lenses to provide vision units for robots, allow an inspector or monitor to tap into critical junctions (e.g., at nodes of a communications network, assembly points at factories, on laboratory countertops, etc.) by visual telepresence. In minutes, he or she can troubleshoot and control those situations almost as if physically present.

The use of micromachines when size precludes the use of conventional machines can effectively streamline standard applications. Old, bulky equipment can be replaced with reliable micromachines that are integrated with the use of neurocomputers and robots. These can be controlled remotely via VR realizations of the environment. In addition, because they can be mass produced, micromachines will be inexpensive compared to their conventional counterparts, and worn-out machines can be replaced easily and quickly. Retrofitting factories and assembly plants with strategically placed, virtually controlled micromachines will be cost-effective and space-saving.

Automated instrumentation for industrial purposes will be networked with imaging, storage, transmission and reception systems to offer research and development (R&D) laboratory units the tools for control-based, on-line process analyses in such areas as electrical conductivity, chromatography, mass spectroscopy and pH. One clear benefit is the faster production of reliable high-quality products without the uncertainties of human analyses.

PLANT DESIGN & MAINTENANCE PROCEDURES

Modern process simulators are becoming increasingly essential for plant procedures and for safety and maintenance training applications. The feedback and display technologies developed for VR applications can be used in valuable by-product offshoots — to alert people, for instance, to dangers that are computer-displayable but invisible to humans.

Diagnostics

It is possible to build diagnostic circuits into engines and machinery. Eventually, engines, machinery and appliances will come not only with customer information packets but also with built-in banks of technical data that can be accessed by computer systems for inspection, diagnosis and repair purposes. Information stored in these is processed to generate images and superimpose them on the equipment or piece of machinery being tested. For example, using a transparent virtual overlay as a guide, a mechanic can check the wiring of a hot rod. Alternately, a jet engine specialist may prefer to extract written specifications from a nonimmersive text-based system and view them through a head-mounted eyepiece while working on an engine's fuel injection system.

The image would display information from many sources about the nature, location, probable causes and possible remedy for any trouble detected. Preventive maintenance tips would be suggested. Dealing with each trouble spot becomes an opportunity to tap into the accumulated expertise of others and learn more about the system as a whole.

Canary in the Coal Mine

There are many different ways to monitor the levels of various elements in our personal and world environments. Particular elements, those that can be dangerous to us or to the ecological balance, can be hooked into systems that provide feedback to users to alert them of the dangers.

Odorless but poisonous gas often reaches high levels in coal mines. Traditionally, canaries were brought along as alert systems. Dead canaries were a sure sign to the miners to get out of there. Computer systems serve this type of monitoring purpose, as well. People sensitive to particular substances that are undetectable to their natural senses can be given jolts or vibrations when the levels of those substances become dangerously high.

Workers examining or cleaning out nuclear plants will be able to "wear" their monitoring devices and receive immediate warning of high levels of radiation. Firemen will want to track locations of each other and sources of danger in burning buildings and will want to use computerized scenarios of potential danger for training purposes.

A Finnish company has developed a helmet sporting ultrasound transducers on the front. These survey the area ahead of the wearer, alternately sending out bleeps and picking up reflections from objects. The returning signals control light-emitting diodes (LEDs) that generate a transparent image of the scene ahead onto the panel in front of the user's eyes. How brightly or dimly the LEDs shine is determined by the density of the object detected; thus, the user can tell if the obstacle or object is solid (such as a boulder) or otherwise (such as floating seaweed). Because the viewing apparatus renders 3-D images, the user can also estimate how far he or she is from the object, making it particularly suitable for firemen and divers, who often have to navigate in smoke or mud. [Dunn92] Such systems will facilitate simultaneous multisite training and instruction for the development of common processes and the establishment of emergency procedures.

In the design stages of manufacturing plants, sophisticated three-dimensional CAD/CAM imaging systems will be used for process design that will support safety and maintenance across disciplines and sites. These can eventually be converted into virtual systems.

For new production plants, the viability of safety and maintenance plans can be viewed and tested during the conceptual planning phase and throughout the construction phases, enabling changes early in each process, thereby avoiding change-order costs and production delays. The use of simulators employing the advanced imaging techniques and feedback technology developed for virtual-reality applications permits ongoing experimentation, training and the exchange of skills and insight without actual exposure to the inherent potential dangers of the processes.

PRODUCT CONCEPT INDUSTRIAL DESIGN

Industrial designers are using virtual clay to mold virtual tools and instruments. Designers work with a 3-D computer graphic model, molding it and folding it, much like a sculptor would do with flexible mesh or a potter with clay, until they are satisfied with it as a product.

The virtual-clay model is then felt and examined by designers at other sites. They either approve it or modify it. Finally, the computed specifics of the approved version are fed back into a system (often a telerobotic factory) to recreate the virtual models as solid models.

Through such integrated high-speed computational facilities, video imaging, voice synthesis and transmission, previously independent design teams, manufacturers and suppliers can be integrated into a distributed system that shortens the concept-to-realization time-frame for product or process development. Most importantly, modifications in the design are made by consensus as soon as detected, and morphing techniques are used to design the new components without clay prototypes. The cost benefits of such early detection and correction are well documented.

The design potential of virtual prototypes extends to light industrial design, as well. It is conceivable that the fashion industry will use some type of projection displays for iterative "fittings" before new styles are actually tailored, and household items will be subjected to "usability" testing by potential customers before purchase. Department stores that offer nonimmersive computer-aided hair and make-up styling sessions will augment their equipment to incorporate some degrees of immersion and extend the marketing idea into clothing areas.

The Virtual Lathe

The virtual lathe has evolved from a piece of software already used for animation purposes. One of the ways a designer begins to create a three-dimensional object is to import a flat-image file into a new file and trace around the edges of the object with an extrusion editor. A "lathe" facility is then used to build a new 3-D object from the outline.

This process has now been made even easier with a virtual lathe system that provides the user with a unique view — one in which the object being carved seems to float right in front of him, like a colorful hologram, instead of just appearing on the monitor. The view and orientation of the object are determined by the user's head movements as tracked by an ultrasonic six-degree-of-freedom position sensor. As a user looks around the object, just as he or she would in the real world, the display changes accordingly.

A customized computer mouse serves as the virtual cutting tip for the lathe. A pencil-like wand sticking out from the front of the mouse is pressed into the object wherever material is to be cut away. The size of the tip can be varied to produce different types of cuts. Animated sparks and sound effects — grinding and spinning — are used to make the process seem realistic to the user, and the volume and intensity of these are coordinated with the amount of virtual material being removed from the object. The illusion is further enhanced because the output is a stereo, relatively clear 960x680-pixel display.

Automobile & Industrial Vehicle Design

Computer conceptual design and rendering systems can cut the time it takes to design an automobile more than half, speeding up product introduction and enhancing its quality and performance — an important weapon in the fight for international market share. Manufacturers of heavy industrial vehicles are outsourcing contracts to VR research groups in universities to drastically cut the lifecycle for the design and development of their new models — sometimes by as much as 90 per cent.

The automobile industry already provides its product concept industrial designers with sophisticated CAD/CAM imaging systems that have solid modeling (3-D) animation capabilities, and designers now fully illustrate a new car's appearance and experiment with ergonomics design before clay models are built. Eventually, as these systems are converted into virtual systems, automakers will be able to not only illustrate a new car design, but also show it in relation to its operational environment and begin to evaluate the automobile's engineering performance before the solid model is made. The clay model car is giving way to a virtual clay model that can be scrapped, modified or enhanced repeatedly early in the process. When thoroughly debugged, this virtual clay model is replaced by a virtual "realization" that can be test-driven over a virtual course.

Virtual prototypes can be shipped from site to site electronically or can be accessed via shared virtual spaces. Early testing and modification of these electronic mock-ups save manufacturers both time and money, e.g., a tester will be able to judge whether a dial or switch is placed too far for a driver to reach, if any view is obstructed, if the seat position is awkward or if the driver's head is likely to hit the roof at every bump in the road. Maintenance problems can be simulated, as well, and personnel can lift up the virtual hood to test maintenance procedures or assess whether parts can be easily reached for repair.

Finally, well before investment is made in a solid model, those persons responsible for final products can drive the test models through virtual reality and initiate changes or approve the design. Thus, at each stage throughout the manufacturing lifecycle, the model is refined, and a final car design quickly evolves. The computer specifications are then fed into a system that controls the manufacturing process, and the virtual car is recreated with real material as a physical car.

The builders of Caterpillar earth moving machines consider it good business to pay fees for supercomputer resources and expertise at the University of Illinois. A design process that previously took 9 months and a great deal of humanpower is now accomplished in less than one month with fewer personnel. [UI93] New cab or shovel configurations are tested by real drivers for possible imbalances or line-of-sight obstructions while handling the virtual bulldozers and trucks under varying conditions.

Applications for Science & Engineering

12

The creative process — the generation of good ideas — depends on mental images. With virtual reality (VR), these mental images can be imposed on users and shared among them.

VR technology provides scientists and engineers with the means for input and feedback that enhance their creative efforts. Intuitive interfacing with large amounts of data is made easier for a user in a virtual environment by allowing interaction with dramatic visualizations that accommodate subverbal queries.

RESEARCH & DEVELOPMENT ACTIVITIES

In engineering research and development, the information content of complex mathematical equations, their solutions and empirical data have to be translated and interpreted into manipulatible, three-dimesional or four-dimensional images. This requires elegant, powerful, high-performance workstations and supercomputer backup capacities. To get the job done, scientists and engineers often put a system together from a number of different machines, one for handling data, one for generating images, one for analysis, etc. Recently, however, machines dedicated to scientific visualizations and capable of combined functions are available and taking their place. [NYT91]

Current physical experimentation is done in such areas as molecular structure, chemical reactions, material strength, kinetics and medicine. This can be enhanced and perhaps even replaced by advanced image processing and virtual-reality models that communicate not only information but expert analysis and interpretation of the information, also. As increasing amounts of data, newly acquired knowledge and expertise are included, the virtual process is continually honed and tested. Researchers explore and interact with the models and with each other to determine the most cost-effective and quality-assured products and processes.

The advantage of bypassing pilot plant projects through the use and visualization of fundamental mathematical models is clear. Rule-of-thumb engineering knowledge will be replaced by highly complex visual structures evolved from strictly controlled, reliable empirical data and computations. All computations and the subsequent rendering into virtual-reality scenarios would be carried out according to the basic tenets of physics, chemistry and engineering sciences that would be inherent to the system.

Advances in image processing will also make themselves felt in chemical research areas requiring surveillance systems, inspection, nondestructive testing, image processing for human/machine interface, robotic vision and remote medical image processing. The time, expense and risk of experiments and field studies are significantly reduced because, during the design and development phases, the models evolve.

Sophisticated mathematical modeling rendered into virtual scenarios will offer safe opportunities for important technological experimentation in many areas, including biological reactions, chemical reactions such as those involving chemical vapor deposits or caustic weapons, as well as environmental concerns such as hazardous waste disposal and consequences of the release of chemicals into the atmosphere.

MOLECULAR MODELING

The display, construction and manipulation of virtual molecular structures are of particular interest and use to chemists and biochemists. It helps to be able to visualize complex, 3-D molecular structures, and today researchers are able to retrieve all kinds of relevant data from scientific databases. Programmed information of atomic types, bonds, electrical charges, coordinates and connectivity is readily available. This is used by the researchers to create virtual molecules of atoms and bonds and fragments of atoms and bonds, which are stored in computer files.

Biochemists have already solved the mysteries of some new proteins — specifically, Copper-Zinc Superoxide Dismutase and Erabutoxin — by virtual means alone, circumventing the need for traditional brass models. [Brooks88] Increasingly, VR applications are being used for enzyme-docking trials and in the development of pharmaceutical products.

Molecules can be displayed in many ways — as wire-frame, ball-and-spoke or space-filling structures. Graceful, ribbonlike structures may intertwine to show, for instance, where the polypeptide backbone of the protein is. A sphere might represent each atom, in which case, the model would resemble a converged mass of soap bubbles. Some models look like erector set configurations; sticks represent bonds between atoms, with a small sphere at the center of each atom. Users report that it is easier to see the structure of a molecule with these ball-and-stick models than with spherical models.

Virtual molecules can be further clarified with text labels, arrows, color or proportional bond thickness and length. With shutter glasses, they may be called up from a personal computer system to float like holograms in front of your eyes. Loading a protein model into a virtual display, a user can put on his or her gear and enter the same virtual environment.

The molecules can be scaled to whatever proportion the observer wishes. The molecules may be scaled up to fill the space — seeming, perhaps, to be 50 feet tall to a user. Within that defined space, a person can "fly" through and around the structure and space, examining it from different perspectives and probing it to evoke change.

If the display is a haptic, force-feedback display, researchers can "experience" atomic-level forces involved, for instance, when a protein and enzyme are linked. A chemist can "feel" torques or attraction or repulsion associated with the binding of drugs and/or enzymes. These "feelings" are usually relayed to the user/chemist through a servomanipulator, a type of hand-held ball device mounted on a mechanical arm. The feedback device is also an input device. It is one means by which the chemist controls the virtual environment and interacts with it.

With atoms as large as beach balls or rods as long as broomsticks, a person plays at altering the molecular structure, joining fragments together to form larger molecules, adding and removing bonds and hydrogen atoms and causing torsional rotations. The program checks any modified structure for unacceptable geometry (e.g., bond lengths and distances) or violation of physical laws.

The program can also provide ways for calculating bond lengths, angles and torsions. Files for equilibrium values and stiffnesses for different types of bonds, angles and torsions can be used and modified to include special conditions. Energy terms can be assigned, evaluated and displayed. In some virtual environments, the user gets haptic feedback from the molecules, e.g., sensations of repulsion, attraction, twists or pressure. Interpreting these, he or she is able to adjust his or her interaction to either solve the problem or gain more knowledge about the configuration of the molecule.

A user can make the molecule turn and see its depth and shape change, highlighted and shaded by the program. Any particular view can be "frozen" in a "snapshot," a computer record of its shape, position and qualities, and configurations can be recalled at a later time for further examination. Extensive investigation into the visualization of protein and nucleic acid molecules is being conducted at the University of North Carolina at Chapel Hill. [Brooks91]

VIRTUAL PLANETS & GALAXIES

A real, manned mission to the red planet has always held great public appeal, perhaps reviving childhood fascinations about Martians. Now, childhood illusion is gaining credibility as a pending reality, but before that, virtual reality and telepresence will play important roles.

To describe Mars as hostile is an understatement. Safely transporting humans to Mars and returning them would be extremely perilous, costly and time-consuming. The terrain is harsh and rugged, its atmosphere is thin enough to boil explorers' blood if they are unprotected, and the average surface temperature is 50 degrees Fahrenheit below zero.

An alternative plan to sending humans to Mars is to launch high-resolution satellites to photograph the surface, followed by a ship carrying robotic explorers. These would perform reconnaissance work, allowing us to walk up mountains and through canyons and observe the environment via telepresence. The first footsteps in the sand of Mars will probably look like a bug's, and he's already been named Attila by the people building him.

The data from these missions can be combined with the various technologies developed for flight simulators and with computer software and graphic displays to create a virtual world based on the mapped Martian surface. Right now, despite persistent difficulties in simulating the force or absence of gravity — and provided you allow yourself to be fooled — it is virtually possible to fly to outer space, take a ride in a roving lunar terrestrial vehicle or view the earth and stars from a perspective in space.

It is the convergence of technologies described in Chapter 1 that will enable people to explore Mars or other planets without leaving Earth. Not only will it enable a visitor to the virtual terrain to stand at a Viking landing site, look around and scan the horizon and see what he or she would see if really there, but such a venture would also allow large numbers of people to study the planet's surface over a long period of time (in parallel). This approach would be less costly than human exploration and, in the event of failure, would not threaten public opinion of the space program.

Scientists have been acquiring highly accurate, detailed data from outer space for decades. A wealth of information has been collected and is being constantly updated. Recently received signals from Venus are the newest additions. Creators of virtual planetary spaces are now mining this resource, channeling vast amounts of these little bits of data into computers to generate digital models — virtual planetary scenarios — that accurately represent the real things.

Virtual Planetary Exploration System

Most notable among research efforts along these lines is the Virtual Planetary Exploration (VPE) system developed by NASA at Ames' Research Institute for Advanced Computer Science (RIACS). There, based on the new paradigm of virtual reality, the concepts, methods and user-based interaction strategies useful in the design of planetary exploration workstations are developed and tested. [McGreevy91]

Most data used to create detailed virtual images that surround a user are retrieved from imaging systems mounted on actual planetary rovers. These real data are sometimes supplemented with data gathered from mapping areas on Earth that resemble those surrounding the Viking 2 lander site — certain parts of Death Valley, for instance. [McGreevy91]

For key planetary sites, data are precomputed to generate realistic images or scenes that are then stored. This has been nicknamed the "Mars National Park" approach because it ventures to collect and display complex planetary scenes in much the same way the U.S. National Park Service does for scenic trails and features. [McGreevy&91] As a user explores the terrain, these realistically detailed scenes are displayed to correspond with those a person would see if walking in the real planetary environment.

Adaptive refinement, i.e., proportionately lowering the complexity of surrounding scenery as the action speeds up, is used to a great extent in the VPE system, but certain recognizable features of the passing terrain usually have to be preserved to help a user navigate. As the user slows down, the resolution of the display improves, and the surrounding scene gradually sharpens.

Panoramic 360-degree images or mosaic-like images displayed in hemispherical form around the user are augmented with audio effects and tactile feedback. As the user navigates around and grabs virtual objects, sounds of pebbles crunching beneath boots and pressure felt on the hand of the user via an instrumented glove serve to enhance the illusion of reality and give the user a sense of presence.

Models of Astronomical Proportions

The scaling features of virtual realizations has encouraged astronomers to begin construction of a virtual galaxy from data collected over many years. The visual scenario will provide researchers with the means to view our galactic system and others from perspectives impossible till now, allowing them to virtually explore and experiment with black holes, super novae and asteroids.

VIRTUAL WINDTUNNEL

The design of modern aerospace vehicles relies heavily on precise engineering and vigorous testing. Before the first flight of the space shuttle, scale models were tested in laboratory windtunnels to help predict how the vehicles would perform under various conditions.

Since that time, computer simulations for aerospace studies (referred to as computational aerodynamics) have been introduced into the design cycle to augment actual physical windtunnel trials. This is because computational aerodynamics can simulate conditions that are difficult or impossible to achieve under physical laboratory conditions.

Steady vs. Unsteady Flows

Steady air flows are easy to calculate because the directional and speed paths scientists use to measure and study them all coincide. Unsteady air flow patterns, such as those around airplanes and three-dimensional objects, pose particular problems. Their calculations often generate immense amounts of data — up to several thousand megabytes — and the complexity of the patterns requires techniques that help researchers visualize them yet remain faithful to classical physical approaches.

Often, 2-D (and even most 3-D) graphic images based on the solution data do not convey a flow's complexity. Also, because flow patterns typically occur over very large areas, the ability to scale is important.

Realizations of Numerically Generated Flows

To address this shortcoming, Steve Bryson and Creon Levit of NASA-Ames Research Center in California have devised a prototype virtual system for exploring air flow patterns around objects. [Bryson&91]

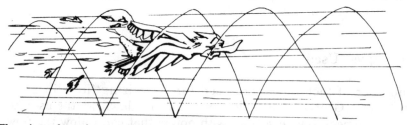

The virtual environment provides realizations of numerically generated, unsteady flowfields. Called the Virtual Windtunnel, the system uses 3-D computer graphics and special input devices to give the user an illusion of being surrounded by a flow.

Advantages over Physical Models

By allowing a scientist inside a computer-generated flow field, the virtual windtunnel combines advantages of a physical windtunnel with those of simulated conditions. Given the illusion of being totally surrounded by aerodynamic flow, a user enjoys a unique perspective of the dynamics of flow past objects. As virtual high-velocity air streams are injected into the flow, a user watches them form complex, asymmetrical patterns like those created when an aircraft loses power or equipment, ices over, encounters enemy fire or suffers windshear stress. Visualizations help a user spot areas that may be sensitized to these types of chaotic flow.

Flow problems that change over time may also be examined, e.g., three-dimensional unsteady flows can be studied in real time as a researcher walks around inside a vortex. Time may be accelerated, run in reverse, slowed down or frozen. By freezing time, a designer can take as long as necessary to intuitively explore complex aerodynamic flows from varied perspectives and under varying conditions.

Another benefit of a virtual over a real windtunnel is that flow within a virtual windtunnel remains unimpeded by the presence of an observer or sensor. In a virtual environment, a user can enjoy freedom of perspective without being defined as a virtual object; thus, flows within the environment proceed without being deflected by his or her presence. In other words, a researcher can examine the virtual flow from almost any perspective without actually disturbing it. This is not the case for physical experiments, where the mere presence of even the tiniest of sensors within the environment can impede flow enough to alter results.

A problem of scale (not encountered in many applications) is accommodated by the virtual windtunnel environment. There, a person can shrink himself or herself to a point of perspective or shrink the whole flow realization to fit in his or her hand. Also, because one virtual environment can be nested within another one, a user of the virtual windtunnel can view other flow simulations by simply changing databases. This greatly facilitates the testing and comparison of various experimental methods for aircraft control.

Techniques Used

A number of techniques are used for visualizing flows in a virtual windtunnel. Generally, at critical places in the flowfield, the user "seeds" the environment, one at a time, with points that can follow the flow. A predefined hand gesture is used to denote the original seed point; another establishes how far it is to trace. An instrumented glove allows a user to direct the stream and manipulate the image. The system recognizes a variety of gestures as commands.

Within the virtual windtunnel, a small, cross-shaped cursor tracks the virtual hand's position. A stream line tracks the position of the hand, representing the path a particle would travel if emitted into the flow.

The seeded points may be designated as bubblers, in which case, a stream of virtual bubbles denotes the flow path, a throwback to scientists' use of hydrogen-bubble tracers in water tunnels. In some applications, paths are not controlled by glove movement. Instead, flow is visualized by programming "smoke" or "dye blob" emitters along each side of a virtual object itself and tracing their paths.

A collection of streamlines or series of points can be grouped as a "rake" that follows a flow path as a set, but one in which each member reacts independently to the pattern it encounters — neighboring streams can appear to diverge, be caught up in the wing-tip vortex or be deflected under the wing. A user can scale the data and then walk around inside the vortex, examining its structure in detail.

External to the virtual environment, a head-tracking device monitors the user's orientation. A pair of CRTs display high-resolution wide-field stereo images of the flow field to the user's monitor. The weight of the monitor is borne by a BOOM, a type of gimbal counterweighted, six-degree-of-freedom motion platform (as described in Chapter 3). Researchers of this project preferred the use of a BOOM over that of head-mounted gear, citing the fact that a BOOM provides users with CRT resolution rather than LCD without the users having to bear the weight of the CRTs.

Goals

The main goal of the windtunnel project is to use virtual-reality technology to solve real problems associated with the interactive demonstration of 3-D flows, especially unsteady ones. Thus, efforts are being made to:

- facilitate and make more precise the testing and control of the geometry, aerodynamic control surfaces and propulsion systems of aircraft;

- integrate the many techniques now being used in the study of aerodynamic flow;

- provide a rich investigative environment in which designers have a wide range of options and the facility to change quickly and intuitively among them.

TELEPRESENT MAINTENANCE FOR NETWORKS

Real-time visualization of what is going on in a network affords engineers the opportunity to adjust the network for more optimal routing and performance in a timely fashion, much like a traffic engineer on the spot might resolve highway congestion. In virtual, electronic landscapes, maintenance engineers can telefly over the links and through the switches to spot problems and optimize the flow of data over the network as a whole. Subsequently, they are better able to anticipate network problems or resolve them more quickly by rerouting before the condition worsens and imposes considerable inconvenience and expense.

Micromachines and robotics are used to identify, diagnose and repair cabling problems. Sensors and robotic features embedded at critical sites along the network monitor traffic information and pass it to humans in a control center, providing them with an accurate perceptual assessment of the state of the network. Engineers at the virtual network management center exercise telepresent control over self-diagnostic features and programmed repair procedures. By telecontrol, human operators are able to override automatic procedures when necessary.

Telemanagement of micro network switches and traffic monitors is also being investigated. Virtual mock-ups facilitate remote operation of the devices' minuscule components and help operators maintain control over them. When traffic on any link of the network or through any switch becomes excessive, it slows the network down. In a visualization of the network, different characteristics of the traffic over a link or through a switch are made distinguishable by width, color or level of animation.

Systems are being developed that animate network data. Others incorporate "intelligent" data management strategies that allow data to work on themselves to produce adaptive data when certain conditions prevail, when an uncharted or incomplete link is found, for example.

The system can be programmed to issue dramatic visible or audible alarms as thresholds are neared or exceeded. Through telepresence, maintenance engineers are alerted by these or other perceptual and sensory clues. As transmission progresses or aborts or is altered, the network visualization changes dynamically to reflect the new states of affairs.

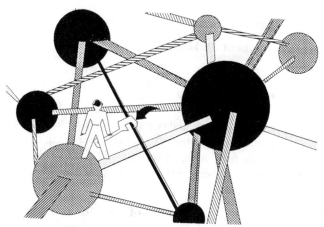

Network repair and preventive maintenance can be facilitated by telemanipulation of the network and its parts from a central virtual control station. By being provided with information that is perceptually meaningful, network engineers are spared the time-consuming and labor-intensive effort it would take to intellectively analyze the complex collection of data itself, freeing them to concentrate on repairing what is wrong.

THE CHEMICAL INDUSTRY

Considering that the profitability of a chemical manufacturing operation depends to a large degree on process operations and control systems, the use of VR design and test procedures will improve a company's competitive position significantly. Access to databanks containing relevant molecular structures, types of reactions and patent information will allow corporate research and development divisions to determine processes available to them and help them discern under which conditions each is to be preferred.

Potential applications for optimizing resources in the chemical industry include those in the areas of:

- chemical properties and thermodynamics;

- dispersion models and liquid release;

- flow analysis, fluid dynamics;

- production and maintenance management;

- design of equipment (e.g., reactors) and separations;

- network optimization;

- control, measurement and analysis of systems;

- energy management and balances.

Hazardous Waste Remediation

By-products of the chemical industry's primary products are very often hazardous waste products that require special handling. Treatment for hazardous waste, which may include toxic, radioactive substances, differs greatly from the process of converting solid (garbage) waste into inert landfill or products.

The defense industries on both sides of the old cold war have created the most hazardous waste, with base closures and nuclear arms cutbacks adding to the numbers and amounts of items to be disposed. The military's record is followed by that of the chemical industry. Both produce products and leave waste. Legislation to minimize the dangers of exposure, accidents and leakage of underground tanks used for storage of these materials has forced them, in particular, to develop means for neutralizing their hazardous waste products and stabilizing hazardous waste sites.

The use of VR technologies facilitates the steps required for efficient remediation of hazardous waste. The use of telerobotic operation for drilling, sampling, analysis and removal of hazardous waste spares human operators the dangers of exposure and allows manipulation of the material that might otherwise be impossible. By enabling an on-site technician to combine abstract data with real data in real time, quick and accurate assessment of potential dangers is possible. Visualization techniques aid in the retroactive analysis of causal factors by allowing a user to compile large amounts of relevant information and process them into easily interpreted images.

DANGEROUS LABORATORY EXPERIMENTS

Many laboratory experiments, even when strictly controlled, are not without danger, and accidents occur frequently. Where there is danger of explosion, such as in the experiment described below, the safety of distance allowed by telepresence and teleoperation is attractive. Virtual realizations would act as safe, intimate interfaces in the study of the processes involved.

Virtual realizations of the actual processes, combined with teleoperated manipulation from remote control centers, would also offer researchers opportunities for observing the reactions in real, reverse and slow-motion times and allow mid-cycle analyses of the reactions involved. An example of the type of experiment that lends itself to realization trials is described below.

Cold Fusion Experiments

Thermonuclear fusion is simply a reaction in which the nuclei of light atoms are heated to extreme temperatures until they fuse with each other and form nuclei of heavier atoms. Fission, by the way, is the other way around, starting with a heavy atom and resulting in two lighter ones. Both types release great amounts of energy.

Fusion is the source of the sun's energy. It is also the basis for the hydrogen bomb, in which the fusion of the nuclei of various hydrogen isotopes (deuterium) results in heavier helium nuclei and the production of energy — a very expensive means of producing energy.

Cold fusion is an unknown type of electrochemical reaction that also releases energy — but purportedly does so from mixtures of distilled water at room temperatures. In other words, cold fusion is an inexpensive, "nonthermo" nuclear reaction. It is currently limited to controlled laboratory experiments, but unfortunately, in 1992, there were a number of fatalities attributed to efforts at reproducing and validating laboratory results.

The basic setup consists of electrodes of the metals platinum and palladium hung into a jar of "heavy" water, i.e., a solution enriched with deuterium, the hydrogen isotopes. When an electric current is sent through the electrodes, the nuclei of the deuterium in the jar supposedly fuse, resulting in heavier nuclei and a surge of energy. When scientists know how much energy (in the form of electrical current) is applied to the system and measure more than that coming out of the system, it is assumed that new energy is generated. Some researchers refer to this as new hydrogen energy.

Results from initial cold fusion studies, though publicized as near-hoaxes in the United States, have shown enough promise to prompt the Ministry of Trade and Industry of Japan to commit $25 million over 4 years toward its development as an unlimited source of cheap energy. Trials are being run with "light" water solutions, as well, and with solid-state fusion tiles or "marbles," little balls of deuterium metal with ceramic coatings.

As is the case for many high-technology innovations, international (and many U.S.) cold fusion projects are being funded by Japanese-backed enterprises. The U.S. Department of Energy does not directly fund much research in the area. However, the Electric Power Research Institute of California has allotted $12 million for SRI, a California research group, to investigate cold fusion as an alternative source of energy. Their preliminary results have been received with less skepticism than expected, and testing will continue.

Military Applications 13

AIR FORCE PIONEERS OF '66

The initial task of Air Force training efforts in the 1960s was to interface the human with a very complex machine, the jet plane. Then, as now, engineers found that there were too many things to keep note of, and the systems available for pilot training were not intuitive. No amount of human "smarts" would be enough to cope with the necessary 75 displays and 300 switches, 9 of which were on the throttle alone. Hundreds of computers were involved, shipping information around on digital busses.

Thus, military spending pushed pilot and cockpit design interfaces ahead of other applications. Super Cockpit, a classified U.S. Air Force project, ranks first on the list of recreating realistic conditions for pilot trainees. The interfaces ultimately designed for that project were so nonintrusive that one pilot-user fainted when he thought he had landed too low and was about to hit a simulated ditch. [Furness91] As systems have become ever more complex since then, the priority remains.

Wearable Cockpits

A way had to be found to streamline, interpret and display this overload of information to the pilot so that he or she could instantly understand it and respond with input of his or her own. This required a paradigm shift from focus on the information glut to creating a visualization for what went on in a pilot's head in that situation. In other words, pictures had to be generated to reflect what the collection of switches meant at any instant. Through a special helmet worn by the pilot, these helpful visualizations of the world were projected into his or her eyes via high-resolution, miniature CRTs. The original aim was for a cockpit that was "worn" rather than sat in or looked at.

That effort led to many advances in other technologies, as well, such as the correlation of 3-dimensional sound to images by earprints, advanced tracking technologies and large LCD screens to be used as virtual cockpit displays. Because of the expense involved, progress on this last point will be slow unless tied to defense and supported by the military. [Ross88]

Extensive and expensive research — up to $1 million for a helmet alone — has always been possible in the military, but as East/West relations ease up, funding for military research expenses will fluctuate and suffer cuts. [Scheffer88] At the same time, it is this very research that will allow us to greatly reduce our forces, yet provide adequate defense because the weapons systems are so much more effective.

TRANSFER OF THE TECHNOLOGY TO INDUSTRY

In 1985, NASA demonstrated its first VR project results to nonmilitary visitors from industry and universities. [McGreevy91] That same year, the military issued its first press release on the results of its efforts in virtual-reality applications.

Since then, interest has been steadily growing, and a number of very human, diverse requests has underscored the need for other applications — firefighters wanting to be able to track each other's locations in burning buildings, mothers wishing to extend the range of experiences to their disabled children, doctors needing more accurate diagnostic and healing tools and businesspersons seeking better ways to compete in world markets.

Hopefully, the trend will continue, and the benefits of experience gained from defense applications and paid for by the taxpayers will apply to other industries. Because of regulations, the expertise and management of VR design and development for defense purposes are not easily transferred out of the military. However, some steps are being taken to respond to calls for such transfer, and a number of groups made up of representatives from like arms of industry and government are forming.

With the blessings of the U.S. military, the first industrially oriented laboratory was set up at the University of Washington in Seattle. Its goals are to share the results of the military's $100-million investment in technology with industry and to train professionals who are able to communicate and effect the transition. [Furness91] In addition, the Defense Advanced Research Projects Agency (DARPA, now just ARPA) is exploring the possibilities of limited support for outside startup companies and research and development (R&D) projects with synergetic goals.

TODAY'S MILITARY AGENDA

Focus on Environments, Entry Points & Connectivity

Military users refer to virtual environments as *synthetic environments*. Envisaged for the future are seamless operating environments as "wearable" as the Super Cockpit and as pervasive and far-reaching as networks allow. Bandwidth does not appear to be an issue; projects being planned assume almost unlimited amounts.

Accommodation must be made and protocol established for getting into these seamless, pervasive environments and interacting within them, once there. Topics being investigated include varied modes of entry and access — via networked simulators, through constructed models or via connections of independent systems to networks.

Connectivity issues involve demands for real-time interactivity and support. Also among the types of issues being studied are whether virtual support should be provided worldwide, deployable during conflict or restricted to tactical purposes.

Collaborations between the military and private organizations include other types of projects such as basic research on the psychological aspects of synthetic environments, parallel computation techniques, the degree to which immersion is necessary for achieving very focused goals and the transfer of technology to support businesses. Work is also being done in conjunction with universities on the adaptation and construction of databases for virtual training purposes and on the development of algorithms and data structures for dynamic, virtual "outdoors," e.g., vegetation, weather, water, etc. How to display land being exploded, virtual pontoons floating or virtual water flowing under varying wartime conditions are some of the questions researchers are trying to answer.

Institutionalization

Most VR conferences and forums center around technical aspects and implementation of its relevant technologies. A 1992 strategy statement published by the U.S. Department of Defense, however, made it clear that issues of policy, management and institutionalization were important considerations as the technology is integrated into the defense acquisition process. This involves the whole lifecycle of an idea, from its inception through its realization and, finally, to its battlefield connections. This is a monumental task for any organization, particularly for the Department of Defense.

There are, within the parent organization, many vertical lines of command, each attempting to bend the technology to serve its own purposes. For instance, environments designed and adapted for the education and training arm of an organization are not necessarily equally appropriate venues for engineering and development purposes or for analysis and operations research. The degrees of accuracy needed and the means of visualizing data differ among the groups, and all groups are subject to regulations that do not provide the flexibility required for shared VR resources within the organization. Meanwhile, around the world, at the laboratory level, things are being done by seemingly unencumbered autonomous groups — anticipating the day when the regulations and networking issues are resolved and results can be implemented and shared.

Still to Be Resolved

There are a number of technical issues to be resolved before joint military networking is practical. Many of the computer systems originally built for SIMNET or built to connect to it are becoming obsolete. These are being replaced at different times, but upgrades and replacements are often incompatible, as are systems belonging to countries other than the United States. So, before ambitious projects can be implemented, international operational standards must evolve from the de-facto ones in place today.

System security is another issue of importance, especially to the military. Many military simulations are designed for use by many people. It must be possible to control user access to the system and control permission to modify programs. Because devices and capabilities are being installed in many places, widespread connectivity is inevitable; however, so will the means for circumventing security be made possible.

Problems of system synchronization and network contention may also impede the ideal of "seamlessness" among synthetic environments. Collision detection and override features must operate according to established protocol, which must be reviewed and adjusted as users gain experience integrating the systems.

Current limitations of HMDs are of concern. Military applications require very realistic images, and computer-generated displays are often not convincing enough. It is still difficult to generate sloppy swamps, detonating mine fields or convincingly threatening enemies. It is also difficult to simulate the effects of radiation or sonar or electromagnetic fields; so, a lot of work is being done by the military to solve these problems.

EVALUATING WEAPONS SYSTEMS

Applications for testing and evaluating weapons are designed to render previous systems obsolete; so, unlike simulations for training purposes, they do not make use of available interfaces. These applications require the construction of unique, expensive and elaborate prototypes of new control panels each time a design is varied.

Now, virtual-reality technology will be enlisted for this stage of weapons development, as well. Realizations of the immediate interfaces — the controls and displays between human crews and the systems they must control — will replace expensive physical mock-ups.

The creation of virtual crew station controls and display units will allow developers to evaluate designs soon after concept, reducing costs significantly. Ill-conceived designs can be modified countless times or scrapped early in the process without incurring the high costs or time involved in constructing physical versions. The system evolves, and the specifications are used to drive construction of the actual system. After actual construction, the virtual model need not be scrapped; it can then be used for training purposes.

BATTLE STAFF TRAINING

Many researchers have been surprised by how quickly people learn when given "hands on" experience in virtual scenarios and cite examples of skepticism turning to enthusiasm after only 5 minutes. The effectiveness of virtually-real scenarios for training purposes was underscored in a casual trial by scientists showing their teenaged children around the laboratory. Soon after sitting in the virtual cockpit of a fighter jet, these novices were able to handle the complicated machine — and were able to "fly" missions within a few hours of slipping into the gear.

Virtual-reality technology is being employed in many weapons systems — in fighter pilot eye-control helmets, for instance, to help weapons lock on to targets. Video tank crews also raise their skill levels by practicing on virtual electronic battlefields and learning to telemanipulate weaponry in the field. Three-dimensional simulation techniques for training purposes generally incorporate actual weapons panels, complete with real buttons and levers, as interfaces between the human crew and the systems they control. These are sometimes referred to as Battlefield Distributed Simulation (BDS) Testbeds.

Mission Planning & Rehearsal

In the Army, shared decision-support environments simulate tactical command and control (C2) operations, and implications of networking tactical planning efforts are important. NASA is particularly keen on how to best incorporate the scientific visualization of various large datasets into simulator databases. Combining efforts has proven effective. For example, data received from planetary fly-bys or from computational fluid dynamics experiments can be fed into the military's virtual realization systems to upgrade scene realism or promote greater understanding or communication among participants.

Current military simulation models for ballistics and propellants or for directed-energy weapons are natural candidates for virtual realizations. Efforts may eventually extend to include interactive investigation in more esoteric areas of lethality, vulnerability and survivability of personnel and missions, as well.

On either a standard CRT or through a head-mounted display device, mission planners display 3-D terrain data and generate flight paths of single or multiple aircraft using an aerodynamic model of aircraft performance. Then, in mission rehearsals, the user signals with a glove to select targets, threats and aircraft viewpoints, which may be modified interactively. Viewing modes are selected by voice command. Varying constraints may be imposed during mission rehearsals to challenge users and record their responses under different conditions.

SUPERIMPOSED INTELLIGENCE

For certain things, human intelligence will always surpass performance by computer systems, even those boosted with sophisticated artificial-intelligence (AI) features. Tasks at which humans excel include pattern recognition and the ability to retrieve facts from large bodies of information with strange and unusual connections among them. The machines and techniques developed for virtual-reality applications can now be enlisted as powerful intelligence amplification (IA) adjuncts to our natural human abilities. [Brooks91]

Visualization and realization techniques help people recognize, translate and interpret complex patterns. Used for cryptanalysis, VR techniques and environments render intelligence data into displayable, manipulatible images that are easy to compare and analyze.

On the Horizon

14

> If I were now to rewrite the book,
> I would offer the Savage a third alternative.
> Between the utopian and the primitive horns of his dilemma
> would lie the possibility of sanity . . . .
> Science and technology would be used as though,
> like the Sabbath, they had been made for man,
> not as though man were to be adapted and enslaved to them.
> Aldous Huxley, 1946, commenting on BRAVE NEW WORLD

WHAT TO EXPECT

Any degree of internalization of how a user interfaces with a virtual world promotes believability in a number of ways — comfort and unburdened movement, a more natural field of vision and the minimization of peripheral interference. Spared distraction, the brain receives a well controlled, true image to override or superimpose upon what is outside.

Current research acknowledges the importance of such "seamless" interfacing. Projects under way, regardless of discipline, aim to achieve it.

Virtual Retinal Display

That the experiential medium of virtual reality relies on the impact of images is evidenced by the expensive, cumbersome optics systems it requires. Even the most lightweight of viewing devices is a piece of "gear," and equipment developers juggle the factors of physical burden, image resolution and cost, having to settle for two of the three.

Now, at the Human Interface Technology (H.I.T.) Laboratory at the University of Washington in Seattle, scientists are investigating writing images onto the retina of the eye. In essence, a person's own retina becomes a screen for images transmitted then through the optic nerves to his or her brain. Laser-light images are scanned and condensed through an "exit pupil" (like funneling a large view through a small window). The tiny, high-resolution image goes right into the eye (through the real pupil). At 10 microwatts, the beams are harmless to the eyes, measuring well under the federal safety guideline for constant exposure to lasers, which is 40 microwatts.

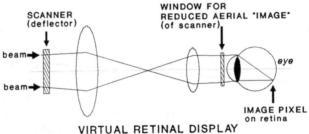

VIRTUAL RETINAL DISPLAY

Modulation of the helium-neon lasers used until recently has been difficult. They are being replaced with very low-power diode lasers that can be independently modulated. Vertical resolution is about 1000 pixels, and horizontal resolution has been improved from 500 pixels across to 1000 pixels. Researchers are also investigating nonlaser light sources and stereoscopic and eye-tracking versions, as well as possible medical applications of the approach.

H.I.T. Laboratory has scheduled a commercial prototype of the device by 1996. Called the Virtual Retinal Display (VRD), it is designed to hang from conventional eyeglass frames and will add less than 1 ounce to the weight of any frame used. Plans for the commercial prototype include specifications for full-color images of a much higher resolution — 3000 horizontal pixels by 2000 vertical. Mass production would make user units quite inexpensive, but powerful graphics engines and ample bandwidth will still be needed to make it work. [Furness91,Kollin93]

Brain Implants

Our brains are difficult territories to map; they are not hard-wired and are constantly changing with use. Yet, neuroscientists have persisted in trying to image what goes on there. Now, aided by new technologies that can process and visualize the millions of signals involved, neurosurgeons are addressing many of the questions that could only be conceived a few years ago.

Sleep researchers are able to tap into the brain waves of sleeping human subjects and classify them. With about 80 percent accuracy, they are able to identify patterns associated with different stages of the sleep process. [LaFee92] Brain surgeons have demonstrated that they are able to evoke responses and provoke images in subjects by stimulating the brain tissue itself. Thus, in one scenario, as brain impulses are channeled as input to the system, stimuli may be directed from the system into a user's brain to further expand or intensify the virtual experience. A few researchers expect that biofeedback techniques could also be enlisted to reinforce virtual effects. Both of these techniques, however, are invasive.

More important, perhaps, are recent breakthroughs in what is called Positron Emission Tomography (PET). These enable researchers to produce functional imaging of the nervous system (as reflected in the brain) from minimally invasive measurements. Initial steps include programming of movement and tying motor skills to images — for example, registering a pianist's PET readings with movements of his or her hands.

User demands are already driving the development of input and feedback devices away from the cumbersome helmets and gloves used today. It is thus conceivable that brain waves will become a venue for direct (but limited) human/system communication. However, all these efforts must be undertaken with extreme caution and responsibility. Many areas of expertise must be involved, especially those of cognitive psychology, modeling, computational neurobiology and ethics.

To many people, dimming the line between virtuality and reality is scary — and second-rate movies don't help. Good ideas are being expounded upon to absurdity, and fears of addiction fuel already provocative debates on ethics and the courage or lack thereof to deal with reality. Indeed, the government is planning a major study of the effects on humans from exposure to synthetic environments. [Dunn92]

For the time being, at least, one deterrent to too much believability is the relatively primitive, cartoon state of the renderings that make up a virtual environment's components and population. It's still hard to take something that looks like Roger Rabbit seriously.

Teleoperated Flight & Reconnaissance

Systems are evolving that allow human pilots on the ground to project their sensory, cognitive and motor skills into the cockpit of a flight vehicle located somewhere else — even aloft — and remotely operate that craft. Unmanned Air Vehicles (UAVs) controlled via telepresent pilots are slated for reconnaissance missions, for designating and specifying targets and for assessing damage after firing.

Because increasingly sophisticated displays and virtual interfaces will render the command and control of such vehicles transparent, operators will function as effectively in telepresence as in real trials. Versions of these systems were used during the Gulf War. Camera and aural sensor aiming systems and tracking systems residing in the pilot's helmet are sensitive to eye movements, and helmet-mounted stereo display systems generate graphic overlays on the view. Audio systems and biocontrollers will also eventually be part of the head-mounted units. [Warhover92]

Intelligence Gathering & Fusion

Teleoperation and robotics applications will spur advances not only in flight research but also in reconnaissance, surveillance and combat planning operations. Swarms of remotely controlled, intelligence-gathering robots will be counted among nations' future military units. These robots may be equipped to direct information from remote sites via satellite- or terrain-mounted devices down to head-mounted displays worn by real military personnel located elsewhere.

Commanders may don personal "private-eye" devices, which can be used in stealth mode for nonintrusive observation of units or personnel in the field. A vibrating mirror and LEDs produce two-dimensional images for this type of device.

Computer-model syntheses of intelligence information are super-imposed on views seen by the personnel, e.g., an etching of enemy troops will appear to be just over the ridge of a hill, a truck is outlined inside a bunker or tunnel or instructions for detonation appear as real-space images when personnel enter strategic locations marked for such, etc. This intelligence information and any action taken as a result of it become part of a dynamically changing database at the battleforce operations center. There, what is gathered can be analyzed, assimilated and, subsequently, disseminated to all appropriate units.

Among the goals of an expanded military network program are joint allied maneuvers, including simulated forces from other countries and simulated warfare with both real and computer-generated forces in virtual battlegrounds. [SCS92] It is not clear yet how a participant is to know whether it is a real adversary that has been hit.

Astronaut Information Systems

Manned space walks will undoubtedly be part of tasks assigned to astronauts for a long time to come, not only for exploration purposes but also for repair and maintenance work. The complexity of many of these human-performed jobs requires that the astronauts have extensive resource material at their disposal. Repairing a malfunctioning telecommunications satellite, for instance, involves a high degree of precision and a number of intricate instructions that reside in equipment manuals or databases. These usually contain diagrams and details necessary for the diagnosis and repair of the equipment. Currently, satellites are retrieved with great difficulty by shuttle crews and dealt with later.

The display technologies advanced by virtual-reality research will eventually make it possible to address many of the problems on-site, in orbit. Systems built into head-mounted units that look like motorcycle helmets will enable astronauts to receive contextual information via transparent images "etched" on the visors or as holograms that seem to float in front of them.

What the astronauts see may be videos or sections of text and procedural diagrams. Voice commands could activate and control the system, allowing a repair crew to work "hands-free," a particular advantage in manually taxing or potentially dangerous situations. Alternate or additional telerobotic manipulations and consultation with experts may be conducted through shared virtual environments that are shuttle- or ground-based.

VIRTUAL WORLDS: THE CUSTOMER CREATOR

Japanese department stores are already installing Matsushita virtual-home design and order facilities in district branches. Customers can visit Tokyo's Shinjuku store, slip into VR gloves and goggles and enter a virtual kitchen recreated from their own ideas or from standard designs fed into the system. There, they can run virtual water, try out the virtual appliances or redesign the setup on the spot with virtual components. Then, if they wish to order, detailed specifications of the components selected are translated by the system into actual plans and a contract. The order is then immediately priced and computer-processed. Interestingly, the design of the original house and kitchen realization done in Japan is western-style. It took the Art Center of Pasadena of California to design and create a virtual Japanese-style house.

A virtual world — even part of one — can be a powerful component of a marketing and distribution plan. Easy transfer of techniques for selling goods via this experiential medium fosters new markets, e.g., applications for cosmetic surgery and beauty aids from VR medical applications.

The Ultimate Subliminal Sales Pitch

Some researchers have expressed the fear that negative values will result from the excessive commercialism and stimulation possible with new technologies, particularly virtual reality. Information services may encourage mental laziness and stagnation by an emphasis placed on convenience coupled with aggressive advertising. Other concerns, ranging from the potential for addiction to virtual stimulation to danger from electromagnetic fields in and around virtual environments, have been raised.

All of these questions and others are being addressed in private and public. Conference sessions such as "Ethics and Simulation in the Service of Society," held in Newport Beach, California in 1992, are becoming increasingly more visible on the international scene. [SCS92]

RESTRICTION-INDEPENDENT FLOW OF KNOWLEDGE

Information is unique as a resource in that it can be shared with the world without being depleted. Virtual-interface technology can facilitate the sharing of new concepts, knowledge and expertise and can stimulate language- and culture-independent transfer of learning. Truly global communication and management of business also become possible through the conceptualization aids of virtual reality. Border-independent, culture-independent transfer of technology and training are effected quickly and cheaply when seamless virtual interfaces help lower the barriers of language and interpretation.

People miles apart can meet in a shared virtual world and join in conversation even if they speak no common language. Shared experiences raise the level of community among people, and shared virtual spaces provide venues for making that happen. Powerful computer systems can facilitate near-simultaneous translations in participants' languages of choice and provide the means for family and friends to convene in virtual places, with language and physical barriers dissolved.

Virtual Global Information Communities

Systems that meet many of the criteria for the effective exchange of information and knowledge already exist in many corporations and among universities around the world. Commercial time-sharing services also provide support. All of these, however, are limited to closed groups of users, they are costly and many are constrained to rigidly defined protocols and interfaces. Through public utilities enlisting the latest technologies, participation of ordinary citizens in the management and dissemination of information can be encouraged. Eventually, the utilities can be expanded and extended on an international scale.

An infrastructure must be established, using a combination of computers, communication networks and satellites, in order to introduce any type of global information utility. Driving the system would be the basic tenet that any citizen in the world should be able to obtain useful information readily, quickly and at low cost, at any time and place.

Japan has already adopted the concept of a global information utility (GIU). Project goals include an expansion of the self-multiplicative production effect of information and the promotion of autonomous group decision making by ordinary citizens in order to minimize their tendency toward a centralized administrative society. Public telephone booths already in place may serve as access points to the utility. [Masuda78/90]

People anywhere in the world, for instance, would tap into computer-aided self-education systems, library and other information services, world news services. They would enjoy unimpeded access to, for example, comparative studies of incomes and pensions with other countries, overseas travel arrangements and competitive games. Time differences would not interfere as the services would be provided round the clock.

Global Interfaces

VR interface technology will play a major role in bringing this about. The same type of system that translates hand gestures into synthesized speech and displays it simultaneously as a comic-strip-like bubble of words, can be adapted for translating speech among participants in virtual environments. In that case, the spoken words are first translated and then floated as a bubble. Persons who are not able to speak can communicate via GloveTalker; their gestures are subsequently translated and converted to either speech or displayed text. A few hundred phrases can be programmed in current versions of the gloves. (See Chapter 4.)

Ideally, the basic language of such utilities or shared programs would be internationally standardized; so would the basic computer language. However, in lieu of this, automatic translation systems of the types described for virtual environments can be embedded in the utility.

Virtual Global Interest Communities

In the early days of electronic bulletin boards, Howard Rheingold wrote delightedly of witnessing and participating in the emergence of interesting virtual communities from a base of computer users with modems. [Rheingold86] Diverse communication groups were established among users, and bonds were formed — not on the basis of being hooked into a common system but purely on the basis of shared human interests.

When global information utilities come into practical application, they will provide a universal venue for many diverse virtual interest groups, ones that transcend systems and constraints. These will promote intercultural exchanges and understanding at whole new levels.

Virtual global interest communities may focus around:

- environmental issues;
- worldwide collection and interpretation of data;
- voting;
- medical intervention;
- instruction (prenatal care, community hygiene, etc.);
- educational facilities;
- recreational interests;
- historical perspective;
- philosophy or religion;
- shared experience (construction, crisis management, etc.).

How successfully these applications are implemented depends on many things — e.g., how much bandwidth is made available, how networks intermesh, how well universal operating standards are established, etc.

PORTABLE SYSTEMS

With lightweight, reconfigurable VR systems, many more applications will be developed not only for military field usage but for personal use at home and away from home. Portable head-mounted image-display generators and head trackers work outdoors, allowing users to operate over large spaces. Extra-large-space and long-distance operations will be facilitated by networked multisensors installed at strategic locations.

Systems are being developed that will provide 6-degree-of-freedom tracking of portable, head-mounted or stuck-on-the-forehead sensors. Satellite tracking and transmission are also being investigated for outdoor, large-area applications. The operating system of a portable model should work with whichever fixed computer system a person otherwise uses so that files may be updated, downloaded, interchanged or stored. Blueprints, instructions, specification manuals and training materials for specific clients are some of the resources a professional may wish to maintain in a portable system. Finished projects may be stored on a parent machine.

For Professional & Personal Use

Small commercial systems are powered by computers held by a belt around a person's waist or arm. Helmets may also incorporate both computer and display systems.

Different types of display systems are used for portable systems. They come with visors for full viewing or with devices positioned by braces for single-eye viewing. Via a see-through or dual-purpose viewer, transparent images appear superimposed on the real world. Alternately, a see-through visor allows a person to activate a nonimmersive television-like screen. A small viewing window appears to float in front and off to the side of the wearer's view. Dual-purpose visors may be switched to opaque mode, in which case a user's view of the real world is blocked out.

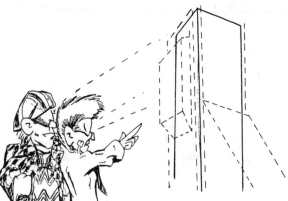

The ability to access and visually navigate through illustrated repair and maintenance manuals and then to call up a display of recommended procedures promotes responsible care of machinery and equipment. Too often, important information is stored far away in bulky, poorly organized technical tomes that defy even a diligent mechanic's efforts to find necessary information. This type of application is already used in the military and in industry.

Because there is choice among the types of display systems, programs that already work via personal or laptop computers lend themselves to adaptation for portable VR-type systems. How-to and self-help guides, e.g., prenatal and postnatal care instructions, fitness training modules and cooking lessons, comprise a large body of this type of information, much of it already digitized.

Medical history records or monitoring devices may be built into personal systems, and the advanced display techniques developed for VR purposes may be incorporated into visual augmentation systems for visually-impaired individuals. (See Chapter 6.) Persons exposed to workplace hazards may also be outfitted with monitoring and regulatory devices. (See Chapter 11.)

EROTICA

Sex leads the list of long-standing culprits in our occidental theories of degeneration. Because the history of human nature succeeds in replacing the Biblical only rarely and very slowly, each milestone along the timeline of sexology seems to take generations.

Up until the 18th century, any sexual intention other than procreation was labeled sinful and criminal. It was not until the mid-1700s that the stigma was removed. Indeed, from some religious points of view, it remains firmly in place today. Then, it took another hundred years before occasions of lust, even within marriage, were exempt from prosecution as crimes — but they stayed high on the list of no-nos.

The 19th century's struggle against man's potential for self-abuse was enacted amidst forensic medicine's classification of vices. This led physicians to encourage almost fanatic attention to every facet of a child's life as a safeguard against the alleged harms of masturbation — part and parcel of a growing belief in a connection being made by scholars between sexuality and insanity. [Bremmer91] But by even acknowledging that masturbation occurred, they had come a long way.

Insanity & the Beastly Passion

Growing interest in the study of human passions was further sparked by a categorization scheme dreamed up by a Frenchman. [Descuret1844] Passions were classified as social, intellectual or the simply beastly. The social passions encompassed human indulgences or hedonism of almost any ilk — love, ambition, greed, nostalgia and suicide. Those deemed intellectual were passions associated with the more artistic, religious or political natures of humankind and included most types of respectable compulsions, such as studiousness, a sense of order, music or collecting.

Finally, libertinism, onanism or anything that smacked of scandal were lumped into a category with gluttony, anger, drunkenness and rage — passions surely arising from what were deemed the darker depths of man.

Toward the end of the 19th century, old medical classifications of vices gave way to the science of sexual psychopathology and the study of perversions. To be fully understood, the sensual human being could no longer be susceptible to bodily harm alone; it had to be compounded by psychological harm. Purity crusades were waged all over the western world, and social interests in the various forms of sexual life developed. [Bremmer91] A shift occurred back to the study of "normal" sex as opposed to the perverse, and sexuality was addressed in contexts other than procreation.

Thus, enlightenment of a sort was brought to the early 20th century. Homosexuals were described as "inverse" rather than perverse, and Freud attempted to render previously perverse drives harmless by staging them as phases in individuals' personal Greek tragedies. Europe adopted sexual policies more liberal than America's and instituted treatment for aberrant behavior. In the new climate, masturbation was still frowned upon — not because it led to physical harm but because it was not a social activity. Medical therapy and social rehabilitation replaced criminal proceedings.

Meanwhile, here in the States, research focused on the sociological implications of sexual practices, and acts were classified as normal if they had any potential as socially redeeming relations. This encouraged further study in the field. In the 1960s, *Playboy* became a forum and articulated new attitudes toward sex and continued to advertise lifestyle changes through the 1980s. Still, though much has been discussed and written, little has been done to investigate scientifically how sexual fantasies correlate with sexual practices or to address the issue of sexual mores. For example, how does poverty affect the levels of promiscuity and prostitution? What is normal at any one time?

Fantasy

Take fantasy — so much a part of our creative lives today and certainly a component of virtual worlds. As recently as 100 years ago, fantasy was blacklisted as leading to perversion — and perversion, it was believed, led to insanity. That the final stage of syphilis closely mimicked the deadly brain disease "dementia paralytica" was proffered as "proof." [Bremmer91]

Today, dallying at the door to the 21st century, most of us can speak about hetero- or homosexuality without too much personal agony. In the United States, though, we do so amidst the social vestiges of a Puritan heritage. There still exists the litter of psychopathologic labels that were affixed by turn-of-the-century doctors to any lusts other than "normal" desire. Many people are quick to label even the notion of sex arcades as perverse and abnormal.

Well, virtual sex (teledildonics, to some) is based quite heavily on the power of fantasy, and the total escapism potential of VR environments inevitably ushers in fantasies of virtual sex. As the subject of parodies on "Saturday Night Live" and alarmist articles in monthly magazines, it has piqued a lot of media attention and public interest.

Actual implementations of the idea, however, remain underdeveloped, and it is not clear whether enthusiasm will wane before applications appear. Regardless of the stance you take, as a social and historical given in our constantly changing climate of sexual policy, the possibility of virtual sex commands our attention.

Of All Things Virtual & Fantastic

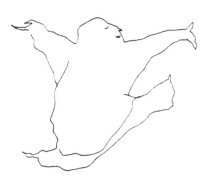

"Absence, say, of Susan's,
Absence of Egeria's
Arms and respective bosoms,
Lips and, ah, posteriors,
Slowly form a presence;
Whose? and, I ask, of what
So absurd an essence,
That something, which is not,
Nevertheless should populate
Empty night more solidly
Than that with which we copulate,
Why should it seem so squalidly?"
BRAVE NEW WORLD

Feedback gloves and body suits that relay the sensation of stimulation are available, and the aspect of being suited up to cavort with cartoon-like characters does not seem to dim people's fascination. Talk abounds of development efforts toward interaction with representations of humans — of the past, present or future — and with fictional or invented creatures. The old query, "With which historical figure would you like to have dinner?" may lead to speculation of interactive virtual trysts.

A result of the development of any new technologies is an increase in our options — across the board and in many areas. While ushering in opportunities for medical, scientific and other applications, VR will hold open enticing doors to virtual sex, as well. Economic interests may then succeed in blurring distinctions between the "private" and "public" of our lives. However, we can always keep in mind that "a new device merely opens a door; it does not compel one to enter." [White62]

Good News & Bad News 15

MADE IN THE U.S.A.

There is a lot of good news. Virtual-reality technology was born in the United States — remember Sutherland as far back as 1965. Technologies that integrate different types of systems challenge the creativity of vibrant minds, and research in VR is providing many such opportunities. VR researchers are motivated to push hard into many areas — interactive display technologies, tracking mechanisms and multicomputer systems that exploit massively parallel approaches to image generation.

Unfortunately, the bad news is that VR is not being vigorously nurtured or well bred. Here in the United States, we have watched valuable results of research and development wind up in other countries, only to be quickly converted into goods for export back to us. Around the world, means are often lacking for research groups to build running systems. Even after good starts, follow-up funds are hard to obtain, and initial vibrancy and excitement are dampened. As an example, long before VR became stylish as a fundable technology, teams at the University of North Carolina at Chapel Hill continued the historical lead of Sutherland, recognizing VR as a legitimate area of work. But they had to build their own computing system because adequate vision and support from outside sources were not available.

Private interest has grown for research areas such as virtual reality, but substantial government support has not been quick, nor has it been strong. Where it does exist, initial seed funds are often followed by lesser, inflexible budget line amounts. Even when the research return on the investment is especially promising, resources can seldom be mustered quickly, and competitive advantage dissipates in bureaucratic discussion.

Advocacy & Ownership

Information and good ideas, in private or public hands, are counted among a nation's most valuable resources, and they are unique in that sharing doesn't deplete them; rather, they are increased. From the perspective of a national economy, this is called the macro-cumulative effect of information. In the case of manufactured goods, high levels of investment in capital equipment usually yield increased production and decreased costs, a mass-production effect. This, in turn, generates further profit and further accumulation of capital and is referred to as the multiplying effect of capital or the self-multiplication of capital.

It is the same for information; however, its cumulative effect is more important. By-products of the self-multiplication of information are upgrades in the value of what is accumulated. As information self-multiplies, its inherent value increases. The process itself teaches us how to better accumulate information — and, subsequently, to accumulate better information. And, as the number of people using the technology in creative ways can never be more than a subset of those who know of its existence, it is in a country's interest to promote widespread knowledge among the population of new technological innovations.

Private and public sectors that communicate and share innovation and information operate at higher levels of understanding. They are able to consolidate priorities and appropriate funds to meet goals in a national context. Some countries have been quick to realize the significance of VR applications and recognize the potential implications of its ownership. In countries competing with us for a technological lead, there is an air of robust advocacy and a government-sanctioned spirit of cooperation toward public and private development of applications.

New knowledge is created independently by preciously few people, and support for them must be strong. They are valued commodities and warrant treatment as such. And in the field of virtual reality, the creative element is a conspicuous driving force.

STARTUP FIRMS & UNIVERSITY GROUPS

With the exception of military applications, most original research in virtual reality and related VR product development is being accomplished by small, startup firms. In an informal survey conducted for this book, the author found that, with the exception of university groups or large think tanks, a majority of companies actively involved in the research and development of virtual-reality technologies employed fewer than 10 people. They are sophisticated — definitely not backyard operations — but they are small.

Startup firms' development efforts are geared primarily toward building equipment, systems and specific applications as products. University research efforts seem to focus more on refining and intermeshing the technologies into convergent working systems.

The Company Store

Most startup firms have difficulty raising capital. As is always the case, the costs of bringing the baby out of the laboratory and into use are high. Thus, in order to obtain seed money to continue their creative work, researchers sometimes sell exclusivity — in the form of licenses with very high price tags. Parties able to spot potential winners early on invest and lock others out. This has been especially hard on other small startups, which need access to particular technologies to survive but cannot afford to play the same game.

Small firms also borrow money. Foreign capitalists, quick to exploit the potential of emerging technologies and aware of this need for funds, have provided loans to many upstart U.S. ventures, quietly establishing inroads and positions of advantage in the companies. The most significant example of this is the 1992 debacle in which the French firm Thomson CSF SA acquired a large number of valuable VPL patents through default of a mere $1 million loan. Previously, licensing for each of the prized patents went for near the amount of the whole loan.

Private Contracts

Perhaps we are banking on the entrepreneurial spirit to prevail and that young, creative minds will survive and thrive without deliberate support policies. Alas, it's not happening. The spirit of creative American entrepreneurs is being dampened in light of full floors of well-funded researchers in other parts of the world using ideas originating here to develop applications and further their own research.

A form of consignment mentality is being fostered. Much of the VR development going on in the United States is targeted to product marketing opportunities, and a lot of the money for this comes from abroad. For some small U.S. firms and laboratories, the only means of meeting the high costs of initial development have come from abroad, notably Japan.

This poses a dilemma. It is inappropriate both to demand full, no-strings support from Washington and to waste valuable development time criticizing other nations — for doing things right. Instead, it is in everyone's interest to quickly find ways to support legitimate research wherever it is being conducted.

We are faced with another problem that was not anticipated. Much U.S. research that is dependent on foreign interests for funding and business is also dependent for system components upon which our own projects depend, as well. Recently, the U.S. government approved sale of the only American manufacturer of critical components of the Trident and Patriot missiles. Another example is active-matrix liquid crystal display (LCD) technology, definitely in the hands of the Japanese, though U.S. researchers contribute to the field. LCDs, as described in Chapter 3, are display devices often preferred for virtual environments over CRTs because of their light weight and flat casings.

One of the challenges technical innovators in the United States face is that, generally speaking, research occupies one world and isolated pockets of industry another. Unless employed in-house, it is almost impossible for creative talent to get to the movers and shakers of industry. Even industries occupying the same world don't share what they're doing, and too few bodies feel responsible for facilitating communication among them. It may be in this area that foreign countries make greater strides than are evident in the United States.

University Funding

University-based researchers have been successful in getting some federal funds. However, doing so is usually a bureaucratic test of their mettle. First, many of the people allocating funds do not possess the technical expertise or vision to spot and quickly evaluate proposals that warrant no-strings-attached support; they must rely on guidelines provided by their respective agencies. So, proposals have to be sprinkled with the right buzzwords — what's hot on government lists — often, in tangential ways that many researchers have difficulty with. Feasibility studies are also required, during which extensive review processes interrupt the flow of research. Even such small issues as coordinating government fiscal years (which start in October) with academic fiscal calendars (which start in July) stall the process.

Last but not least, exhaustive reporting and bureaucratic paper requirements detract from the quality and amount of time researchers are able to dedicate to their real work. Usually, when all is done, less than half the amount allotted is actually available to the researchers. Administrative expenses and university overhead costs cut deeply into the funds. Many of the government agencies' concerns are legitimate. However, in the course of things, a lot of good work is jeopardized, delayed or forced to find a home elsewhere.

OTHER MAJOR PLAYERS: GERMANY, FRANCE & JAPAN

Overseas, more money and resources are made available for VR research and development than are allotted here in the United States, where small firms often take on consignments from foreign companies just to stay in business. Germany and France are pulling ahead of us in the types of applications being developed and in funds being allocated for research, and overall support in Japan for the advance of VR applications is of a magnitude greater than we have managed so far. [Lanier91] In the United Kingdom, growing research and entrepreneurial activity has produced many of control devices used for VR today.

Surprisingly, until fairly recently — the late 1980s — Japan was unaware of the importance of the technologies converging into systems for virtual environments. With the exception of a few individuals who were studying here in the States, almost no resources were devoted to it. Now, within just a few years, *each* of Japan's many (over 10) consortia spends more annually on virtual-reality research and development than does the entire United States.

In Japan, because all major companies are involved as part of a national agenda, there is extensive knowledge-sharing across industry and government sectors. This, combined with long-term planning (50-100 years), contrasts with a U.S. short-term, bottom-line approach — and in the long run, gives Japan substantial competitive advantage. An urgency to reap financial gains very soon after introducing commercial products only clouds the vision of manufacturers and undermines their long-term competitive stance. It makes it easy for them to postpone projects that might be interesting but less likely to generate immediate profit. [Duga92]

Both Japanese and U.S. economies have been hurt by current economic slumps; however, prognoses for their recoveries differ. In the United States, reaction to the slide of the economy is belated and only mildly proactive. In Japan, the pattern of this downturn does not match that of previous ones; so, in what was criticized internally as a late response, the Japanese government has taken a very proactive stance. [Miyoshi92]

Buying the Company

Interested parties have found another way to acquire technologies they need — they simply buy companies outright. A small sampling of whole U.S. companies going abroad between 1989 and 1992 includes:

- military/space equipment — Fairchild Industries' Space & Defense Electronic Units sold to Matra, France.

- 8-inch silicon wafers — Monsanto's Silicon Division bought by Huels, Germany.

- semiconductor equipment — Materials Research Corporation bought by Sony, Japan.

- advanced ceramics — Norton Co. bought by Compagnie de Saint-Gobain, France.

- computers — Honeywell Federal Systems, Inc. bought by Groupe Bull, France.

- industrial robots — Cincinnati Milacron's Robot business sold to Asea Brown Boveri, Switzerland.

- semiconductor equipment — Hercules Corporation's Semi-Gas Unit bought by Nippon Sanso, Japan.

- ultrapure polysilicon — Union Carbide's Polysilicon business bought by Komatsu, Japan.

- M-1 tank transmissions — General Motors' Allison Division sold to ZF Friedrichshafen, Germany.

Source: compiled by the Economic Strategy Institute reported in THE WALL STREET JOURNAL, November 3, 1992.

INTELLECTUAL PROPERTY ISSUES

In 1978, a U.S. federal copyright law established protection for certain kinds of property deemed "original work." This is usually assumed to mean an author's or developer's unique intellectual or artistic treatment of something, the most familiar of which is the printed word. It now also extends to software and computer creations. But copyright law does not precisely define "original work," and infringements of intellectual property rights are difficult to track and prove. This holds especially true internationally unless the creator of an original work has gone to inordinate lengths to properly register in as many countries as might be involved. Even then, chances of enforcing the law are slim.

Present copyright coverage does not extend to ideas but may protect the way those ideas have been put together in a unique creation — and it can apply to simultaneous creations. So, designers and developers of virtual applications have a serious responsibility not only to maintain dated documentation of the progress of their own designs but to stay abreast of what others in their field are doing, a sensible idea in any event.

Establishing and following a policy of marking and documenting anything considered a trade secret can be very important. Cases have been thrown out of court because legitimate, original owners who want to prosecute secret stealers cannot prove *their* claim. In the United States, it is not necessary to formally register original work with the Copyright Office for protection; however, a basic requirement is that all versions of the work display a clear, visible declaration of copyright intention, along with the year of declaration.

NUMBER OF PATENT APPLICATIONS

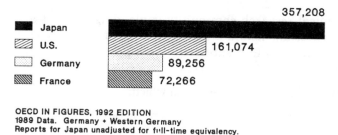

357,208

Japan

U.S.   161,074

Germany   89,256

France   72,266

OECD IN FIGURES, 1992 EDITION
1989 Data. Germany = Western Germany
Reports for Japan unadjusted for full-time equivalency.

It is evident that companies here and abroad are becoming attuned to the possibility of suits for infringement of intellectual and invention property rights. Two large Japanese insurers are studying international laws as bases for new offerings — policies that cover clients' liabilities for infringement of patents, copyrights or trademarks.

PLEA FROM THE RESEARCH COMMUNITY

People working with virtual reality are sensitive to the plight of their colleagues in artificial intelligence, who got tossed about in the wake of promises and beat down by the expectations of the marketplace. Keenly aware of this as they travel along equally nightmarish paths, today's VR researchers avoid sensationalism and tend to downplay claims. No one will hear bandwagon boasts about virtual reality imitating or supplanting human thought. Instead, researchers maintain, *this* technology aims only to empower or extend our human capabilities — intelligence amplification (IA) rather than simulation. [Brooks91]

Real applications, however, no matter how sophisticated, never keep up with our active imaginations, and an impatient market makes it doubly difficult for researchers to exercise patience and maintain the scientific validity of their work. They are often placed in the position of having to humbly solicit government and industry funds and jump through bureaucratic hoops for legitimate educational and medical applications — fully aware that capital would flow much more easily if they became involved in bizarre or quick-turnaround deals.

At some laboratory sites, research efforts have been curtailed primarily because of lack of enthusiasm and funds from the private and public sectors. In order to bring funds in to support their work, some scientists are tempted to shift their focus to what they consider sexy-but-less-than-noble projects.

The Ideal Climate

The technical research community is pleading to start a real dialogue between government and industry, in hopes that virtual-reality research will be recognized and supported as a potentially valuable national resource.

The ideal climate would be one in which:

- Both government and industry encourage domestic markets for the technology.

- People with vision hold responsible positions in funding agencies.

- Adequate funds (with fewer strings attached than now) are available for computer systems research in universities.

- Government coalitions with universities and industries establish the superhighways in the sky (high-bandwidth channels) necessary to provide shared resources to as many people as possible.

- Friendly interface technologies are available to all — to spur as many practical applications as possible.

Researchers feel that the above steps would help the U.S. research community reinforce its position of leadership as originators and innovators of the technology. [Brooks91] They would promote creative applications development here and secure for the U.S. a large portion of the world market share.

Glossary

3-D three-dimensional; a display, medium or performance giving the appearance of height, width and depth.

#-D sometimes used for systems in which any number of dimensions is being displayed, e.g., *6*-D system in which three forces and three torques are demonstrated.

6-DOF 6 degrees of freedom; six different measurements that can be assigned to any one movement. E.g., any one movement may entail changes in as many as 3 spatial positions (horizontal, vertical and depth) and 3 degrees of orientation (rotation, yaw and pitch). The capability for assessing all six for each movement is incorporated into many devices, such as six-degree-of-freedom tracking mechanisms.

absolute values position and orientation within a virtual space as measured from a single, constant point of origin, e.g., one "corner" of the virtual space; used for tracking purposes. If object is moved, previous measurements are ignored, and new position and orientation measurements are taken. (See relative values.)

actuator usually mechanical (hydraulic) or electric means used to provide force or tactile feedback to a user.

adaptive refinement taking advantage of a reduced level of a user's interactivity with the system (e.g., walker slows to a halt) to increase the level of detail of his or her immediate surroundings; an inversely proportional trade-off between levels of activity and detail in a virtual-reality scenario.

add-on product	peripheral equipment or software enhancement that is sold separately from a system and can be added to a system to upgrade its performance or provide added features; called application processors by AT&T for telephone services (such as voice mail).
ad hoc	for a specific purpose or situation; done "on the fly" as needed.
algorithm	a formula for a sequence of steps to solve a problem or do computation to make something happen; a mechanical or recursive computational procedure.
amplified intelligence	empowerment or extension of human capabilities or intellect rather than computer simulation of human cognitive processes; term coined by Frederick Brooks. (See artificial intelligence, augmented reality.)
animatronic	electronically created and generated and manipulated to appear "alive."
application	a unique set of software instructions designed to solve a particular problem or perform a particular task. Electronic spreadsheets and word-processing packages are applications. Groups of applications comprise an information system.
Argonne Remote Manipulator	referred to as ARM; hand-held grip system often used for feedback to a user in applications involving forces or torques; hand-held control and input device with six-degrees-of-freedom movement.
ARPA	Advanced Research Projects Agency of the U.S. government; formerly Defense ARPA (DARPA).
artificial intelligence (A.I.)	computer programs that try to efficiently perform task-oriented computations (e.g., memorizing lists) or to simulate cognitive aspects of human behavior (e.g., figuring out which lists to memorize); an attempt to represent, process and transfer knowledge. (See amplified intelligence.)
artificial reality	simulated, computer-generated spaces; a combination of computer and video systems; term coined by Myron Krueger for title of groundbreaking book. [Krueger83]

aspect ratio ratio of width to height; usually 4:3 screen area of televisions and computers; must be consistent among displays (screen, paper or microfilm) or image is stretched to fill area, i.e., a square image on one might appear rectangular on another if aspect ratios differ.

attribute an adjective, quality, distinct feature or characteristic of a person, place or thing; piece of data containing a single item of information about something.

augmented reality as opposed to "virtual" reality; enhanced perception; when a person chooses to rely on the real world as a frame of reference but uses a transparent (rather than opaque) display or other nonintrusive means to augment it, e.g., schematic superimposed on view of car engine. (See amplified, artificial intelligence.)

author (VR) designer or programmer of virtual environments. An expert enlisted from an outside discipline is sometimes called a collaborative author.

automated interpreting telephony instantaneous translating system designed for two-way telephone communication; takes input spoken in one language, converts it into computer-readable form, translates it into another language, transmits it and then synthesizes it into spoken output at another site.

bandwidth the particular range of electrical frequencies (consequently, the types of communications) that can be handled by a communications device.

"barf" zone instances when nausea occurs because rates of display are too fast or too slow or when synchronization fails.

binary code groups of electronic signals comprised of only two kinds of digits, zeros ("offs") and ones ("ons") that can be read by a computer; as opposed to decimal, which is based on 10 digits, zero through nine.

biocontrollers (biosensors) devices that detect and process most bioelectrical signals, e.g., electrical activity of muscles, eye movement, etc., into digitized signals.

bi-ocular displaying same image to each eye; sometimes done to conserve computing resources when depth perception is not critical. (See stereoscopic.)

bit on and off signal to the computer represented by 0 or 1; smallest unit of memory in a computer; part of a byte, which is usually comprised of 8 bits.

bladders tiny air bags embedded in the lining of gloves or body suits, controlled by a computer to inflate or deflate in synch with the program; transmit sensations of pressure or tangibility to a wearer coming in contact with a virtual object in a virtual setting; used with micropins.

blob computer-generated, bloblike character created at Carnegie Mellon University; programmed to appear to have emotion and act independently. [Bates92b]

BOOM Binocular Omni-Orientation Monitor; for VR purposes, a floor-standing device consisting of two rings mounted in such a way (at right angles to each other) that a monitor used to view virtual environments remains suspended in a horizontal plane between them regardless of its platform motion; similar to device used on a ship to suspend a compass.

broadband a multifrequency transmission facility (usually coaxial cable) that simultaneously carries a number of channels (e.g., voice, data, video), each assigned to a different frequency so that interference will not occur.

buffer immediately accessible computer space used for temporary storage of data, e.g., a holding bay for text sent faster by the computer than the printer can print.

byte common unit of computer storage — 8 bits (digital signals) of information; usually equals 1 character. One bit of each "octet" may be a "parity" bit used for software error detection and correction.

CAD Computer-Aided Design; computer use for architecture or product design.

CAE Computer-Aided Engineering.

CAM Computer-Aided Manufacturing; when CAD output operates machinery that makes products.

CAT scan Computer-Aided Tomography; x-ray map of body.

CD-ROM Compact-Disk Read-Only Memory storage device; holds about a bookcaseful of text; valuable delivery media but store no information about/by users. Writeable optical type is called WORM (Write-Once Read-Many times). Programmable type (i.e., with small amount of update-able storage) is called CD-PROM.

clue conflict a kind of motion sickness caused when the body tries to interpret conflicting clues being received by the senses; sometimes attributed to faulty calibration of eye devices. (See "barf" zone.)

collision detection computer ability to calculate if a user shares spatial coordinates with a virtual object, i.e., if the object were real, whenever there would be contact. Software code is written so that, when virtual collision is detected, feed-back alerts the user, and/or the virtual object appears to be modified or moved.

conceptual mentally conceived (e.g., idea, plan, thought or design).

convolve to filter and intertwine signals (e.g., sounds) and render them three-dimensional; used in VR applications to recreate sounds that give directional cues.

coordinates sets of numbers that determine the location of a point in a space of given dimension; numbers given to position a point, line, curve or plane; the "x, y" set that relates a point to vertical and horizontal axes.

CPU Central Processing Unit (computer); the main part of a computer that interprets and executes commands as they are received; part containing logic and computa-tional circuitry — sometimes all on one chip.

cross-sensory substitution substitution of one sensory stimulus for another, e.g., seeing instead of hearing, smelling instead of tasting. In VR scenarios, signals for one are converted into signals for another and displayed as such, e.g., speech is con-verted into a visual display of text that can be read.

CRTs Cathode-Ray Tubes; around since end of 19th century; glass display terminals or TV screens; heavy and bulky for many purposes, sometimes replaced by LCDs. Images are produced by electrons shot onto a light-emitting phosphor screen.

cyberspace	term coined by William Gibson, science fiction writer to describe computer-synthesized, 3-D spaces; fantasy site of "consensual hallucination." The terms "cyberspace" and "virtual reality" are often interchanged, but some researchers make a distinction between them based on usage or equipment requirements. Most often, virtual reality involves "experiences," and cyberspace is used more for visualizing information and accessing it.
cyberspace representation	another term for three-dimensional visualization or VR realization (virtualization).
cyborg	robotic humanoid modeled directly from digital readings of a real actor and transformed into a photorealistic, animated "twin" such as those shown in the action films *Terminator 2* or *Robocop*; spiritless character produced via illusionary metamorphosis.
DARPA	Defense Advanced Research Projects Agency of the U.S. government; now ARPA, without the D.
data	organized facts and figures; facts and figures from which conclusions may be drawn.
database	data collected and stored in ways structured to facilitate access to information; contains records and fields.
data efficiency	selection and use of only those types of data that effectively address a particular problem; elimination of nonessential data.
data sonification	assignment of sounds to digitized data; may involve filtering to give illusion of localized sound.
data spatialization	assignment of orientation (yaw, pitch) and position coordinates (x, y, z) to digital sounds assigned to data.
decision-support system	a system designed to help users make better business decisions in specific areas; appropriately structured database and set of software tools that facilitate the study of management decisions and factors considered in arriving at each; software for analysis and computation of factors influencing decisions.
dedicated machine	computer or other device designated and reserved for one specific purpose.

dextrous master — mechanical structure for (hand) input; constructed of little pneumatic pumps, motors, pulleys, cables, strain gauges, calibration devices and position sensors; used in place of or with glove for telerobotics with force feedback; sometimes referred to as a robotic hand.

digital, digitized — converted or rendered electronically into digits (usually binary 0s and 1s) that can be processed and displayed by computer.

display technology — system or program needed to electronically generate computer pictures and images.

domain — particular area of expertise; specialty; field of study.

Doppler effect — an apparent increase in the frequency of sound (or light) as its source approaches an observer and a decrease as it moves away (analogous to an approaching/passing train); named after Austrian physicist.

effectors — interfacing devices used in virtual environments for input/output, tactile sensation and tracking, e.g., gloves, bladder and pin arrangements, audio units.

endoscope — slender, tube-like instrument inserted into a body cavity or organ for medical examination; special tip transmits images back to viewing device.

environment (virtual) — space in which a user of VR technology imagines him- or herself and within which interaction takes place; computer-generated display world or scenario.

EPCOT — Experimental Prototypical Community of Tomorrow.

exoskeleton — mechanically linked structure for control of and feedback from an application. (See dextrous master.)

experiential prototyping — application where a designer is building something (a building or automobile, usually larger than a human being) that needs to be explored and tested before committing to construction; meant to improve communication among persons involved with the project and to allow them to test and revise iterations before physical production so that final result closely meets specifications. (See prototyping, virtual prototyping.)

expert system   computer program relying on knowledge or reasoning to emulate the performance of a human expert; contains encoded rule statements (in a knowledge base or rule base) that reflect individual or gathered expertise in a field and then performs "reasoning" via a rule interpreter in order to reach a decision, come to a conclusion or give up (if unable to do either of the former).

fiber-optic transmission   sending large amounts of data as light pulses through slender glass filaments; expensive but accurate, reliable and fast, especially over long distances.

fission   production of energy resulting from the splitting of the nucleus of a heavy atom into the nuclei of two lighter ones. (See fusion.)

flogiston chair   reclining chair designed for long-term, information-intensive work; positioned for minimal stress so that occupant can comfortably view an image projected overhead and manipulate it via a mouse on a pad mounted on the chair's arm. Some versions are installed with motion platform and feedback devices. [Park92b]

flow   continuous movement or circulation; smooth motion that is characteristic of fluids.

force   a power that is made operative when faced with resistance or exertion; operative strength.

force feedback   an inference of a sense of resistance to a user; sensation from actuators of not only contact but also how much force is involved (as distinguished from tactile feedback).

frame   one of many still images that, displayed sequentially at a prescribed speed, convey motion, e.g., one shot in a roll of film.

frame buffer   temporary, immediately accessible computer storage facility.

fusion   formation of nuclei of heavy atoms from lighter ones, accompanied by a release of energy. Thermonuclear fusion results from applying extreme heat to lighter atoms. Cold fusion purports to effect the formation of heavier nuclei and energy in laboratory setups at room temperature. (See fission.)

gesture recognition
interpretation by the computer of hand (or body) movements as commands for action.

gimbal
a device consisting of two rings mounted in such a way (at right angles to each other) that an object remains suspended in a horizontal plane between them regardless of motion of the platform supporting it; used on a ship to suspend a compass and in the laboratory to hold devices such as the monitor for viewing virtual environments (nicknamed BOOM).

glove input
preset movements of the hand and joints that are monitored through a glove fitted with fiber-optic sensors running along the fingers and translated into computer commands that are reflected in a virtual environment.

graphics (computer)
pictures or drawings either created by or entered into the computer by scanning or photographing; can be stored, retrieved and manipulated electronically; usually perceived as geometric or line-based (as opposed to pixel-based).

hand gesturing
predetermined hand movements or sets of hand movements registered by an input glove to cause changes in or manipulate a virtual environment; single movements or sets (combined as gestures) that are interpreted as commands to the program generating the images.

hand input device
hand-held or hand-controlled gadget used to relay precoded signals to the VR program.

haptic
pertaining to sensations of touch, pressure, temperature, twist, etc., mediated by skin, muscle, tendons or joints; representing tactile senses (though not limited to them).

haptic display
computer-generated display designed to appeal to the haptic senses, i.e., one in which things seem to push, pull, radiate or sensate in different directions with varying degrees of strength; objects within the virtual world with assigned force fields, torque, friction, heat and pressure, which are made noticeable to a person interacting with them.

hardware
physical devices at each location of a computer system and the network links between locations.

HDTV

High-Definition TeleVision; system for transmission of of very high resolution television signals. Current NTSC standard in the United States and Japan is only 525 lines and 60 pictures per second.

head-mounted display (HMD)

headpiece or head-held brace with viewing or optical devices (located or suspended in front of a user's eyes).

hologram

an image made on high-resolution film that captures patterns of light waves emanating from an object when illuminated by a laser. When light shines through this special film, the light patterns are reproduced, giving a 3-D effect.

hypermedia

information in the form of text, diagrams, moving diagrams (animation), images, moving images (television), speech, sound or computer programs; information under the control of a computer and the means for a user to navigate through it in valuable ways. Hypermedia are frequently used for complex documents, such as training manuals, safety manuals and other large documents stored on optical disks.

image

a manual, mental or computer-generated reproduction of the appearance of someone or something; a picture or drawing; usually perceived as being pixel-based.

image primitives

lines, polygons, curved shapes and surfaces.

imaging system

hardware and software designed specifically to efficiently capture, store, manipulate, transmit and display images from either direct computation, real environments, models or documents; renders realistic pixel-based representations; *not* computer graphics. Commercial applications are video systems, cameras and optical disks.

immersive graphics

encompassing, multidimensional displays (pictures, sounds, tactual effects) wrapped around so that all senses seem immersed and the line between the real and illusionary worlds disappears.

incompatible systems

systems controlled by different types of software that won't work together.

inference	applying rules to facts to come up with new facts; reasoning by deduction.
information	random collection of unsynthesized material; different from data, which is information organized for analysis, and knowledge, which encompasses material that is empirical, inferred or interpreted.
information system	business system designed to support decision making within an organization and to provide flexible access to an organized, consistent collection of data; set of related applications.
interactive	has features enabling a user to influence or manipulate the course of action; allows conversant interdependency between user and system.
interface	whatever is used — a piece of equipment or choice of menu(s) to connect a user with a computer program; whatever is used (often an interface card inserted into the computer unit) to connect a computer to an external device such as a printer, modem or network.
I/O device	Input/Output device used to present or receive data via computer.
ISDN	Integrated Services Digital Network; new type of large bandwidth, completely digital voice, data and signaling system based on international standards; acronym subject of many jokes (It Still Does Nothing, etc.).
kinesthesis	feelings derived from muscles, tendons and joints and stimulated by movement and tension.
knowledge	understanding gained through experience or study; the cognitive, intellective sum of what is perceived, discovered or inferred; broader in range than information.
knowledge base	electronically recorded knowledge that, instead of being tacitly or verbally transmitted, is accessed and transmitted via electronic interface; aggregated, accumulated knowledge that is cloned, enhanced, augmented, stored or transmitted for use in problem solving. A.I. rules are used to encode knowledge and store it in knowledge bases so that inferences may be drawn from it. Expert systems are examples of encapsulated knowledge.

laparoscope	slender, tube-like instrument inserted through small incision and used for minimally invasive abdominal examination and surgery; special tip transmits images back to viewing device.
latency	lag between user motion and tracker system response; time lapse, sometimes measured in frames; delay between actual change in position and reflection by program; similar to delayed response time.
LBE	Location-Based Entertainment; systems installed at fixed, usually commercial locations (e.g., arcades).
LCD	Liquid Crystal Display (LCD), a type of flat screen; used in calculators and digital watches. An electric field is applied to a surface of liquid crystal molecules, causing them to become so oriented that they act as polarized light filters; considered an advantage over CRTs, but both may be replaced by active matrix displays that require little power but which are still prohibitively expensive and difficult to manufacture. Passive matrix displays are another alternative.
LEDs	ceiling- or fixed-mounted Light-Emitting Diodes; in VR applications, little things used as beacons in combination with imaging sensors (usually mounted on headgear) for tracking purposes; also placed at the ends of joint sections in instrumented gloves to aid measurement of the degree of bending.
lifecycle	complete range of stages in the development of a plan or product from concept to market or implementation.
megabyte	MB or Meg; approximately 1 million bytes; precisely 1024 kilobytes or 1,048,576 bytes.
metallic distortion	measurable amount of noise interference or degraded performance in electromagnetic trackers when used near large metallic objects or operating equipment.
micromachine	very tiny devices comprised of infinitesimally small motors, levers, gears, switches and pulleys — basically, conventional machines miniaturized; a small silicon chip holding very tiny components of a machine.

micropins	groups of tiny pins embedded in the lining of gloves or body suits, connected to a computer and synchronized to move with the program, transmitting sensations of pressure, texture or tangibility to a wearer coming in contact with virtual objects; used with bladders.
MIDI	Musical Instrument Digital Interface; a standard code that accepts as commands different types of signals, including biocontroller signals, which it then implements to control electronic instruments, e.g., music synthesizers, word processors, household devices, etc.
mimesis, mimetic	imitation or representation of nature; exhibiting mimicry of something real; term used to describe how the behavior of artificial or fictional characters mimics real life.
MIRT	Mario Interactive Real Time; Nintendo's video game.
model (VR)	graphics database of the colors and coordinates for polygon-shaped pieces of the virtual world; a computer-generated simulation of something real.
modem	MOdulator/DEModulator, device usually used with a computer and telephone line to convert (modulate) digital data into analog tones and vice versa.
morphing	computer-generated illusion of metamorphosis created by photorealistic computer graphics and animatronic effects.
mouse	hand-held, hand-driven input and pointing device for use with personal computers and workstations.
MRI	Magnetic Resonance Imaging; image of the body derived from magnetic energy readings; generally for medical use.
multicomputer	a class of network-connected parallel machines with multiple computing nodes, each having its own memory for data and commands.
multi-dimensional	having many dimensions such as physical size, scope or purpose.

multimedia	combined text, images, full-motion video and sound; requires lots of bandwidth and computing power.
NASA	National Aeronautics and Space Administration; a division of the U.S. federal government.
networked immersion environment	network-connected sites of VR activity; sum of all remote sites hooking into shared virtual spaces, e.g., Virtual Art Museum, military training networks, etc.
node	point of connection to a network — a switch, another computer site, a terminal, etc.
NPSNET	network of workstation simulators established at the U.S. Naval Postgraduate School (Monterey) for research, training and educational purposes; government-owned utility slated to be connected to SIMNET databases.
NTSC	National Television System Committee; establishes official standards for video transmission signals.
number crunching	repetitive, iterative mathematical calculations.
numeric-intensive	requiring extensive mathematical calculations; number-crunching.
object (virtual)	computer-generated, three-dimensional image within a virtual environment; representations within the virtual space with which a user interacts.
object deformation	still limited ability of a system to calculate and display images that reflect elasticity, e.g., pulling or stretching a layer of virtual skin or other nonrigid object (so that it appears to distort rather than move).
object-oriented	conceptually grouped into autonomous units; any intelligible thing that can be perceived by the mind.
operating system	basic set of software instructions that run a computer (e.g., DOS or OS/2); computer supervision software; provides support for applications programs and interfaces used with the system.
paradigm	an example or conceptual model used to illustrate new approaches or ways of thinking.

parameters measurement factors or determined bounds.

pixels short for picture elements; dots on a computer screen that make up letters or pictures. The number of pixels per inch determines the sharpness of the image. (For volumetric renderings, "boxels" are used.)

pod enclosed capsule, car or booth in which a user sits.

polygon flat, closed shape made of three or more straight lines; many-sided figure; smallest piece of a virtual display.

position sensor electromagnetic or optical device that translates a user's head or hand movements into coordinates that can be deciphered and used by a computer program to determine location and orientation of the user within a space; a tracking device.

power glove VPL version of the data glove for home use.

procedure defined activity or sequence of executions addressing *how* something will be done, not *what* is to be done; different from process.

process defined activity or sequence of executions relating to *what* is to be done, not *how* it will be done; the repeated execution of logical tasks identified in terms of input and/or output; different from procedure.

projected reality a slave image of a user's motions is projected along with other images onto a large screen, where the user can observe himself or herself as if within the scene; sophistication between 3-D and total immersion.

programmer a person who prepares or writes a computer program.

proprioceptor a sensory receptor in muscles, joints and tendons that respond to stimuli from within the organism in real life, from external devices in VR environments.

prototyping a technique for building a quick, rough version of a desired system or parts of that system; developing an original or model on which final versions are formed. Prototyping allows users and designers of systems a chance to spot flaws and invent ways to improve the system or to explore a system that is not fully understood.

puppet
image of a user as visually represented in a computer-generated space; slave image of person using the system.

quantum leap
an abrupt, dramatic change or step up, especially in level of knowledge and information.

radiosity
grades of color values and lighting, such as the diffuse reflections found in building interiors.

RAM
Random-Access Memory; primary electronic memory in a computer where programs and data are stored while the computer is on; *not* ROM, Read-Only Memory, whicht stores information permanently. RAM can be overwritten but loses the information when the computer is turned off; allows fast access from anywhere to its information. Conventional, extended and expanded memories are types of RAM.

ray tracing
the simulation of light effects.

RB1/RB2
Reality Built for 1; VPL product of 1980s, one of first commercial real-time, on-line, single-user systems; allows user to interact with virtual objects. Reality Built for 2 (RB2) is the same as RB1 but for 2 persons. It allows two users to interact not only with objects defined in the environment but with each other, as well; software works with newer product, MicroCosm.

reality engine
computer system with software for generating virtual objects and worlds and enabling user interaction.

Reality Net
an experimental service to support long-distance linkages of simultaneous users to a remote common virtual space; individual, long-distance hook-ups where people can communicate and collaborate even though they are not at the same physical location.

realization (VR)
actualization of an image in a virtual environment; turning data into displayable objects; virtualization.

real-space database
a register of real-world-based coordinates for virtual objects that rely on a position relative to the real world for meaning and context; collection of specific altitude, latitude and longitude coordinates assigned to the virtual objects (and the only ones at which those virtual objects can be found).

real-space imaging	graphics dependent on real-world coordinates; images registered with real locations.
real time	the actual time something occurs; for problem-solving with computer, the time between putting data in and receiving a solution; used when response to input to a computer is fast enough to affect subsequent input.
real-time imaging	graphics or images synchronized with real-world time and events.
relative values	values for position and orientation *relative* to previous position and orientation within a virtual space; calculated anew from zero each time virtual object is moved. (See absolute values.)
rendering	translation into another form, e.g., converting signals into a picture; yielding or reducing to another state or interpretation; what you see is what you *set* [IBM91]; performing pixel-oriented calculations for display.
rendering algorithm	mathematical formula for generating images from data.
resolution	measure of image quality, usually expressed in dots per inch (dpi); more dots equals sharper image; sometimes used to measure halftone quality in lines per inch (lpi);
RGB	the primary colors, Red, Green and Blue; additive colors used by color monitor displays. The combinations and intensities of these three colors are used to represent the whole spectrum.
risk factoring	determining and weighing those features of a plan or environment that contribute to its success or failure.
ROM	Read Only Memory; data stored in unerasable, non-alterable form (e.g., a chip built into the machine to hold important, nonchanging information such as the computer's operating system); *not* Random-Access Memory (RAM), which is usable for one session only and disappears when machine is turned off.
scale	reduce or increase size proportionately with regard to a fixed measurement.

scanner
a device similar to a copy machine but connected to a computer; a device that contains software to convert an image into machine-readable code; similar to facsimile. Images are sensed electronically or optically (via a finely focused beam of light or electrons) and converted into digitized form for transmission, modification or integration via a computer program.

scene view
virtual display viewed on a large screen or through a terminal window rather than with immersive devices.

shuttered goggles
stereoscopic glasses for viewing three-dimensional, computer-generated images; usually battery-operated; also called shutter glasses.

SIMNET
simulation network of nonimmersive battleground environments started at the Institute for Simulation & Training, University of Central Florida for U.S. army military communication and training purposes; funded by ARPA. (See NPSNET.)

simulation
a process or apparatus to generate test conditions that approximate real or operational conditions, e.g., the use of flight simulators for pilot training purposes; a setup that mimics or is used to pretend something else.

simulation code
software that controls both the actions performed by a user and the behavior of objects, sounds and forces in the virtual world. It also controls scaling of the virtual environment and things within it. Simulation code for some applications allows users to grab and pick up virtual objects.

six degrees of freedom
(See 6-DOF.)

software (tool)
coded programs that tell a computer what to do in order to perform a specific task; a set of logical, detailed instructions for operating a computer.

spatial data file
computer-readable file of information on locations of virtual things relative to real-world scenes or locations.

spatial sound
notes and tones appearing to emanate from different, varying distances; reproduced in virtual-reality audiospheres to enhance realism; type of surround-sound.

speech recognition   recognition of a human voice as input to a computer; transcribing whatever is spoken, analyzing the sound patterns and then converting them into digitized text.

speech synthesis   rendering digitized signals (text) into electronic speech.

startle response   an indicator of whether telepresence or virtual displays achieve the goal of believability; e.g., will the human operator of a robot flinch if something attacks it?

stereoscopic   imparting a 3-D effect; each eye receiving a slightly different image so that, when viewed together, what is seen appears to have depth. (See bi-ocular.)

stylus   a pen-like input device used with a graphics tablet to enter data into a computer.

Sutherland, Ivan   started the whole field in 1965 with visions of "the screen as a window into which one looks into a virtual world," one that would "look real, sound real, feel real" [Sutherland65]; built first head-mounted gear in Utah in 1968.

synthetic environments   term used by some government agencies for virtual environments; among 1992 Department of Defense's seven strategic thrusts for science and technology.

tactile feedback   feedback directed through or simulating the sense of touch or physical feel; sense of contact distinguished from force feedback, which reflects magnitude of force.

teledildonics   simulated sexual encounter via telephone hookup of one computer to another; computer-generated environment providing tactile feedback via a shared program; described in [Rheingold91].

teleoperation   getting things done via robot or telepresence; sometimes referred to as telemanipulation.

telepresence   word coined by Marvin Minsky; "remote" presence; medium that gives a person the sense of being placed physically within remote, computer-created scenes; a psychological experience resulting when simulator technology works well enough to convince users they are immersed in virtual worlds [Rheingold91].

texture mapping filling in polygons with stored, ready-made textured patterns; substituting mottling, grain or construction material surface effects for single colors within individual polygons; used instead of independently created patterns to conserve computing resources.

thermocouple a device usually consisting of two dissimilar metals joined in such a way that, by applying power to them, heat can be moved from one to the other.

three dimensional (See 3-D.)

torque turning or twisting force; rotation around an axis.

transputer a powerful processor chip containing a computer, memory capacity, I/O channel and communication protocol; suitable for problems that can be broken down into independent subproblems that can be solved simultaneously.

vaporware computer-industry slang for software products that are yet to be demonstrated or delivered ("hyperware" for hardware products); products of wishful thinking; preannounced ploys to seize market share and buy time for development; widespread across the industry.

variable something likely to change and upon which something else may depend; an unknown with no fixed quantity.

VIEW Virtual Interface Environment Workstation; developed by the Aerospace Human Factors Research Division of NASA's Ames Research Center (VIEW Laboratory).

virtual prototype a realization of an intended design or product to illustrate the characteristics of the product or design to users before actual construction; usually used as an exploratory tool for developers or as a communications prop for persons reviewing proposed designs.

virtual reality (See VR. See Preface, pg. ix.)

virtualization the process by which a human interprets a patterned sensory impression to be an object in an environment other than that in which it physically exists. [Ellis91]

visualization (VR)   taking data (usually scientific), exploring its meaning and making it more comprehensible by presenting it in an intuitive simulation; used primarily for physics, chemistry and medical applications.

vortex   whirlpool-like, fluid flow rotating around an axis.

VPL   Virtual Programming Language (Laboratory, Inc.), one of the first commercial ventures for developing and producing control devices (e.g., DataGlove) for virtual environments; founded by Jaron Lanier.

VR   Virtual Reality; also referred to as artificial reality; a digital model of an environment; term coined by Jaron Lanier; virtual "worlds" predicted by Ivan Sutherland in 1960s; the convergence of computer simulation and visualization that attempts to eliminate separation between a user and a machine. (See Preface, pg. v.)

Waldo   nickname for remote, teleoperated robot or device.

"what-if"   hypothetical scenario used to project and explore possible outcomes of courses of action under varying sets of conditions, e.g., *What* would happen to the bank rate *if* no one defaulted on loans? ... *if* Argentina invaded the Falklands? ... *if* your mother-in-law moved in? ... all three?

WIMP   acronym for widget, icon, mouse and pull-down-menu approach to graphical user interfaces.

workstation   a single-user microcomputer, usually with high-resolution graphics capability and high-speed capacity, capable of running applications independently or with other computers via a network. Workstations are generally considered more powerful than personal computers (PCs); however, many high-end PCs now match or exceed low-end workstations and are less expensive. Today's PC approaches in power the large IBM mainframes of the 1980s.

Places & Players

Virtual reality (VR) is emerging from an embryonic, noncommercial state into what appears to be a frenzied marketplace. It is not the aim here to include comprehensive entries for the hundreds of vendors and services that already exist in the field; they should be obtained from frequently updated sources. The purpose of this section is to give you a general inkling of what kinds of things are going on and who is becoming involved.

Likewise, estimates of investments and revenues in the field of VR today are impossible to assess; the latter range anywhere from $5 million to $50 million annually. Regardless, forecasters predict outstanding growth in both the levels of activity and in investment in VR.

Relevant information is presented according to specialty: displays; tracking; input and control devices; software; integrated systems and support software; audio; animation and entertainment; product distribution; publications; research and consulting; conference management; and degree courses, educational systems and support. Included for each area of concentration is a listing of a few representative companies and research teams — arranged simply by how long they've been in business. An asterisk placed by an entry indicates that the group has been visible in more than one area.

Note: Jaron Lanier, founder and former CEO of Virtual Programming Languages, Inc. (VPL), is now strongly committed to the application of VR technology to medicine, with particular emphasis on surgical simulation. This encompasses a number of interesting projects, including an independent investigation of surgical tools and their design. Mr. Lanier is also developing VR authoring tools and VR-related software. He remains involved with the future of virtual reality in entertainment, particularly as it influences theatrical form, virtual music and musical instruments.

DISPLAYS

Tektronix, Inc. P.O. Box 500, M/S 46-943
TEK Beaverton, Oregon 97077, U.S.A.
503-627-5064

Founded 1946. Incorporates liquid-crystal shutter technology with high-resolution monochrome CRTs; full-color, 1″ display systems for HMDs and VR applications; battery-powered stereo glasses and stereo displays for desktop applications. Worldwide sales and service.

StereoGraphics, Corp. 2171 E. Francisco Boulevard
San Rafael, California 94901, U.S.A.
408-378-7693

Founded 1980. CrystalEyes stereoscopic eyewear and infrared emitter, CrystalEyes Video projection systems and CrystalEyes VR. Electronic stereoscopic displays. Images generated from computers or video cameras for medical, entertainment and industrial video applications. Facilities for mass viewing of 3-D projections onto screens.

Polhemus Laboratories, Inc. Two Winter Sport Lane
Williston, Vermont 05495, U.S.A.
802-660-9544

Founded 1983. Binocular, eyeglass-based "Looking Glass." Lightweight, off-the-head fiber-optic display system, neither LCD nor CRT. No radiation or voltage exposure to wearer. High-resolution (1280x1024 pixels) color image formation; stereo capabilities. Not to be confused with Polhemus, Inc., which is a separate company also founded by William Polhemus but later sold internally, then to Kaiser Industries.

Virtual Programming Languages, Inc.* 3977 East Bayshore Road
VPL Research, Inc. Palo Alto, California 94303, U.S.A.
415-988-2550

Founded 1985. EyePhones, DataGloves & Microcosm systems. Originally started by Jaron Lanier, now under French ownership. (See "Input & Control Devices" below.)

Imaging & Sensing Technology Corp. Westinghouse Circle
IST   Horseheads, New York 14845, U.S.A.
                                            607-796-4352

Founded 1988. Small, high-performance, 10-50mm CRTs.
Fabrication, electronics design, computing and optics expertise.
Head-mounted, 640x480 resolution monochrome VR display
with 30-degree field of view. Color technologies available.
Specialist displays for military applications. Man-wearable sys-
tems design and production.

Fakespace, Inc.   4085 Campbell Avenue
                             Menlo Park, California 94025, U.S.A.
                                            415-688-1940

Founded 1989. Stereoscopic displays and interfacing systems
software. BOOM with 1-million-pixel display; teleoperated,
motion platform (Molly) for transmission of images from
remote sites. System design, prototyping and service. Products
in use in science and engineering.

Virtual Reality, Inc.*   485 Washington Avenue
VRI   Pleasantville, New York 10570, U.S.A.
                                            914-769-0900

Founded 1992. Parent company of Technology Innovation
Group (TIG, founded 1988), specialist in military and aerospace
VR and simulation tools. Related-technology products for
commercial medical, educational and entertainment markets.
High-resolution, wide field-of-view HMDs; systems offering vari-
ous levels of immersion. Research and prototyping.

Virtual Research   3193 Belick Street, Suite #2
VR   Santa Clara, California 95054, U.S.A.
                                            408-748-8712

Founded 1992. "Flight Helmet" stereo display units with dual
NTSC inputs, stereo headphones and 13-foot integrated cable.
Easy to put on; adjustable with single knob; balanced; weighs
under 4 pounds.

n-Vision, Inc.
800 Follin Lane, Suite 270
Vienna, Virginia 22180, U.S.A.
703-242-0030

Founded 1993. Datavisor. High-performance head-mounted stereo color display unit based on CRTs + Tektronix LCD shutter devices; infinity focus; geometry correction; adjustable for monoscopic or monochrome display; 1280x960 pixels per eye.

TRACKING

W. W. Gaertner Research*
140 Water Street
Norwalk, Connecticut 06854, U.S.A.
203-866-3200

Founded 1966. Head, hand and foot tracking systems. Image generators and HMDs. Tools for VR system integrators. Research and consulting approach couples hardware and database/systems software. Course development and database modeling for VR, simulation and training.

Polhemus, Inc.
1 Hercules Drive
Colchester, Vermont 05446, U.S.A.
802-655-3159

Founded 1970. 3Space Isotrak & Fastrak Systems. Electromagnetic, real-time, 3-D tracking and digitization for high-end VR graphics, animation and medical/biomedical applications. Digitizer enters geometries into database. CAD interfaces. Low latency, high accuracy and resolution. Range to three meters. (See Polhemus Laboratories, Inc.)

Ascension Technology Corporation
P.O. Box 527
Burlington, Vermont 05402, U.S.A.
802-655-7879

Founded 1986. "Flock of Birds" motion tracking devices and booster transmitters providing full-body tracking over room-sized areas. Pulsed DC magnetic fields minimize environmental sensitivities. Simultaneous tracking (of up to 30 targets). Multiprocessing used for fast updates, low lag.

Gyration, Inc.*   12930 Saratoga Avenue, Bldg. C
                                  Saratoga, California 95070, U.S.A.
                                  408-973-7078

Founded 1989. Gyroengine and Gyropoint. Motion-sensing
devices and developer kits. Optically-encoded miniature spin
gyroscope to translate angular movement into digital output.
Hand-held computer pointer combining mouse and tracker for
interactive multimedia use. Non-VR-specific products for car
navigation, robotics, mining, aircraft and defense use.

Shooting Star Technology   1921 Holdom Avenue
                                 Burnaby, B.C. V5B 3W4, Canada
                                 604-298-8574

Founded 1989. Fast 6-DOF tracker. Direct reading measures
angles on multiply-jointed arm and computes geometry. No
noise, no filtering. Universal compatibility; RS232c port access;
single-letter commands.

MULTIPOINT Technology Corp.*   319 Littleton Road, Suite 201
                                 Westford, Massachusetts 01886, U.S.A.
                                 508-692-0689

Founded 1991. Z 3D Mouse, Developer's Toolkits and Z-Ware
for AutoCAD. 6-DOF, 3-input device for manipulating objects.
Combination of 2-D mouse and trackball. Programmers' aids,
platform-specific software and interfaces. Telephone support.

INPUT & CONTROL DEVICES

Virtual Programming Languages, Inc.*   3977 East Bayshore Road
VPL Research, Inc.   Palo Alto, California 94303, U.S.A.
                                 415-988-2550

Founded 1985. DataGloves, Microcosm & EyePhones. Started
by Jaron Lanier; owned since 1992 by French firm Thomson
CSF SA. Pneumatic tactile feedback, force-sensitive, force-
feedback gloves fitted with micro-actuators producing force
feedback to multiple fingers; suitable for desktop development.

EXOS, Inc.

2A Gill Street
Woburn, Massachusetts 01801, U.S.A.
617-933-0022

Founded 1988. Dextrous HandMaster, Clinical Hand Master System, GripMaster/Ergo Quantifier. Medical measurement and rehabilitation products using robotics sensing technologies. Assessment of hand function, wrist motion and distribution of force on the hand; study of interaction of hand with tools, objects; exoskeletal monitoring of finger-joint motion for controlling machines or robots in laboratory or VR environments.

CIS Graphics and Image Processing

1 Stiles Road, Suite 305
Salem, New Hampshire 03079, U.S.A.
603-894-5999

Founded 1988 U.S., 1972 Germany. Geometry-ball force/torque sensors for 3-D object movement, 6-degrees-of-freedom. Data processed in real time via serial link.

BioControl Systems, Inc.

430 Cowper Street
Palo Alto, California 94301, U.S.A.
415-329-8494

Founded 1989. BioMuse biosignal computer processors, working devices using biological signals from the human nervous system as volitional controllers for hardware or software applications. Interfaces for operating surgeons to control endoscopic cameras. 2-D, 3-D eye-controlled mouse, joystick. Mapping of nervous system for identical projected robot movement in real time. Aids for disabled persons to communicate via eye tracking and control. Connections to music synthesizers. Wearable, wireless versions available. Development consultancy available.

flogiston Corporation

462 Capehill
Webster, Texas 77598, U.S.A.
713-280-8554

Founded 1989. Suspension or fix-mounted chair designed for minimal stress body posture. Embedded sensors. Computer interfaces, e.g., controls and HMDs, within chair structure. Combined with motion platform for generic cyberspace simulation. Turnkey VR systems and environment design services.

Spaceball Technologies, Inc.
600 Suffolk Street
Lowell, Massachusetts 01854, U.S.A.
508-970-0330

Founded 1991. 3-D input device providing 6-DOF position and orientation control. Finger pressure used to push, pull or twist a ball mounted on hand rest to control images and viewpoint.

Greenleaf Medical Systems
GMS
2248 Park Boulevard
Palo Alto, California 94306, U.S.A.
415-321-6135

Motion Analysis and Gesture Control Systems. GloveTalker. Clinical motion and functional assessment program using the DataGlove and DataSuit. Products and applications for rehabilitation training and preparation, e.g., retraining stroke victims. Alternative communications devices that are programmed and interfaced with system so that phrases can be evoked by gesture.

Also: **Gyration***
Multipoint Technology Corporation*
University of North Carolina, Chapel Hill*

INTEGRATED SYSTEMS & SUPPORT SOFTWARE

University of North Carolina, Chapel Hill*
Graphics & Image Group/Microelectronic Systems
Sitterson Hall
CB #3175
Chapel Hill, N. C. 27599-3175, U.S.A.
919-962-1758

Across-the-board research program on enabling VR technologies — multiprocessor image-generation hardware, displays, tracking devices. Database management software and techniques. Test applications in image-guided surgery, radiation treatment planning, architectural modeling, molecular structures and user-driven microscopy. Students at graduate levels. Software library (VLIB) available on request.

Division, Ltd.*
19 Apex Court
Woodlands, Almondsbury
Bristol BS12 4JT, U.K.
+44.454-61-5532

Division Incorporated
400 Seaport Court, Suite 101
Redwood City, California 94063, U.S.A.
415-364-6067

Founded 1992 U.S., 1989 U.K. Integrated, standalone platforms for immersive VR applications; UNIX V or MS-DOS. Distributed, object-oriented system model linked for multiuser cooperation. Upwardly compatible entry-level toolsets for building VR worlds and objects. Parallel VR supercomputer for volume visualization and telepresence applications. Support includes peripherals and training options.

Telepresence Research*
TELEPRESENCE

320 Gabarda Way
Portola Valley, California 84028, U.S.A.
415-854-4420

Founded 1991. Application development and system integration for telepresence and mobile-robot technologies, immersive environments. Focus on entertainment, learning/exploration, training simulation, scientific visualization and remote presence. Hardware, software, design strategies and tools. Consultancy, prototyping, development and installations.

Also: **Virtual Reality, Inc.***

AUDIO

COVOX
COchlea VOicing eXtractor

675 Conger Street
Eugene, Oregon 97402, U.S.A.
503-342-1271

Founded 1975. Text-to-speech adaptor that attaches to printer port of IBM PC compatibles. Digital audio recorder with playback amplifier and voice recognition. Half-size card fits in slot of IBM PC compatible. Voice-recognition software compatible with aii sound cards. 24-hour bulletin board service. Installed base of voice-recognition products.

The Voice Connection, Inc.
Voice Connexion

17835 Skypark Circle, Suite C
Irvine, California 92714, U.S.A.
714-261-2366

Founded 1982. Voice recognition, voice synthesis and real voice I/O systems. Standalone modules with 1000-word recognition, text-to-speech synthesis; allows speaker-dependent words and phrases. Uses serial port or batteries. Half-size PC-compatible card for voice recognition and synthesis; 500 words, unlimited text to speech. Subsets for hard drive. Home automation link and hand-held computers available. Technical support.

Crystal River Engineering, Inc.
CRI

12350 Wards Ferry Road
Groveland, California 95321, U.S.A.
209-962-6382

Founded 1987. Systems delivering 3-D sounds over conventional headphones. Virtual acoustic displays for basic research, aerospace and VR applications. Digital audio processing system (Convolvotron), low-cost version (Beachtron) and 3-D audio workstation for high-end VR applications (Acoustetron). Technical and software support provided.

Visual Synthesis, Incorporated
VSI

4126 Addison Road
Fairfax, Virginia 22030, U.S.A.
703-352-0258

Founded 1990. Data sonification and spatialization; real-time 3-D sound, imaging of audio phenomenon, sonic-imaged analysis. Currently workstation platform. "SoundCube" development environment for 3-D audio-imaging applications. Sound libraries and interfaces between host systems and digital control systems. Features for high-level library, editing and formats from external systems (e.g., Sun, Apple, NeXT, etc.). Porting, environment engineering and customer support.

SOFTWARE

Most companies include supporting software, conversion facilities or installation advice for the products and services they provide. In addition, many in-house and 3rd-party products are being developed.

Dimension International

Zephyr One, Calleva Park
Aldermaston, Berks RG7 4QW, U.K.

Founded 1983. Visualization and virtual-world development "superscape" software for VR applications. Interactive creation and editing systems. Networking versions and developer toolkits for interfacing products with 3rd-party applications. Virtual-object control language of over 400 commands to attribute "intelligence" to objects within virtual worlds. Hot-line support, training and consultancy. +734.81-0007

University of Virginia

User Interface Group
Computer Science Dept., Thorton Hall
Charlottesville, Virginia 22903, U.S.A.
804-982-2211

Founded 1989. Basic research. Interaction techniques, perceptual psychology, software techniques for VR applications. "VR at $5 a Day" experimental system. Student researchers at B.S., M.S. and Ph.D. levels.

The Vivid Group*
VIVID

317 Adelaide Street West, Suite 302
Toronto, Ontario M5V 1P9, Canada
416-340-9290

Founded 1986. Mandala VR System Amiga, VR System PC. Software production and custom installation. Manipulation of user image within virtual world surrounding user; interactive to user touch. Interactive virtual music performances and consultation.

StrayLight Corporation*

150 Mount Bethel Road
Warren, New Jersey 07059, U.S.A.
908-580-0092

Founded 1991. VR software for IBM PCs and compatibles. Photorealistic rendering of complex scenes. Shading, reflections, shadows, textures and bump maps. Imports files from AutoCAD, 3d-Studio, animation and other CAD packages.

Also: **Division, Ltd.***
          University of North Carolina, Chapel Hill*

ANIMATION & ENTERTAINMENT

Mr. Film

228 Main Street, Suite R
Venice, California 90291, U.S.A.
310-396-0146

Founded 1983. Automated choreography for production of series cartoons and creation of animated characters.

Pacific Data Images, Inc.

1111 Karlstad Drive
Sunnyvale, California 94089, U.S.A.
408-745-6755

Digital effects for the entertainment and advertising industries. Creation of images combining photography and animatronics. Computer-created images for real-time interaction. Morphing. Performance animation technology.

StrayLight Corporation*

150 Mount Bethel Road
Warren, New Jersey 07059, U.S.A.
908-580-0092

Founded 1991. *CyberTron* and location-based (arcade) entertainment systems based on the concept of virtual reality. Strong link to CAD and animation databases. Custom program software and client support.

RESEARCH & CONSULTING

Stanford Research Institute Int'l.
SRI

333 Ravenswood Avenue
Menlo Park, California 94025, U.S.A.
415-859-4006

Founded 1946. Think tank. Research only; no physical products. Capabilities covering most areas of VR sensing, displays and software.

Machover Associates Corp.
MAC

199 Main Street
White Plains, New York 10601, U.S.A.
914-949-3777

Founded 1976. Provider of business, technical, marketing and financial advice to users, vendors and investors in VR-related areas; 35 years' specialty in computer graphics, including VR display technologies; strong consultant credentials, experience.

Spectrum Dynamics, Inc.*
SD

3336 Richmond Avenue, Suite 226
Houston, Texas 77098-3022, U.S.A.
713-520-5020

Founded 1990. VR systems integration and product distribution. Programming, consulting, systems integration and product maintenance. Reseller of majority of VR products from most vendors.

SophisTech Research*

6936 Seaborn Street
Lakewood, California 90713, U.S.A.
310-421-7295

Founded 1991. Provider of information, consultancy and strategic planning. Publisher of *Virtual Reality Sourcebook*, quarterly listing vendors, products, seminars, publications and resources; electronic PC edition available; round-the-clock pay-per-minute information line; product and system development; marketing; presentations; systems integration help.

Virtual Environment/Teleoperator Research Consortium M.I.T.
VETREC

77 Massachusetts Avenue
Cambridge, Massachusetts 02139, U.S.A.
617-254-2534

Founded 1992. Collaboration drawing members from various departments and research groups at M.I.T. and outside university and business groups for investigation of virtual environment technologies and training techniques; special projects accepted.

Also: **W. W. Gaertner Research, Inc.***
         VIVID*

PUBLICATIONS

The numbers of books being published on virtual reality and related topics are growing — as evidenced by the bibliographical sources used for this book alone. Numerous papers are being published by independent research and commercial groups, and subscription services that mail overseas are available. Listed here are three examples of the types of VR-dedicated publications being offered through subscription. Announcements and reviews of most new publications can usually be found in good subscription magazines.

CyberEdge JOURNAL

#1 Gate Six Road, Suite C
Sausalito, California 94965, U.S.A.
415-331-3343

Founded 1990. Virtual-reality subscription newsletter distributed in 14 countries. Current news on VR, artificial reality, telepresence, tactile feedback and force feedback devices, 3-D sound. Information services and fact verification for researchers and press journalists, some at no cost.

VR NEWS

Cydata Limited
P.O. Box 2515, London N4 4JW, U.K.
+44.81-292-1498

Founded 1991. 16-page subscription newsletter. Worldwide coverage, 20 countries. Information exchange for subscribers; no advertising content. News and analysis of all aspects of VR.

MIT PRESENCE

55 Hayward Street
Cambridge, Massachusetts 02142-1399, U.S.A.
617-253-2889

Founded 1992. Quarterly subscription journal for serious investigators of teleoperation and virtual-reality systems; scholarly presentations and discussions of designs and multidisciplinary (engineering, computing and psychological) implications of the technologies involved. Each issue contains two sections, the first devoted to research papers and the second to contributions and review articles. Strong editorial board.

DEGREE COURSES, EDUCATIONAL SYSTEMS & SUPPORT

Many institutions around the world are incorporating VR-related courseware into their curricula. In the United States, the **Institute for Simulation & Training** at the University of Central Florida in Orlando and the **CAD Institute** in Phoenix, Arizona, offer accredited degree courses. **Harvard University's School of Architecture** is expected to offer a degree program incorporating design techniques within virtual environments.

Generally, in the United States, products for educational systems are being developed and supported by independent research groups, e.g., **AutoDesk, Inc.** in Sausalito, California, the **Human Interface Technology (H.I.T.) Laboratory** at the University of Washington in Seattle, the **Massachusetts Institute of Technology (M.I.T.) Media Laboratory** in Cambridge, the **University of North Carolina (Chapel Hill)** and **Virtual Reality, Inc.** of Pleasantville, New York.

TYPICAL COMMERCIAL SYSTEMS

Typical commercially available systems can be classified as "high-end," "mid-range" or "low-end" products. Prices and sophistication of applications generally match these descriptions. For example, typical of high-end systems is the Power Visualization Series from IBM. One unit may cost anywhere from $600,000 to $2 million. Customers for these systems include car companies, banks and research laboratories.

Mid-range systems are typified by VPL's RB2, "Reality Built for 2," the oldest of presently marketed systems. These run about $430,000 per 2-person unit. NASA's VIEW System is a mid-range platform used by the military.

Low-end systems are the type used for arcade video-game attractions. Single-user versions of RB2, each of which costs about $50,000-$60,000 per CD-ROM unit, are typical of this category.

Sales of interactive video control devices and head-mounted stereoscopic displays are bringing the low end even lower. Initial devices for home use are expected to be in the few-hundred-dollar range.

PRODUCT DISTRIBUTION

Spectrum Dynamics, Inc.*   3336 Richmond Avenue, Suite 226
SD   Houston, Texas 77098-3022, U.S.A.

Founded 1990. VR product distribution and systems integration. Distributor and value-added reseller of majority of VR
products. Product maintenance, programming, consulting and
systems integration.

CONFERENCE MANAGEMENT

Numerous VR exhibitions, conferences and symposia are held, sponsored
by various organizations. Proceedings are usually available for purchase.
A few of those presenting annually in the United States are listed here.

Aligned Management Association   P.O. Box 23220
AMA   San Diego, California 92193, U.S.A.

Founded 1991. Continuing education conferences serving the
health sciences; transformation of medicine through communication. Events bringing together new technologies and health
practitioners. Organizer of "Medicine Meets VR."

SIG-Advanced Applications, Inc.   1562 First Avenue, Suite 286
"Virtual Reality Systems"   New York, New York 10028, U.S.A.

Meckler Conference Management   11 Ferry Lane West
"Virtual Reality"   Westport, Connecticut 06880, U.S.A.

Conferences are also staged regularly in Europe.

Additional Sources of Information

Ben-David, Joseph, *The Scientist's Role in Society*, University of Chicago Press, Chicago, 1984.

Bunzel, Mark J. & Sandra K. Morris, *Multimedia Applications Development Using DVI Technology*, McGraw-Hill, Inc., New York, 1992.

Ellis, Stephen R., M. K. Kaiser & A. J. Grunwald (Eds.), *Pictorial Communication in Virtual and Real Environments*, Taylor and Francis, London, 1991.

Huxley, Aldous, *Brave New World*, Harper & Row, Publishers, Inc., London, 1932.

Huxley, Aldous, *Brave New World* and *Brave New World Revisited*, excerpt from author's foreword, reprinted by permission of HarperCollins Publishers, Inc., New York, 1946.

Krueger, Myron, *Artificial Reality II*, Addison-Wesley, Reading, Massachusetts, 1991.

Martin, James, *Hyperdocuments & How to Create Them*, Prentice-Hall, Inc., Englewood Cliffs, 1990.

Parsaye, K., M. Chignell, S. Khoshafian & H. Wong, *Intelligent Databases: Object-Oriented, Deductive Hypermedia Technologies*, John Wiley & Sons, Inc., N.Y., 1989.

Pimentel, Ken, & Kevin Teixeira, *Virtual Reality: Through the New Looking Glass*, Windcrest Books, TAB imprint, McGraw-Hill, New York, 1993.

Salvadori, Mario, *Why Buildings Stand Up: The Strength of Architecture*, W. W. Norton & Company, New York, 1990, afterword, p. 303.

Weizenbaum, Joseph, *Computer Power and Human Reason: from Judgment to Calculation*, W. H. Freeman & Co., New York, 1976.

Academic Journals & Conference Proceedings

Applegate, L. M., J. I. Cash, Jr. & D. Q. Mills, "Information Technology and Tomorrow's Manager," *Harvard Business Review*, Volume 66, Cambridge, November/December 1988, p. 6.

Bates, Joseph, A. Bryan Loyall & W. Scott Reilly, "Integrating Reactivity, Goals, and Emotion in a Broad Agent," in *Proceedings, Fourteenth Annual Conference of the Cognitive Science Society*, Bloomington, Indiana, July 1992.

Blanchard, C., S. Burgess, Y. Harvill, J. Lanier & A. Lasko, "Reality Built for Two: A Virtual Reality Tool," in *Proceedings, ACM SIGGRAPH 1990 Symposium on Interactive 3D Graphics*, March 1990.

Csuri, Charles A., "Art and Animation," *IEEE Computer Graphics & Applications*, Volume 11, Number 1, January 1991, p. 30.

Csuri, Charles A., & Michael Haggerty (Eds.), "The Art of Artificial Reality," *IEEE Computer Graphics & Applications*, Volume 11, Number 1, January 1991, p. 8.

Fisher, S. S., E. M. Wenzel, C. Coler, & M. W. McGreevy, "Virtual Environment Interface Workstations," *Proceedings, Human Factors Society 32nd Annual Meeting*, Anaheim, California, 1988.

Grinstein, Georges, "Notes on Multisensory Visualization Systems," *IEEE Computer Graphics & Applications*, Volume 11, Number 3, May 1991, p. 18.

Haggerty, Michael, "Virtual Reality Dominates Siggraph," *IEEE Computer Graphics & Applications*, Volume 11, Number 5, September 1991, p. 14.

Haimes, R., & M. Giles, "VISUAL3: Interactive Unsteady Unstructured 3-D Visualization," paper AIAA-91-0794, *Proceedings, American Institute of Aeronautics 29th Annual Aerospace Sciences Meeting*, Reno, Nevada, 1991.

Masuda, Yoneji, "A New Era of Global Information Utility," *Proceedings, Eurocomp*, London, 1978.

McDowall, I. E., M. Bolas, S. Pieper, S. S. Fisher & J. Humphries, "Implementation and Integration of a Counterbalanced CRT-Based Stereoscopic Display for Interactive Viewpoint Control in Virtual Environment Application," in *Proceedings, SPIE Conference on Stereoscopic Displays and Applications*, J. Merrit & Scott Fisher (Eds.), 1256, 1990.

Narasimhalu, A. D., & S. Christodoulakis, "Multimedia Information Systems: The Unfolding of a Reality," *Computer*, Volume 24, Number 10, October 1991, p. 6.

Nugent, William R., "Virtual Reality: Advanced Imaging Special Effects Let You Roam in Cyberspace," *Journal of the American Society for Information Science*, September 1991, p. 609.

PRESENCE: Teleoperators and Virtual Environments, Massachusetts Institute of Technology (MIT) Press, Cambridge, Massachusetts, Volume 1, Number 1, Winter 1992.

Proceedings, International Society for Optical Engineering Conference, "Image Understanding and the Man-Machine Interface," "Microsensors & Catheter-Based Imaging Technology," "Optical Storage Technology and Applications," Los Angeles, 1988.

Proceedings, Medicine Meets Virtual Reality, "Discovering Applications for 3-D Multi-Media Interactive Technology in the Health Sciences," San Diego, California, June 1992.

Richardson, D. C., "Three-Dimensional Structure of Cu, Zn, Superoxide Dismutase," in *Superoxide and Superoxide Dismutases*, A. M. Michelson, J. M. McCord & I. Fridovich (Eds.), Academic Press, New York, 1977.

Tsernoglou, D., & G. A. Petsko, "Three-Dimensional-Structure of Neurotoxin from Venom of the Philippines Sea Snake," *Proceedings, National Academy of Sciences, U.S.A.*, Volume 74, Number 3, March 1977, p. 971.

Tsernoglou, D., & G. A. Petsko, "Molecular Graphics: Application to the Structure Determination of a Snake-Venom Neurotoxin," *Science*, Volume 197, Number 4311, September 1977, p. 1378.

Research Papers

Department of Computer Science, University of North Carolina, Chapel Hill, N.C.

Brooks, Frederick P., Jr., Ming Ouh-Young, James J. Batter & P. Jerome Kilpatrick, "Project GROPE — Haptic Displays for Scientific Visualization," *Computer Graphics*, Volume 24, Number 4, August 1990.

Holloway, Richard, Hunry Fuchs & Warren Robinett, "Virtual-Worlds Research at the University of North Carolina at Chapel Hill," *Proceedings*, Computer Graphics '91, London, U.K., 1991.

Project Summaries

Department of Computer Science, University of North Carolina, Chapel Hill, N.C.

"Head-Mounted Display Research," departmental report, July 1991.

"Head-Tracker Research," department report, July 1991.

"PIXEL-PLANE 5, A Heterogeneous Multicomputer for Graphics," departmental report, July 1991.

Course Papers

Department of Computer Science, University of California, Los Angeles, California.

Hsieh, Ifang, "VPL and Its RB2," UCLA course material, December 1991.

Quan, Elizabeth, "Battling with Cyborg: A Computer Image," UCLA course material, December 1991.

Ramos, Paul M., "Virtual Interface Environment Workstation (VIEW), a Virtual Reality System," UCLA course material, December 1991.

Trade Publications & Articles

Alexander, M., "Virtual Reality Still Unrealistic," *Computerworld*, Volume 25, Number 25, June 24, 1991, p. 20.

Anzovin, Steven, "Pathways," *Compute*, October 1991, p. 97.

Brown, G., *The Daily Telegraph*, U.K., November 17, 1988.

Bylinsky, G., "The Marvels of Virtual Reality," *Fortune*, Volume 123, June 3, 1991, p.138.

Carlson, S. "Virtual Mars?" *The Humanist*, Volume 51, March/April 1991, p. 43.

Davis, Dwight B., "Reality Check," *Computer Graphics World*, June 1991, p. 49.

de Groot, Marc, "Virtual Reality," *UNIX Review*, Volume 8, Number 8, August 1990, p. 32.

D'Ignazio, F., "Digital Smoke and Mirrors," *Compute*, Volume 13, Number G22, January 1991.

Ditlea, Steve, "Another World inside Artificial Reality," *PC/Computing*, November 1989, p. 91.

Ditlea, Steve, "Inside Artificial Reality," in *Science Supplement 1991*, Grolier, 1990, p. 102.

Farley, L., "Making Sense of Change: Strategies for Educational Technologists," *The Computing Teacher*, April 1992, p. 8.

Ferrington, G., & K. Loge, "Virtual Reality: A New Learning Environment," *The Computing Teacher*, April 1992, p. 16.

Frazer, L. "Remote Eyes, Remote Hands," *Ad Astra*, Volume 2, October 1990, p. 24.

Fisher, Scott S., & Jane Morrill Tazelaar, "Living in a Virtual World," *BYTE*, July 1990, p. 215.

Glines, C. V., "Brain Buckets," *Air Force Magazine*, Volume 69, Number 8, 1986, p. 86.

Hamit, Francis, "New SIMNET Modes Revealed at the SCS Multiconference," *CyberEdge Journal*, Mill Valley, California, March 1992.

Horn, M., "Seeing the Invisible," *U.S. News & World Report*, Volume 110, January 28, 1991, p. 56.

InfoWorld, Volume 13, Issues 22 & 28, 1991.

Jacobson, Linda, "Virtual Reality: A Status Report," *AI Expert*, Volume 6, Number 8, August 1991, p. 26.

Johnston, Stuart J., "The Expensive World of Virtual Reality: Not Just Another Pretty Space," *InfoWorld*, February 1990, p. 50.

Kelly, Kevin, Adam Heilbrun & Barbara Stacks, "An Interview with Jaron Lanier," *Whole Earth Review*, Fall 1989, p. 108.

Laurel, Brenda, "Virtual Reality Design: A Personal View," in *Multimedia Review*, Meckler Publishing Corp., Connecticut, summer 1990.

Laurel, Brenda, "Strange New Worlds of Entertainment," *Compute*, Volume 13, November 1991, p. 102.

Levy, Steven, "Jaron Lanier is the Wizard of Virtual Reality," *Rolling Stone*, June 14, 1990, p. 92.

MacWorld, Volume 8, Numbers 1, 6, 5, 9 & 11, 1991.

McAvinney, Paul, "Telltale Gestures," *BYTE*, July 1990, p. 237.

National Geographic World, "A New World at Your Fingertips," Volume 192, August 1991, p. 8.

Newquist, Harvey P., III, "A Computer-Generated Suspension of Disbelief," *AI Expert*, Volume 6, Number 8, August 1991, p. 34.

Park, Brian, "VR at Syracuse," *Workstation News*, Volume 3, Number 5, May 1992.

Peterson, I., "Looking-Glass Worlds," *Science News*, Volume 141, January 4, 1992, p. 8.

Peterson, I., "Exploring the Virtual Wind," *Science News*, Volume 139, Number 398, June 2, 1991.

Rheingold, Howard, "Travels in Virtual Reality," *Whole Earth Review*, Summer 1990, p. 80.

Robinett, Warren, "Electronic Expansion of Human Perception, *Whole Earth Review*, Fall 1991.

Saffo, Paul, "Virtual Reality Is Almost Real," *Personal Computing*, June 29, 1990, p. 99.

Seaborn, Margaret, "The Many Faces of Mario," *Workstation News*, Volume 3, Number 5, May 1992.

Stedman, N., "Fields of Dreams," *Video*, Volume 15, May 1991, p. 30.

Stewart, Doug, "Through the looking glass into an artificial world — via computer," with bibliographical references, *Smithsonian*, Volume 21, January 1991, p. 36.

Stewart, Doug, interview with Jaron Lanier for *Omni*, Volume 13, January 1991, p. 44.

Stix, G., "Reach Out," *Scientific American*, Volume 264, Fall 1991, p. 134.

Stone, J., "Turn on, Tune in, Boot up," *Discover*, Volume 12, June 1991, p. 32.

Turcan, P., *The Guardian*, U.K., March 17, 1988.

VR Monitor, Frank Dunn, Ed., Matrix Information Services, Lathrup Village, MI, May/June 1992.

Wright, Jeff, "Altered States," *Computer Graphics World*, December 1989, p. 77.

Cable News Network, *Technology Week*, "Mars Life," Journal Graphics STW #83-4, Cable News Network, Inc., 1991.

References

[ABC91]   American Broadcasting Company, *Prime Time*, "Virtual
               Reality," Journal Graphics Prime #211-3, September 1991.

[ADAM92]   reference to *Animated Dissection of Anatomy for Medicine*,
               an interactive, multimedia encyclopedia of anatomy with
               accompanying medical database; ADAM Software, Inc.,
               Marietta, Georgia, 1992.

[Airey&91]   John M. Airey, John H. Rohlf & Frederick P. Brooks, Jr.,
               "Towards Image Realism with Interactive Update Rates in
               Complex Virtual Building Environments," in *Computer
               Graphics*, Volume 24, Number 2, p. 41.

[Barasch92]   Douglas S. Barasch, "The Mainstreaming of Alternative
               Medicine," *The New York Times Magazine*, Part 2, New
               York, October 1992.

[Barker&92]   Bruce Barker & Robert Goodwin, "Audiographics: Linking
               Remote Classrooms," *The Computing Teacher*, April 1992.

[Bates92a]   Joseph Bates, "Virtual Reality, Art and Entertainment,"
               PRESENCE: Teleoperators and Virtual Environments,
               MIT Press, Cambridge, Volume 1, Number 1, 1992, p. 133.

[Bates92b]   Joseph Bates, "The Nature of Characters in Interactive
               Worlds and the Oz Project," *Virtual Realities: Anthology of
               Industry and Culture*, Carl E. Loeffler, Ed., 1993.

[Biedny91]   David Biedny, "Reviews — 3-D Graphics," *MacWorld*,
               Volume 8, Number 9, September 1991, p. 222.

[Bremmer91]   Jan Bremmer, Ed., "A History of Sexology," *From Sappho
               to De Sade*, Routledge, London, 1991.

[Brooks91]   Frederick P. Brooks, Jr., Prof. Electrical Engineering, Com-
               puter Science Department, University of North Carolina,
               Chapel Hill, North Carolina; at U.S. Senate Hearing on Vir-
               tual Reality, Washington, D.C., 1991.

[Brooks&90]   Frederick P. Brooks, Jr., Ming Ouh-Young, James J. Batter & P. Jerome Kilpatrick, "Project GROPE — Haptic Displays for Scientific Visualization," *Computer Graphics*, Volume 24, Association of Computer Machinery, August 1990.

[Brooks88]   Frederick P. Brooks, Jr., "Grasping Reality through Illusion — Interactive Graphics Serving Science," Keynote Address, ref. to [Tsernoglou&77] and [Richardson77], 5th Conference on Computers and Human Interaction, Washington, D.C., May 1988.

[Bryson&91]   Steve Bryson & Creon Levit, "The Virtual Windtunnel: An Environment for the Exploration of Three-Dimensional Unsteady Flows," *Proceedings, Visualization '91*, IEEE Computer Society, G. M. Neilson & L. Rosenblum, Eds., , San Diego, California, October 1991.

[BusWk93]   "Micromachines," *Business Week*, Science and Technology, McGraw-Hill, Inc., New York, April 26, 1993, p. 94.

[Carpenter92]   Calvin L. Carpenter, "Plugging in to the Information Age," *The Computing Teacher*, April 1992, p. 38.

[CNN92]   Cable News Network, *Technology Week*, "VR for the Disabled," Cable News Network, Inc., July 1992.

[Descuret1844] J. B. F. Descuret, *La medicine des passions*, 3rd Edition, Liege, 1844; cited in *From Sappho to De Sade*, Jan Bremmer, Ed., Routledge, London, 1991.

[Drucker88]   Peter F. Drucker, "Management and the World's Work," *Harvard Business Review*, Volume 66, Number 5, Cambridge, September/October 1988.

[Duga92]   Jules J. Duga, personal communication, Battelle Memorial Institute, Columbus, Ohio, 1992.

[Dunn92]   *VR Monitor*, Frank Dunn, Ed., Matrix Information Services, Lathrup Village, Michigan, 1992.

[Ellis91]   Stephen R. Ellis, "Nature and Origins of Virtual Environments: A Bibliographical Essay," *Computing Systems in Engineering*, Volume 2, No. 4, Pergamon Press, U.K., 1991, p. 321.

[Farmer92]   Randall Farmer, *Habitat* project, LucasFilms, 1992.

[Forbes92]   *Forbes* Magazine, October 12, 1992.

[Furness91]   Thomas A. Furness, Director, Human-Interface Technology Laboratory, Washington Technology Center, University of Washington; at U.S. Senate Hearing on Virtual Reality, Washington, D.C., 1991.

[Gannon89]   R. Gannon, "Micromachine Magic," *Popular Science,* March 1989, pp. 88, 143.

[Goldfarb91]   Norman Goldfarb, "Virtual Reality: The State of the Art," *MicroTimes,* October 14, 1991, p. 62.

[Graham92]   Ellen Graham, "Classrooms without Walls," in *The Wall Street Journal,* May 18, 1992.

[Greenleaf92] Walter. J. Greenleaf, "The DataGlove and DataSuit Technology for Medical Applications," *Medicine Meets Virtual Reality,* University of California, San Diego, June 1992.

[Haavind92]   Robert Haavind, "Software's New Object Lesson," *Technology Review,* MIT, Cambridge, February/March 1992.

[Holloway&91] Richard Holloway, Henry Fuchs & Warren Robinett, "Virtual-Worlds Research at the University of North Carolina at Chapel Hill," *Proceedings, Computer Graphics,* London, October 1991.

[IBM91]   "Visualize the Future ... Today," POWER Visualization System, International Business Machines, Inc., Product Marketing, Hawthorne, New York, July 1991.

[Kelso&91]   M. Kelso & J. Bates, "Live Simulation of a Model for Dramatic Virtual Worlds," Working Paper, Oz Project, School of Computer Science, Carnegie Mellon University, Pittsburgh, Pennsylvania.

[Kollin93]   Joel Kollin, "The Virtual Retinal Display," unpublished paper and personal communication, Human-Interface Technology Laboratory, Washington Technology Center, University of Washington, Seattle, 1993.

[Krueger83]   Myron Krueger, *Artificial Reality,* Addison-Wesley, Reading, Massachusetts, 1983.

[LaFee92]   Scott LaFee, "Futuristic Use of Technology a 'Virtual Reality' for the Disabled," *The San Diego Union Tribune,* March 29, 1992.

[Lanier91]   Jaron Lanier, then President, VPL Research, Redwood City, California; at U.S. Senate Hearing on Virtual Reality, Washington, D.C., 1991.

[Laurel91]   Brenda Laurel, excerpt from *Computers as Theatre,* Addison-Wesley Publishing Co., Reading, Mass., 1991.

[Loeffler92]   Carl Eugene Loeffler, "Networked Virtual Reality," STUDIO for Creative Inquiry, Carnegie Mellon University, Pittsburgh, Pennsylvania, 1992.

[Loomis92]   Jack M. Loomis, "Distal Attribution and Presence," *Proceedings, Western Simulation Multiconference*, Society for Computer Simulation, Newport Beach, California, 1992.

[Louis&90]   K. Louis & M. B. Miles, *Improving the Urban High School: What Works and Why*, Teachers College Press, N.Y., 1990.

[Lubove91]   S. Lubove, "Fooling the Inner Ear," *Forbes* Magazine, Volume 147, February 18, 1991, p. 110.

[Lusted&92]   Hugh S. Lusted & R. Benjamin Knapp, "Biocontrollers: A Direct Link from the Nervous System to Computer," *Proceedings, Medicine Meets Virtual Reality*, University of California at La Jolla, San Diego, June 1992.

[Machover93]   *written communication*, Dr. Carl Machover, Machover Associates Corporation, White Plains, New York, 1993.

[Masuda78]   Yoneji Masuda, "Future Perspectives for Information Utility," *Proceedings, Computer Communication*, 4th International Conference, Kyoto, Japan, 1978.

[Masuda90]   Yoneji Masuda, *Managing in the Information Society*, Basil Blackwell, Ltd., Oxford, U.K., 1990.

[May&87]   D. May & R. Shepherd, "The Transputer," *Neural Computers*, NATO ASI Series, Springer Verlag, Berlin, 1987.

[McCormick&87] B. H. McCormick, T. A. DeFanti & M. D. Brown (Eds.), "Visualization in Scientific Computing," *Computer Graphics 21*, Volume 6, November 1987.

[McGreevy91]   Michael W. McGreevy, "Virtual Reality and Planetary Exploration," *on_line*, Volume 13, Number 8, Ames Computer Systems and Research Division, Ames Research Center, Moffet Field, California, August 1991.

[McGreevy&91]   Michael W. McGreevy & Lewis Hitchner, Ames Research Center, Research Institute for Advanced Computer Science, Moffet Field, California, cited in [McGreevy91].

[Ming&89]   Ming Ouh-Young, D. V. Beard & F. P. Brooks, Jr., "Force display performs better than visual display in a simple 6-D docking task," *Proceedings, Robotics and Automation*, IEEE, Scottsdale, Arizona, Volume 3, 1989, p. 1462.

[MIT92]   *PRESENCE: The International Journal of Teleoperators and Virtual Environments*, MIT Press, Cambridge, 1992.

[Miyoshi92]   Masaya Miyoshi, "Why the Japanese Economy Will Bounce Back," *The Wall Street Journal*, New York, December 28, 1992.

[Murphy92]   Ronald Murphy, "Distributed Defense Simulation: The World of Virtual Reality," Keynote Address, Western Simulation Multiconference, Society for Computer Simulation, Newport Beach, California, 1992.

[Nugent91]   William R. Nugent, "Virtual Reality: Advanced Imaging Special Effects Let You Roam in Cyberspace," *Journal of the American Society for Information Science*, September 1991.

[NYT91]   "Abe Peled's Secret Start-Up at IBM," *The New York Times*, December 8, 1991.

[Park92]   Brian Park, "The Projection Workstation," *Workstation News*, Volume 3, Number 6, June 1992.

[Paul92]   Howard A. Paul, D.V.M., "Image-Directed Robotic Surgery," *Proceedings, Medicine Meets Virtual Reality*, University of California, San Diego, June 1992.

[Pausch91]   Randy Pausch, "Virtual Reality on Five Dollars a Day," *Proceedings, Human Factors in Computer Systems*, ACM SIGCHI, New Orleans, Louisiana, 1991.

[PTel87]   *Annual Report*, Pacific Telesis, 1987.

[Rheingold86]   Howard Rheingold, *Cognitive Connections*, Prentice-Hall, Inc., Englewood Cliffs, 1986.

[Rheingold91]   Howard Rheingold, *Virtual Reality*, Summit Books, Simon & Schuster, New York, 1991.

[Richardson77] D. C. Richardson, "Three-Dimensional Structure of Cu, Zn, Superoxide Dismutase," *Superoxide and Superoxide Dismutases*, edited by A. M. Michelson, J. M. McCord & I. Fridovich, Academic Press, New York, 1977.

[Ross88]   P. W. Ross, "720x400 Matrix Ferroelectric Display Operating at Video Frame Rate," *Proceedings, International Display Research*, IEEE, New York, 1988, p. 185.

[Satava92]   Colonel Richard M. Satava, M.D., "Virtual Reality Surgical Simulator, the First Steps," *Proceedings, Medicine Meets Virtual Reality*, University of California, San Diego, June 1992.

[Scheffer88]   T. J. Scheffer, "Liquid Crystal Displays — Where are they going?" *Proceedings, International Display Research*, IEEE, New York, 1988, p. 184.

[SCS92]   *Proceedings, Western Simulation Multiconference*, Society for Computer Simulation, Newport Beach, Calif., 1992.

[Selkowitz&86]   S. E. Selkowitz, K. M. Papamichael & G. M. Wilde, "A Concept for an Advanced Computer-Based Building Envelope Design Tool," *Proceedings, International Daylighting Conference*, Long Beach, November 4-7, 1986, p. 496.

[Sutherland65]   Ivan E. Sutherland, "The Ultimate Display," Information Processing Techniques Office, *Proceedings, International Federation of Information Processing (IFIP) Congress 65*, p. 506.

[Sutherland68]   Ivan E. Sutherland, "A Head-Mounted Three-Dimensional Display," Harvard Computation Laboratory, *Proceedings, Fall Joint Computer Conference*, Thompson Books, 1968, p. 757.

[Tsernoglou&77]   D. Tsernoglou, G. A. Petsko, J. E. McQueen, Jr. & J. Hermans, "Molecular Graphics: Application to the Structure Determination of Snake Venom Neurotoxin," *Science*, Volume 197, 4311, September 30, 1977.

[Tufte83]   Edward R. Tufte, *The Visual Display of Quantitative Information*, Graphics Press, Cheshire, Connecticut, 1983.

[Tufte90]   Edward R. Tufte, *Envisioning Information*, Graphics Press, Cheshire, Connecticut, 1990.

[UI93]   University of Illinois-Caterpillar, Inc. collaboration reported on Cable News Network, Inc., *Business News*, June 2, 1993.

[VPL91a]   *Virtual World News*, "All the News That Can Possibly Fit on Four Pages...," VPL Research, Redwood City, California; Volume 3, No. 1, U.S. Edition, Summer 1991.

[VPL91b]   *ibid. Virtual World News.* The Gesture Control System is being developed by GMS and researchers at Cal State University at Northridge, California.

[Walter90]   R. Walter, "Elements of a Cyberspace Playhouse," in *Virtual Reality: Theory, Practice and Promise*, New York, Meckler Press, 1990.

[Warhover92]   R. Warhover, Reference #A92-011, Army Aviation Systems Command, St. Louis, Missouri, 1992.

[Warner&92]   Dave Warner, Jeff Sale, Stephen Price & Doug Will, "Remapping the Human-Computer Interface for Optimized Perceptualization of Medical Information," *Proceedings, Medicine Meets Virtual Reality*, University of California, San Diego, June 1992.

[Weizenbaum76] Joseph Weizenbaum, *Computer Power and Human Reason*, W. H. Freeman and Company, New York, 1976.

[Wenzel&90] Elizabeth M. Wenzel, Scott H. Foster, Frederic L. Wightman & Doris J. Kistler, "Realtime Digital Synthesis of Localized Auditory Cues over Headphones," *Proceedings, Applications on Signal Processing to Audio and Acoustics*, IEEE ASSP Workshop, New Paltz, New York, 1989.

[White62] Lynn White, Jr., *Medieval Technology and Social Change*, Classic Volume, Oxford University Press, New York, 1962.

[Zaliznyak91] Diana Zaliznyak, "Reality Built for Two and Architectural Walk-Throughs," UCLA course material, December 1991.

[Zuboff88] Shoshana Zuboff, *In the Age of the Smart Machine*, Basic Books, New York, 1988.

ABOUT THE AUTHOR

L. Casey Larijani is a technical writer and consultant living in Manhattan. Previously director for James Martin Research and managing editor for *High-Productivity Software*, Ms. Larijani is well-versed in a wide variety of computer systems and their applications to business and education. She has traveled extensively abroad and has taught at secondary and college levels.

Index